ROMANTIC GARDENS

Romantic Gardens

NATURE, ART, AND LANDSCAPE DESIGN

ELIZABETH BARLOW ROGERS

ELIZABETH S. EUSTIS

JOHN BIDWELL

THE MORGAN LIBRARY & MUSEUM · *New York*

in association with DAVID R. GODINE, PUBLISHER · *Boston*

and the FOUNDATION FOR LANDSCAPE STUDIES · *New York*

This book published in 2010 by
David R. Godine · *Publisher*
Post Office Box 450
Jaffrey, New Hampshire 03452
www.godine.com

This exhibition is underwritten by the Johansson Family Foundation.

Generous support is provided by Janine Luke and Melvin R. Seiden, as well as by The Bodman Foundation, Charles C. Butt, The Chilton Foundation, the Heineman Foundation for Research, Educational, Charitable and Scientific Purposes, Inc., and Deutsche Lufthansa AG.

The catalogue is made possible by The Foundation for Landscape Studies; the Graham Foundation for Advanced Studies in the Fine Arts; Patrick and Elizabeth Gerschel; Furthermore, a program of the J. M. Kaplan Fund, Inc.; the German Consulate General in New York; the Consulate General of the Republic of Poland in New York; and the Andrew W. Mellon Fund for Research and Publications.

LIBRARY OF CONGRESS CATALOGING-IN-PUBLICATION DATA
Library of Congress Cataloging-in-Publication Data

Rogers, Elizabeth Barlow, 1936-
   Romantic gardens : nature, art, and landscape design / Elizabeth Barlow Rogers, Elizabeth Eustis, John Bidwell.
-- 1st ed.
      p. cm.
   ISBN 978-1-56792-404-6
1. Gardens. 2. Landscape design. I. Eustis, Elizabeth S. II. Bidwell, John, 1949- III. Title.
   SB451.R638 2010
   712--dc22
                              2010001418

ISBN 978-1-56792-404-6

COVER: Humphry Repton, *View of the Welbeck Estate*, detail, in *Sketches and Hints on Landscape Gardening*, London, 1794
PAGES 2–3: Jean-Honoré Fragonard, *Le Petit Parc* (No. 10)
FRONTISPIECE: Caspar David Friedrich, *Moonlit Landscape* (No. 64)
PAGE 10: Johann Heinrich Wilhelm Tischbein, *Goethe in the Roman Campagna*, 1787, Städel Museum, Frankfurt am Main

The Morgan Library & Museum

FOUNDATION *for* LANDSCAPE STUDIES

FIRST EDITION, 2010

PRINTED IN CHINA BY C&C OFFSET

✒ Contents

❧ Foreword

This exhibition demonstrates the many ways in which the philosophical principles and aesthetic ideals of the Romantic movement influenced landscape design in Europe and America toward the end of the eighteenth and for much of the nineteenth century. Romanticism covers a lot of ground: spanning centuries and crossing borders, it has shaped nearly every kind of human expression—not just art, music, and literature but also architecture, fashion, and interior decoration. The full effect of this wide-ranging cultural movement is even more apparent out of doors—in parks and gardens intended to enhance the appreciation of nature as a liberating force, a fount of inspiration, a source of spiritual sustenance, and a refuge from the rigors of a newly emerging industrial society. Cultural critics decried the constraints of formal gardens and argued for new styles of design in theoretical tracts and lavishly illustrated landscape albums—an impressive array of publications attesting to the artistic and intellectual ferment of the Romantic era. It is the purpose of this exhibition to trace the transmission of these ideas in books and prints, to recognize their origins in literary manuscripts, and to show how they were interpreted by the leading artists of the period.

The Morgan Library & Museum is fortunate to have strong holdings in garden history along with the artistic and literary resources to explore its cultural context. Mrs. J. P. Morgan, Jr. (1868–1925), collected the work of botanical artists and landscape architects such as Humphry Repton, whose manuscript proposals for the redesign of two English estates entered the Morgan with the rest of her collection as gifts of her sons, Junius S. Morgan and Henry S. Morgan. Gifts from Paul Mellon, the bequest of Julia P. Wightman, and recent acquisitions made on the Gordon N. Ray Fund have made it possible to compare styles of garden design in England, France, Germany, and China. We have outstanding material for the study of Romanticism in the books and manuscripts of Dannie and Hettie Heineman, donated by the Heineman Foundation. For splendid drawings by Romantic artists, we are indebted to the continuing generosity of Eugene and Clare Thaw.

The first and last items in this exhibition, and many others in between, are loans from Elizabeth Barlow Rogers, who has also made important contributions as co-curator of the catalogue and author of the introductory essay. A collector, scholar, educator, author, and parks activist par excellence, she was the founding president of the Central Park Conservancy and served as administrator of Central Park from 1979 to 1995. She is president of the Foundation for Landscape Studies, which sponsors research in the field and publishes the journal *Site/Lines*, a forum for the dissemination of research and critical commentary on garden history and related topics.

I am immensely grateful to the many donors whose generosity to the Morgan and excitement about this project have made the exhibition and catalogue possible: to the Johansson Family Foundation; Janine Luke and Melvin R. Seiden; The Bodman Foundation; Charles C. Butt; The Chilton Foundation; and the Heineman Foundation for their generous support and to The Foundation for Landscape Studies; the Graham Foundation for Advanced Studies in the Fine Arts; Patrick and Elizabeth Gerschel; Furthermore, a program of the J. M. Kaplan Fund, Inc.; the German Consulate General in New York; the Consulate General of the Republic of Poland in New York; and the Andrew W. Mellon Fund for Research and Publications for generously underwriting the catalogue.

The exhibition was organized by John Bidwell, Astor Curator of Printed Books and Bindings, who wrote a portion of the catalogue. Most of the catalogue is the work of Elizabeth S. Eustis, who has curated other exhibits on kindred themes and teaches in the Landscape Institute at the Boston Architectural College. She has also lent two items to the exhibition. Vanessa Bezemer Sellers wrote the account of Dutch garden design (No. 18). Karen Banks, Publications Manager, supervised the production of the catalogue, which was edited by Patricia Emerson, Senior Editor, designed by Jerry Kelly, and illustrated with photographs secured by Marilyn Palmeri and Eva Soos in the Morgan's Photography and Rights Department. Conservators Maria Fredericks, Frank Trujillo, and Reba Snyder prepared material for photography and installation in the exhibition. I am very grateful for their efforts as well as for the advice and assistance provided by co-publishers David Godine and the Foundation for Landscape Studies.

Several institutions very kindly agreed to lend to the exhibition. For their participation in this project, I would like to express my appreciation to staff members of the Avery Library, Columbia University; the Cooper-Hewitt, National Design Museum; Frances Loeb Library, Graduate School of Design, Harvard University; Fürst-Pückler-Museum Schloss Branitz; Stiftung Fürst-Pückler-Park Bad Muskau; the Library of Congress; the Metropolitan Museum of Art; the New York City Department of Parks & Recreation; the NYC Department of Records/Municipal Archives; the New York Public Library, Astor, Lenox and Tilden Foundations; the Olana State Historic Site; and the Department of Rare Books and Special Collections, Firestone Library, Princeton University. Registrars John D. Alexander and Erin Hyde secured the loans for the exhibition. Special mention should be made of Cord Panning, who helped to coordinate the loans from German institutions.

The Morgan's holdings, supplemented by these loans, have given us the means to illustrate the greatest achievements of Romantic landscape design along with lesser-known ventures that show how the new styles were developed and transmitted. Of course we cannot claim to have presented a comprehensive account of these stylistic innovations, which were adapted in a multitude of variations to accommodate different cultural priorities, social agenda, and financial resources, not to mention the exigencies of climate and terrain. But we have been able to trace the most significant lines of influence beginning with private estates in England and converging in one of the greatest public parks in the world, here in New York City. I think that it is singularly appropriate that this exhibition should take place in New York, where one can enjoy the Romantic amenities of Central Park and learn what made them possible by viewing books, manuscripts, and works of art in the galleries of the Morgan Library & Museum.

WILLIAM M. GRISWOLD
Director, The Morgan Library & Museum

ELIZABETH BARLOW ROGERS

"The Genius of the Place" The Romantic Landscape, 1700–1900

THE ROMANTIC ETHOS

Romanticism transformed human consciousness and social behavior so deeply and thoroughly that we speak of the Romantic movement as a revolution in Western culture. Although not consciously formulated as such until the final years of the eighteenth century,[1] Romanticism was, like all large shifts in cultural values, a continuing process over an extended period. Its preconditions were established in the early 1700s, and its influence, which reached its peak during the first half of the nineteenth century, still asserts itself in certain societal, personal, and aesthetic attitudes today.

Defining Romanticism is much more difficult than defining Classicism. Usually considered Romanticism's opposite, Classicism is typically associated with rationality, order, balance, rules, and ideal models. Romanticism, on the other hand, gives primacy to emotion and the senses, prizing intuition and inspiration and putting a premium on the dramatic, spectacular, fantastic, and mysterious. Consciousness of the self is its hallmark. The theater of the mind, where imagination has free rein, is its sphere of action. Moreover, it grants the individual unprecedented social and political importance, championing original genius, personal sentiment, and individual liberty.

Democratic in spirit, the Romantic era saw the overthrow of absolute monarchy. Aristocratic privilege gave way to an allegiance to the state and the concomitant rise of nationalism and patriotic sentiment. The Romantic era was also one of tremendous economic change. It encompassed the Industrial Revolution, the rapid enlargement of cities, the rise of commerce, and the social and political empowerment of the middle class.

Finally, and most important for our purposes here, Romanticism defined a profoundly new attitude toward nature. Its exponents considered the natural world in spiritual and aesthetic terms as well as from cosmological and scientific standpoints.

With these thoughts in mind, the following propositions are intended to state the several and often contradictory tenets, tendencies, and attributes that form the complex ethos called Romanticism.

Romanticism holds that there is no such thing as self-evident truth discoverable by rational deduction or induction, only personal feeling, which may be shared yet remains unique to each individual.

Romanticism is rooted in the notion that the individual can gain knowledge and understanding through the senses as well as through the mind.

Romanticism ranks sentiment above logic.

Romanticism forsakes moderation for fervor.

Romanticism champions personal religious values over ecclesiastical authority.

Romanticism is contemptuous of court life and aristocratic privilege, defending individual rights and the dissolution of the bonds of servitude.

Romanticism prizes memory and mood, giving license to nostalgia, affection, and melancholy and adding a new depth of meaning to history, family ties, and death.

Romanticism promotes unsophisticated primitivism and the abandonment of social convention.

Romanticism is drawn to things rural, common, and aged: the rustic cottage and the old mill, the graveyard beside the country church, and the peasant's time-honored toil.

Romanticism has a penchant for the faraway and the exotic.

Romanticism nostalgically cherishes classical antiquity and the Middle Ages.

Romanticism values modernity; it embraces the novel and puts faith in civilization's progress.

Romanticism eschews norms in favor of diversity and eclecticism.

Romanticism chooses spontaneity as its modus operandi; the sketch, the letter, and the journal entry are its typical modes of expression, often serving as the means of capturing and preserving the emotion of the moment as a future subject.

Romanticism prefers nature in its wilder and dramatic guise; the blasted oak, the mountain torrent, the rocky coast, and the snow-crowned peak are its hallmarks.

Romanticism celebrates nature's tranquility and bounty.

Romanticism sees the universe as dynamic and organic rather than as mechanistic and foreordained.

Romanticism is constant change, a continual becoming rather than a perpetual state of being.

Romanticism is transcendental belief; in the face of scientific rationalism, technological innovation, materialism, and secularization, it holds nature divine.

Romanticism believes the only valid psychology is that of the individual, that nature is humanity's benign nurse, best teacher, and artistic muse.

In summary, the Romantic ethos is a compound of various and often opposing beliefs and preferences. For all its fluidity and multiplicity of contradictory perspectives, it is characterized first and foremost by a new sense of the meaning of the individual, society, and nature as well as their relationship to one another.

Yet Romanticism is not a single movement coloring all societies with the same brush. Indeed, nations, like individuals, have temperaments, and these are brought to bear on international culture in different ways. While it is possible to say that the inspiration and consolation of nature is a paramount and universal theme for Romantic philosophers, writers, and artists, Romanticism as a response to nature is by no means the same thing everywhere, nor is it an unvarying phenomenon during each decade of the 200-year time frame discussed here. Distinctions must be made between

Romanticism's divergent inflections according to indigenous predisposition.

Distinctions must also be made among the ways in which various arts considered here—literature, painting, and landscape design—are capable of expressing Romantic ideals. Romantic artists and writers are unfettered in their ability to celebrate nature's raw power. By contrast landscape designers operate within boundaries of domestic and civic space. For this reason they must contend with the preexisting conditions of a specific site.

Landscape designers can, however, borrow certain principles from painters and poets. Indeed, the Picturesque style imitates the ruggedness, ruins, and rusticity found in much eighteenth-century landscape painting. Typical Picturesque tropes are vegetation verging toward the wild; naturalistic rockwork; rude structures made of tree branches, moss, and thatch; pretend hamlets; faux hermitages; cascades; grottoes; fallen abbeys; and exotic features, such as "Turkish" tents and "Chinese" bridges and teahouses. These are often depicted in guidebooks offering suggested itineraries for touring gardens or parks (Nos. 7, 14, 42, and 45).

In addition, pattern and model books—such as *Magazijn van Tuin-sieraaden* (1802–9) by Gijsbert van Laar, a pictorial survey of a wide variety of garden buildings, gates, bridges, and sculpture as well as all manner of garden furniture, decorations, and possible layouts—provided examples for landscape designers (No. 18 and Fig. 1). Gardens designed in this manner are gardens of sentiment; each Picturesque feature is meant to elicit an intended response. In this regard monuments to national and literary heroes are sometimes integrated into Picturesque landscapes.

Moreover, in discussing Romanticism, we cannot discount the influence of the classical heritage of Italy, particularly the ancient ruins in and around Rome and Naples. But the attraction of Italy for Romantics did not result, as it did for many of their contemporaries, in Neoclassicism. It was, rather, a poetic attraction to the ruins of Roman antiquity and the Renaissance—in other words, an emotionally imaginative response to a vanished *past*—that brought many artists, literary figures, and tourists alike to Italy. Some, including Goethe, also sought the tangible heritage of Greece at Paestum and in Sicily. For artists especially, a sojourn in Italy was long considered a necessary prelude to one's subsequent career. Thus we find English painters—ranging from numerous topographical watercolorists to the mystical Samuel Palmer—French artists, such as Charles-Joseph Natoire, Jean-Honoré Fragonard, and Hubert Robert, the German Johann Christian Reinhart, and the American Thomas Cole all going to Italy not only to be schooled in the techniques of the old masters but also for that country's abundant opportunities for depicting the charm of ruins (Nos. 9, 10, 11, and 12).

In addition to being a direct source of artistic capital, Italy—especially the ruin-strewn Roman Campagna as found in the landscapes of the seventeenth-century French artists Claude and Poussin—was a potent secondary font of inspiration and influence. This was true not only of the fine arts but also of landscape design. As we shall see below, because of his interest in architecture and his pivotal position within contemporary intellectual circles, Lord Burlington was a seminal figure in this regard. His tour of Italy with his protégé William Kent—considered by some to be the originator of the naturalistic style of garden design in England—was of great importance to the British nobility who soon began to embellish their country seats. For example, several of the numerous small temples at Stowe, the most important garden of the age, were built as allusions to antique classical themes. Moreover the numerous engravings of Roman ruins, both real and imaginary, by their eighteenth-century Italian contemporary Piranesi were more than souvenirs for Grand Tourists to take home; they were also testaments to the elegiac beauty of vanished empire (Fig. 2).

In its mature phase, the Picturesque and the poetically classical are only an incidental part of the Romantic landscape. By the nineteenth century, artists, poets, and landscape designers sought to incorporate into their works views of distant scenery and an expanse of sky whose spaciousness and hourly and seasonal mutability were capable of stirring the spirit. Park makers, such as Prince Pückler-Muskau

and Frederick Law Olmsted, employed considerable ingenuity in order to produce seamless transitions from both the domestic and the urban landscape to the rural countryside. Like their peer poets and painters, they believed in nature's sublimity as the true domain of the human heart and mind.

Fig. 1. Illustration in Gijsbert van Laar, *Magazijn van Tuin-sieraaden*, Te Zalt-Bommel, 1831(?), collection of Elizabeth Barlow Rogers

Fig. 2. Giovanni Battista Piranesi, *Tempi del sole e della luna*, illustration in *Le magnificenze di Roma*, 1751, collection of Elizabeth Barlow Rogers

* * *

Speaking in very broad generalities, we can characterize Romanticism in England as a predominantly literary and artistic phenomenon. In France, on the other hand, it is both philosophical and theatrical in nature. For Germans, Romanticism is introspective and all-encompassing, with a mystical dimension that is rooted in a profound attachment to folk, fatherland, and forest. American Romanticism is essentially religious, rooted in Transcendentalist belief in Nature's inherent divinity.

These statements, however, deserve immediate qualification and amplification, for Romanticism is truly an international movement, and the above traits are shared in varying degrees among various cultures. The ethos of a historical period is broadly pervasive, not localized, arising spontaneously in many places. In addition, the currents and countercurrents of influence flowed as freely then—and only slightly more slowly—between countries as they do now.

For example, while English poetry and landscape theory chauvinistically celebrated English naturalistic design, the English garden became an eagerly accepted model that was appropriated by other cultures and translated into a native idiom. In turn, the Transcendentalist perspectives of German philosophy influenced English and American thought. Jean-Jacques Rousseau was much more than a French *philosophe;* the influence of this self-proclaimed citizen of Geneva was far-flung. His view of the garden as the arena of prompted meditation and reverie permeated Western culture at the same time that his revolutionary philosophy of the rights of man nourished the ideal of democracy as a system of governance. In America, even as the abundant sublimity of nature became a source of spiritual ecstasy for some, the country's natural riches stirred another kind of faith in others. The notion of a divinely ordained continental conquest and the concomitant commercial exploitation of the country's mineral ores, forest timbers, lakes, and rivers represent the alternate Romantic notion of human progress. This economic ideal stimulated the immigration of many people from

several countries, and over time their attitudes and philosophies inevitably commingled with a more distinctly American version of Romanticism.

These caveats are intended to make us mindful of the danger of being too categorical with regard to a broadly pervasive movement in Western culture. Nevertheless, viewing Romanticism through different cultural prisms will yield a more nuanced view of this multifaceted phenomenon.

ROMANTICISM IN ENGLAND

One important strain of the Romantic movement in England is Englishness itself—an Englishness that cherishes the green pastoral countryside with its hedgerows, fields, and grazing cattle (Fig. 3). This gentle landscape has been immortalized by the words of Shakespeare, Thomson, Wordsworth, and numerous other poets. The country has its wilder reaches as well, and once travel became less difficult and dangerous, these became destinations for travelers and subjects of Romantic poetry and artists' sketches.

A fascination with myth and antiquity was a decided part of eighteenth- and nineteenth-century England's mental landscape. Pastoral Arcadia and the notion of a vanished Golden Age, combined with Virgilian themes of nature and empire, seeded the Romantic imagination. Like the classical ruins of Italy, the country's moldering medieval monasteries were seen through romantic and nationalistic eyes as metaphors of England's own antiquity (No. 39 and Fig. 4). They were memorialized in verse and painting because of their poetical and artistic decay. Significantly, their restoration in accordance with today's ethos of historic preservation would have symbolized a return to a system of values that was being discarded by mid-eighteenth-century libertarians. Indeed, the efforts of Whig lords to promote parliamentary rule formed an important cornerstone of English Romanticism. They deemed the landscape itself emblematic, and they sought to promote the notion that their naturalistically designed estate parks, visually uniting their great houses with bucolic pastures, streams, fields, and hedgerows, were expressions of the political ideals of a freedom-loving nation.

John Locke, the 3rd Earl of Shaftsbury, and Joseph Addison

Philosophically underlying this dual ideal of a symbolically unfettered domestic landscape and a restrained monarchy was Locke's espousal of political freedom as a fundamental principle. Locke's belief that all knowledge must come through sensory experience—not, as Descartes suggested, by means of pure reason—profoundly nourished the new attitude toward landscape design, which can be said to have been the seedbed in which Romanticism was to flower.

The application of Locke's theory of sensory awareness can be ascribed to his follower, Anthony Ashley Cooper, 3rd Earl of Shaftsbury. Significantly, Shaftsbury invoked the "Genius of the Place,"[2] the spirit that interacts with the human mind, eliciting emotion, nurturing memory, and fostering awareness of God, the Great Genius of creation. Shaftsbury advocated grottoes, cascades, and other dramatically charged landscape forms as a means of stimulating mental association with nature's mysteries. At the same time, his contemporary Joseph Addison enunciated a proto-Romantic theory in which the "pleasures of the imagination which arise from the actual view and survey of outward objects . . . proceed from the sight of what is *great, uncommon,* or *beautiful*." Anticipating late-eighteenth-century proponents of the Picturesque, he said, "[T]here is something more bold and masterly in the rough careless strokes of Nature than in the nice touches and embellishments of art." For him, "[T]he beauties of the most stately garden or palace lie in a narrow compass [whereas] in the wide fields of Nature, the sight wanders up and down without confinement, and is fed with an infinite variety of images, without any certain stint or number." For this reason, landowners might look at properties in a new light, for according to Addison, "Fields of Corn make a pleasant Prospect, and if the Walks were a little taken care of that lie between them, if the natural Embroidery of the Meadows were helpt and improved by some small Additions of Art, and the several Rows of Hedges set off by Trees and Flowers, that the Soil was capable of receiving, a Man might make a pretty Landskip of his own Possessions."[3]

Addison's suggestion helped give rise to the *ferme ornée,* exemplified in the Leasowes, the country seat of William Shenstone (1714–1763),

Fig. 3. John Constable, *Wivenhoe Park, Essex,* 1816, Widener Collection, National Gallery of Art, Washington, DC

Fig. 4. Fountains Abbey, near Ripon, North Yorkshire, England, photograph by Elizabeth Barlow Rogers

and Woburn Farm, the estate of Philip Southcote (1698–1758), where fields were melded with scenery of a more contrived sort.[4] His endorsement of the apparent artlessness of Chinese gardens, which "conceal the Art by which they direct themselves,"[5] supplied landowners with another rationale for irregular layouts with winding paths.

James Thomson

Unconstrained by such theories of gardenmaking, the Scottish poet and ardent patriot (he wrote the hymn "Rule Britannia") James Thomson (1700–1748) was able to prefigure Romanticism more closely in *The Seasons*, a four-part poem published in its entirety in 1730, in which he rhapsodically carries the theme of nature's soul-stirring power to new heights (No. 13).

Of "Philosophic Melancholy" he begs:

> Oh bear me then to vast, embowering shades!
> To twilight groves, and visionary vales!
> To weeping grottoes, and prophetic glooms!
> Where angel-forms athwart the solemn dusk,
> Tremendous sweep, or seem to sweep along;
> And voices more than human, thro' the void
> Deep-founding, seize th' enthusiastic ear.[6]

With exultant rapture, the poet then greets winter:

> See WINTER comes, to rule the varied year;
> Sullen, and sad, with all his rising train,
> VAPOURS, and CLOUDS, AND STORMS. Be these my
>   theme,
> These, that exalt the soul to solemn thought,
> And heavenly musing. Welcome, kindred glooms!
> Congenial horrors, hail![7]

Alexander Pope

Thomson's contemporary Alexander Pope (1688–1744) also invoked mythic presences in nature to assist him in singing a song of rapture in "Windsor Forest."

> Thy forests, Windsor! And thy green retreats,
> At once the Monarch's and the Muse's seats,
> Invite my lays. Be present, Sylvan Maids!
> Unlock your springs, and open all your shades.[8]

Pope did not feel that Newtonian science ran counter to this emotional attitude toward nature; if anything his woodland muses confirmed the Deist view of a universe whose mechanical operation was ordered by a supreme being. In his memorable epitaph of the father of the Enlightenment, Pope proclaimed, "Nature, and Nature's Laws lay hid in Night, God said: *Let Newton be,* and All was Light."

Although no one would consider Pope a Romantic poet, his influence on the creation of actual landscapes in which Nature was the guiding force was revolutionary. With missionary zeal, he encouraged his countrymen—many of whom eagerly sought his advice—to forsake the geometrical Anglo-Dutch gardens that were fashionable during the reign of William and Mary (1689–1702). His *"Epistle to Lord Burlington"* (No. 6) sounded the clarion call for a new manner of gardening:

> To build, to plant, whatever you intend,
> To rear the Column, or the Arch to bend,
> To swell the Terras, or to sink the Grot;
> In all, let Nature never be forgot.
> But treat the Goddess like a modest fair,
> Nor over-dress, nor leave her wholly bare;
> Let not each beauty ev'ry where be spy'd,
> Where half the skill is decently to hide.
> He gains all points, who pleasingly confounds,
> Surprizes, varies, and conceals the Bounds.
> Consult the Genius of the Place in all;
> That tells the Waters or to rise, or fall,
> Or helps th' ambitious Hill the heav'n to scale,
> Or scoops in circling theatres the Vale,
> Calls in the Country, catches opening glades,
> Joins willing woods, and varies shades from shades,
> Now breaks or now directs, th' intending Lines;
> Paints as you plant, and, as you work, designs.
> Still follow Sense, of ev'ry Art the Soul,
> Parts answ'ring parts shall slide into a whole,
> Spontaneous beauties all around advance,
> Start ev'n from Difficulty, strike from Chance;
> Nature shall join you, Time shall make it grow
> A Work to wonder at—perhaps a STOW.[9]

Pope's own garden at Twickenham was famed for its remarkable three-chambered grotto, which was conceived as a place both to soothe and stimulate the mind. Its walls were studded with mineral specimens, shells, and mirrors to reflect and multiply the view. Pope was proud to claim that in creating this eighteenth-century version of a classical nymphaeum, with its artificial stalactites, imbedded minerals, and dripping water, he had "strictly followed Nature." Here he was able to engage in reverie, literary pursuit, or conversation with his constant stream of visitors. The garden itself, like others of the early eighteenth century, retained a fundamentally axial plan even as a new experimental approach to the organization of space was developing (No. 4).

Lord Burlington

Although a Catholic Tory, Pope was a friend of several Whig lords who shared his interest in garden design. The most prominent was Richard Boyle, 3rd Earl of Burlington and 4th Earl of Cork (1694–1753), an amateur architect and the center of a coterie of classicists who sought to further Palladian architectural principles and Virgilian values of rural life among England's landed aristocracy. At Chiswick, Burlington built a small-scale version of Palladio's Villa Rotonda; over a twenty-year period beginning in 1725 he created a surrounding garden that combined the artfully irregular with elements of the old geometrical order (Fig. 5).

The contrived quasi-naturalistic design of the garden at Chiswick is not unlike that found in the architect Robert Castell's depictions of one of Pliny the Younger's (ca. A.D. 61–112) two Roman villa gardens. Like other architects inspired over the course of time by the two letters Pliny wrote describing these pleasant retreats, Castell gave graphic expression to his design hypotheses. *The Villas of the Ancients* (1728), a sumptuous book of engravings commissioned by Lord Burlington (No. 3), presents a series of architectural plans of buildings and gardens with accompanying descriptions. These inevitably embody the ideas of Burlington and his circle to as great a degree as they do the descriptions of Pliny. Thus we have the author discoursing on garden history as a progression from the utilitarian selection of plants "grateful either to the Sight, Smell, or Taste, and refreshed by Shade and Water . . . within a fixt Compass of Ground," to "a Manner of laying out the Ground and Plantations of Gardens by the Rule and Line," to one illustrative of "the present Manner of Designing in *China,* . . . where, tho' the Parts are disposed with the greatest Art, the Irregularity is still preserved; so that their Manner may not improperly be said to be an artful Confusion, where there is no Appearance of that Skill which is made use of, their *Rocks, Cascades,* and *Trees,* bearing their natural Forms."[10]

Though it is not certain, it is likely that Castell had seen the copy of Matteo Ripa's (1682–1746) copperplate views of Chinese gardens, which Lord Burlington had acquired by sometime after 1724. Father Ripa had resided at the Manchu court of the Kangxi emperor, and his engravings were among the first illustrations of their kind to reach the West (No. 2). They depict landscapes in which winding paths thread their way through asymmetrical garden layouts and mountainous scenery (Fig. 6). Castell's interesting conflation of

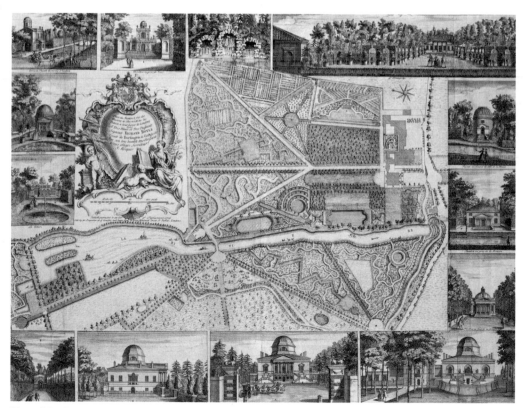

Fig. 5. John Rocque, *Plan du Jardin et Vuë des Maisons de Chiswick,* illustration in Thomas Badeslade, *Vitruvius Brittanicus,* volume 4, London, 1739, Royal Academy of Arts, London

Fig. 6. Matteo Ripa, Views of Jehol, Jehol, China, 1713(?), The Morgan Library & Museum

Fig. 7. Courtyard garden and maze, detail in Laurens Scherm, *Waare af-beelding van 't koninglyk lust-hof van zyn britannische majesteit, Willem de derde, op 't Loo,* ca. 1700, collection of Elizabeth Barlow Rogers

the geometrical and the irregular is especially apparent in his plan of Pliny's Tuscum garden.

Horace Walpole

Horace Walpole (1717–1797), writing a half century later, chauvinistically, and with libertarian zeal, spurned all foreign influences on the English garden, which in his view could only be a product of a free nation. He drew a critically biased distinction between it and the gardens of France, whose strict geometries he censured as symbols of monarchial authoritarianism (No. 15). In his "Essay on Modern Gardens," he heaps scorn on Pliny, asking rhetorically with regard to Tuscum, which he likens to the English gardens built in the prior century, during the reign of William and Mary, and now out of fashion: "and what was the principal beauty of that pleasure-ground? Exactly what was the admiration of this country about threescore years ago; box-trees cut into monsters, animals, letters, and the names of the master and the artificer"[11] (No. 1 and Fig. 7).

For Walpole the revolutionary modern garden truly originated at Stowe, the seat of Richard Temple, first viscount of Cobham. His essay lavishes the following encomium on William Kent (1685–1748):

> At that moment appeared Kent, painter enough to taste the charms of landscape, bold and opinionative enough to dare and to dictate, and born with a genius to strike out a great system from the twilight of imperfect essays. He leaped the fence, and saw that all nature was a garden. He felt the delicious contrast of hill and valley changing imperceptibly into each other, tasted the beauty of the gentle swell, or concave scoop, and remarked how loose groves crowned an easy eminence with happy ornament, and while they called in the distant view between their graceful stems, removed and extended the perspective by delusive comparison.[12]

It goes on to proclaim how Kent achieved his signal victory of articulating this first unalloyed naturalistic landscape design idiom in Stowe's Elysian Fields:

> Thus the pencil of his imagination bestowed all the arts of landscape on the scenes he handled. The great principles on which he worked were perspective, and light and shade.... His buildings, his seats, his temples, were more the works of his pencil than of his compasses. We owe the restoration of Greece and the diffusion of architecture to his skill in landscape....
>
> [Because of Kent's] dealing in none but the colours of nature, and catching its most favourable features, men saw a new creation opening before their eyes. The living landscape was chastened or polished, not transformed. Freedom was given to the forms of trees; they extended their branches unrestricted, and where any eminent oak, or master beech had escaped maiming and survived the forest, bush and bramble was removed, and all its honours were restored to distinguish and shade the plain. Where the united plumage of an ancient wood extended wide its undulating canopy, and stood venerable in its darkness, Kent thinned the foremost ranks, and left but so many detached and scattered trees, as softened the approach of gloom and blended a chequered light with the thus lengthened shadows of the remaining columns.[13]

In his subsequent development of the Grecian Meadow at Stowe, Lancelot "Capability" Brown, still at the beginning of his long career as England's most sought-after landscape designer, expanded the Kentian landscape, showing how to put into practice Pope's advice to Lord Burlington to "scoop in circling theaters the vale" and then "conceal its bounds."

Stowe was the cynosure of the age and a must-see for every tourist with an interest in landscape, including Thomas Jefferson. We should note, however, that although Stowe may foreshadow the Romantic garden, Kent and Brown cannot truly be considered Romantic designers. Stowe is rather an emblematic landscape in which seemingly unbounded meadows and vales and an irregularly shaped lake, curving paths, and casual arrangement of trees were intended to signal the ascension of parliamentary governance and the disempowerment of monarchy by the Whig party in the years following the Glorious Revolution. In addition, at the dawn of Britain's imperial expansion, the numerous small temples adorning Stowe's landscape were invested with symbolic meanings evoking national ambition (No. 7 and Fig. 8). Further inspiration for the landscape at Stowe and other contemporary great estates was the idyllic scenery of vanished antiquity found in the paintings of Claude Lorrain and Nicolas Poussin purchased by young nobles on the Grand Tour. In their Arcadian overtones and naturalistic layouts, these gardens may be considered harbingers of the mature Romantic landscape (Fig. 9).

Fig. 8. The Temple of British Worthies, Stowe, photograph by Elizabeth Barlow Rogers

Edmund Burke

Reinforcing Locke's premise of the relationship between the senses and the mind, the philosopher and political theorist Edmund Burke (1729–1797) gave precise categorical definitions to the corresponding effects on the senses of varied kinds of stimuli. In his 1757 treatise on aesthetics, *A Philosophical Enquiry into the Origin of Our Ideas of the Sublime and the Beautiful,* he equated the Sublime with those scenes that, because of their awesome size, sharp colors, startling sounds, associations with the unknown, and abrupt irregularities, cause a sensation best described as admiring terror or fearful wonder. Beauty, on the other hand, was seen to excite "the passion of love, or some correspondent affection" and was to be found in such qualities as smallness, smoothness, delicacy, soft hues, melodious music, gently undulating surfaces, and curving lines.

Even before Burke had codified the tenets of the Beautiful and the Sublime, young Horace Walpole had found himself enthralled by the scenery of Savoy that he saw on his Grand Tour in 1739.

Fig. 9. Claude Lorrain, *Pastoral Landscape: The Roman Campagna,* ca. 1639, The Metropolitan Museum of Art, New York

Precipices, mountains, torrents, wolves, rumblings, Salvator Rosa . . . . But the road, . . . the Road! Winding round a prodigious mountain, and surrounded by others, all shagged with hanging woods, obscured with pines, or lost in clouds! Below, a torrent breaking through cliffs, and tumbling through fragments of rocks! Sheets of cascades . . . hasting into the roughened river at the bottom! Now and then an old footbridge, with a broken rail, a leaning cross, a cottage, or the ruin of a hermitage! This sounds too bombastic and too romantic to one that has not seen it, too cold for one that has.[14]

William Chambers

Such proto-Romantic fantasies found their greatest exponent in the Scottish architect William Chambers (1723–1796). Chambers had visited China in 1744 and 1748 as a representative of the Swedish East India Company. Assigning to the Chinese some of his more bizarre garden visions in his *Dissertation on Oriental Gardening* (1772), he praised their manner of combining the "pleasing, horrid, and enchanting. . . . Their enchanted scenes answer, in a great measure, to what we call romantic, and in these they make use of several artifices to excite surprize."[15] In addition to associating the Chinese garden with eerie wind sounds emitted from cavities and the display of monstrous animals, Chambers went so far as to include such thrill-inducing artifacts as "temples dedicated to the king of vengeance, deep caverns in the rocks, and descents to subterraneous habitations, overgrown with brushwood and brambles, near which are placed pillars of stone, with pathetic descriptions of tragical events, and many horrid acts of cruelty, perpetrated there by robbers and outlaws of former times"—elements that would subsequently find their way into the Romantic novel.[16] Indeed, he maintained of the Chinese that "Their surprizing, or supernatural scenes, are of the romantic kind, and abound in the marvellous."[17]

Chambers was not, however, primarily a sensationalist but rather a well-respected architect and tutor to the Prince of Wales. Trained in France, he practiced a conservative style of Palladian-influenced Neoclassicism. Still, he wished to make a name for himself by promoting the fashion for *chinoiserie*, which he did in 1757 by publishing simultaneously in English and French *Designs for Chinese Buildings, Furniture, Dresses, Machines and Utensils*.[18] Essentially ornamental rather than functional, the models he depicted in this lavish folio volume were for the most part intended to serve as ornamental garden features (Fig. 10). As court architect to Augusta, Dowager Princess of Wales, Chambers was able to demonstrate at Kew Palace his notion of the garden as a collection of exotic and antique features. His *Plans, Elevations, Sections, and Perspective Views of the Gardens and Buildings at Kew, in Surrey*, published in 1763, depicts the still-extant ten-story-tall pagoda and other structures, including the Ruined Arch, the Temple of Bellona, and the Temple of Aeolus (No. 20).

Thomas Whately

Drawing upon the aesthetic principles Burke had expounded earlier, Chambers's contemporary Thomas Whately (d. 1772), a government official and landscape connoisseur, helped promote garden design as one of the liberal arts in his *Observations on Modern Gardening* (1770). Like Burke, Whately advocated what some landscape historians now term *associationism*—the correspondence of scene and mood, a theory in which sensory impression and emotion go hand in hand. Thus, ruins in the landscape

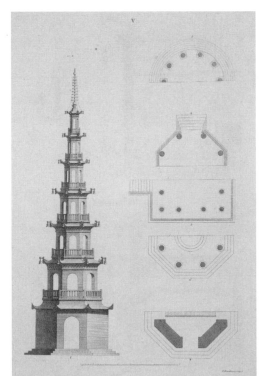

Fig. 10. Architectural rendering of a pagoda in William Chambers, *Plans, Elevations, Sections, and Perspective Views of the Gardens and Buildings at Kew*, London, 1763, collection of Elizabeth Barlow Rogers

were thought to inspire poetic thoughts of vanished ages. Dark-toned vegetation turned the mind into paths of somber reflection, bright green meadows soothed the agitated soul, sunny fields reminiscent of harvest revels raised the spirits to the level of gaiety, still brooks and placid lakes spoke of peace and serenity, and loud tumbling waterfalls induced the thrilling fear associated with the Sublime. Whately thus pointed the way for naturalistic scenery alone, rather than for temples and other objects placed in the landscape, to serve as prompts to certain ideas and reflections. Nature itself was thus ready to assume the role of primary design model.

"Capability" Brown

None illustrated this shift better than Lancelot "Capability" Brown (1716–1783), who was at this time England's most famous "improver," a term derived along with his moniker from his frequent statement to his numerous clients that their estates were capable of improvement. Brown dispensed with allusions to classical antiquity within the landscape; his designs are also devoid of monuments, statues, faux ruins, temples, and other objects associated with political values, historical events, or renowned personages. More aligned with Burke's definition of Beauty than of the Sublime, his lawns are gently rolling and smooth-surfaced, his paths gracefully curvilinear, and

his lakes placid and sinuous in outline. Brown planted trees in irregular clumps and belts while banishing ornamental parterres and shrubberies. His expansive views were achieved by melding park and garden with their agrarian surroundings by means of the ha-ha, a ditch or sunken fence that the eye traverses without disruption. This innovation also prevented cattle and sheep from straying into the domestic precinct. By making the landscape thus appear as a continuum from the steps of a lord's great house to his fields and hedgerows and thence to the belt of trees at the far border of his property, Brown became a precursor of a subsequent generation of Romantic landscape designers who saw space itself as an element—perhaps the most important element—in their work (Fig. 11).

Richard Payne Knight and Uvedale Price

By the time Brown had reached the height of his fame, eighteenth-century English landscape theory was abundant, passionate, and vituperative, and the much-admired improver became the subject of some very unflattering prose. His landscapes were considered by some to be insipid and formulaic. Richard Payne Knight (1750–1824) in *The Landscape: A Didactic Poem* (1794) and Uvedale Price (1747–1829) in *Essay on the Picturesque* (1794) and *An Analytical Inquiry into the Principles of Taste* (1805) rail

Fig. 11. Lancelot "Capability" Brown, Blenheim Lake, photograph by Elizabeth Barlow Rogers

Fig. 12. Salvator Rosa, *Bandits on a Rocky Coast*, The Metropolitan Museum of Art, New York

Fig. 13. Meindert Hobbema, *Village with Water Mill Among Trees*, ca. 1665, The Frick Collection, New York

against what to their eyes was Brown's blandness. Ignoring certain practicalities, they wondered why landscapes could not be designed as if they were painted pictures, with compositional interest in foreground, middle ground, and background. The term *Picturesque* also served as an intermediate category between the Beautiful and the Sublime to accommodate those degrees of rustic wildness found in nature that, while not as awesome and thrilling as the Sublime, have some of its romantic flavor. Designed landscapes could appropriate this aesthetic category as an ideal, and such was the ardor with which Knight and Price promulgated their views that the term fell into common usage and property owners began to think of their land as having the potential for Picturesque transformation.

While proponents of the Picturesque admired Claude's idyllic depictions of the ruin-studded scenery of the Roman Campagna, like Walpole, they held up as a model Salvator Rosa, whose theatrical scenes of wild and tumultuous nature populated by hermits and *banditi* were vastly appealing to their Romantic sensibilities (Fig. 12). They also found inspiration in the works of the seventeenth-century Dutch masters Jacob van Ruisdael and his pupil Meindert Hobbema, whose paintings of rutted lanes, humble cottages, water mills and shaggy, broken-limbed trees served as precursors of the rustic Picturesque (Fig. 13). Moreover, these artists' atmospheric, seemingly mutable, luminous, and darkening cloud-filled skies also heralded the Romanticism of John Constable. Price held the following aesthetic characteristics to be the principal elements of Picturesque landscape design: chiaroscuro effects; roughness of texture, surface, and outline; partial concealment; and variety. Comfort and good maintenance counted for very little with Knight and Price, and some landowners were understandably reluctant to subscribe to the notion of negligence as a means of achieving Picturesque estate grounds or to prefer rutted lanes to Brown's well-graded curvilinear drives (No. 26).

William Gilpin

By the time Price and Knight were writing their diatribes against Brown, the Reverend William Gilpin (1724–1804), another theorist of the Picturesque, had firmly implanted its criteria in the minds of most educated English landholders. The inherent impracticalities of some of the landscape design recommendations of these proponents were of no particular concern to those capable of enduring the hardships of travel in quest of nature's own Picturesque landscapes.

Because an understanding of the Beautiful, Picturesque, and Sublime offered the traveler a new means of critical appreciation, Grand Tourists had gradually shed their disdainful aversion to the discomforts and dangers of crossing the Alps in order to reach Italy. They learned to view majestic snow-capped peaks and vertiginous precipices with wary awe rather than fearful horror. Even before the Napoleonic Wars, which curtailed English travel on the Continent, Gilpin may be said to have begun a "see-England-first" trend with his several tour books intended to educate the traveler in the principles of the Picturesque as an approach to viewing the scenery of the wilder parts of western England, Wales, the Lake District, and the Highlands. To illustrate his prescriptions on how to compose scenes within the periphery of vision, he employed oval-shaped aquatints (then a new printmaking method) in several works.[19] He is known to have carried a handheld apparatus known as a Claude glass, which reflected the view in a slightly convex dark-tinted mirror, giving a frame, tone, and depth of shade to the scene that was being observed. According to him, it "combined two or three different colours; and if the hues are well sorted, they give the object of nature a soft, mellow tinge, like the colouring of that master"[20] (see Nos. 22 and 23).

Theorists of the Picturesque, such as Gilpin, Price, and Knight, were sometimes ridiculed for their finicky discrimination among different kinds of scenery. Thomas Rowlandson's illustrations in William Combe's satire, *Tour of Dr. Syntax, in Search of the Picturesque*, provide a Don Quixote–like caricature of the protagonist (No. 25). In a similar vein, Jane Austen poked gentle fun at the raging fashion for the Picturesque. In *Northanger Abbey*, the heroine, Catherine Morland, who is walking with Henry Tilney and his sister Eleanor, is confused and amazed by the language of the Picturesque.

> *They were viewing the country with the eyes of persons accustomed to drawing, and decided on its capability of being formed into pictures, with all the eagerness of real taste. . . . It seemed as if a good view were no longer to be taken from the top of an high hill, and that a clear blue sky was no longer a proof of a fine day. . . . a lecture on the picturesque immediately followed, in which his [Henry's] instructions were so clear that she soon began to see beauty in every thing admired by him. . . . He talked of foregrounds, distances, and second distances — side-screens and perspectives — lights and shades; — and Catherine was so hopeful a scholar, that when they gained the top of Beechen Cliff, she voluntarily rejected the whole city of Bath, as unworthy to make part of a landscape.*[21]

Fig. 14. William Radclyffe after David Cox, *Rhaiadyr y Wenol, near Capel Curig*, illustration in Thomas Roscoe, *Wanderings and Excursions in North Wales*, London, 1836, collection of Elizabeth Barlow Rogers

In spite of Austen's irony, the search for the Picturesque remained a popular pursuit. The wild scenery of England's western counties and of Wales continued to draw Romantics seeking the Sublime well into the nineteenth century, and lavish travel books brought views of ruined abbeys, cataracts, and castles into the homes of armchair travelers (Fig. 14).

Humphry Repton

A more sensible and middle-ground approach toward improving with taste—"taste" being the favorite expression for the aesthetic aspirations of the day—was taken by Humphry Repton (1752–1818), who assumed Brown's mantle as England's leading landscape designer after the latter's death in 1783. Understandably, his intention was not to proselytize in the manner of Knight and Price, but rather, like Brown, to please clients and obtain commissions.

Brown, unfortunately, left no written documents describing his theories and design practices. Repton, on the other hand, was a talented watercolorist who produced numerous beautifully illustrated manuscript and printed volumes. His Red Books, so named for their red morocco leather bindings, were unique works intended to demonstrate to a particular client how his property could be redesigned according to the principles of taste. To demonstrate this, he first painted a watercolor of the landscape as it would appear when transformed. He then concealed the lower portion of this image with flaps, leaving visible only the background and sky. Folding the flaps to hide what was beneath, he painted the existing unimproved site on the outside. The defects of its scenery were dramatized when his clients lifted the flaps and beheld their estates as they would appear when transformed by Repton (Nos. 27 and 28; Figs. 15 and 16).

Repton also understood the importance of the printed book to the success of his practice and finances as well as to the rise of his reputation. *Sketches and Hints on Landscape Gardening* (1795) was followed by other works, including *Observations on the Theory and Practice of Landscape Gardening* (1803), and a final collection of thoughts gathered from a busy lifetime, *Fragments on the Theory and Practice of Landscape Gardening* (1816). These books are notable in that, although they contain beautiful colored engravings of gardens designed by Repton, complete with overlay flaps like his Red Books, they are not simply descriptions with depictions of existing and proposed scenery but practical treatises with clear prescriptions on how to achieve various ends.

The Picturesque and Romanticism

The exact chronological boundaries of the Picturesque are difficult to define, and the differentiation of the Picturesque as a category separate from the Beautiful and the Sublime is even more vexed. It can best be considered as both an intermediate position and a mediating reconciliation of these two aesthetic oppositions. Sometimes the Picturesque landscape leans more toward the Beautiful, sometimes more toward the Sublime. Often it is a combination of both, its defining characteristic being that the actual scene, whether designed or simply observed, reflects the same compositional principles as a good landscape painting.

What then makes for the Picturesque? Tranquil views characterized as Beautiful are Picturesque if they conform to the artist's means of engaging the eye to traverse from foreground to middle ground to background within a unified compositional whole. The same discriminatory mode of viewing Sublime nature's dramatic power can also produce impressions categorized as Picturesque. The predilections of artists and tourists seeking the Picturesque do in fact seem to tend more toward the raw and the wild scenery of the romantically Sublime than to the serenely Beautiful. Craggy cliffs, distant mountains, moldering monasteries, wind-tossed trees, raging torrents, and crashing waves are the principal tropes of the genre.

Fig. 15. Water at Wentworth, Yorkshire, illustration with overlay down in Humphry Repton, *Observations on the Theory and Practice of Landscape Gardening,* London, 1803, collection of Elizabeth Barlow Rogers

Fig. 16. Water at Wentworth, Yorkshire, illustration with overlay up in Humphry Repton, *Observations on the Theory and Practice of Landscape Gardening,* London, 1803, collection of Elizabeth Barlow Rogers

The Picturesque can be considered to prefigure the Romantic movement while at the same time remaining an important part of its development—a necessary phase fostering the appreciation of the inherent qualities of natural and designed landscapes without relying on landscape painting as the teacher of the eye. It must therefore be seen as an essential prelude to a more complete and unified emotional response to nature in which the self-examined mind, collating simultaneous sensory impressions, experiences something beyond visual satisfaction. Here, where unadorned landscape scenery begins to elicit soul-stirring emotion, lies the threshold of true Romanticism. The notion of comprehensive sensory awareness leading to intimations of divinity—the transcendental union of nature and the human mind—forms the moral core of Romanticism. Put another way, the Picturesque is didactic, a set of instructions for enjoying and creating scenic views. To enter into the realm of Romanticism, the Picturesque must become something personal and experientially unique for each individual. To articulate the ways in which the human soul could be raised to new heights of awareness would take the pen of a great Romantic poet.

William Wordsworth

In "Lines Written a Few Miles Above Tintern Abbey" William Wordsworth (1770–1850) contrasted the respective emotions engendered by two walks taken beside the River Wye near the ruined Cistercian monastery, the first in 1793, the second, five years later, in the company of his sister Dorothy. William and Dorothy Wordsworth were hardly the travelers in search of the Picturesque that Gilpin had in mind when he wrote the scenic guide *Observations on the River Wye*. Their immersion in nature was a spiritual rather than an aesthetic enterprise. Indeed, in this great poem Wordsworth made no critical observations, for his focus was inward, not outward, and instead of analyzing scenery, he analyzed his emotions. In the beginning, recollecting his previous walk, he allowed that they were at that time generated purely by the senses.

The sounding cataract
Haunted me like a passion: the tall rock,
The mountain, and the deep and gloomy wood,
Their colours and their forms, were then to me
An appetite: a feeling and a love,
That had no need of a remoter charm,
By thought supplied, or any interest
Unborrowed from the eye.

Against this picture of turbulent and thrilling nature, he presented a quieter, yet equally passionate, deified vision of the Sublime in which the mind itself was the organ of perception. Counseling Dorothy, "my dear, dear Friend," to share with him the serene knowledge of a powerful, dynamic, invisible spirit pervading all of life, he wrote:

I have learned
To look on nature, not as in the hour
Of thoughtless youth, but hearing oftentimes
The still, sad music of humanity,
Not harsh nor grating, though of ample power
To chasten and subdue. And I have felt
A presence that disturbs me with the joy
Of elevated thoughts; a sense sublime
Of something far more deeply interfused,
Whose dwelling is the light of setting suns,
And the round ocean, and the living air,
And the blue sky, and in the mind of man,
A motion and a spirit, that impels
All thinking things, all objects of all thought,
And rolls through all things. Therefore am I still
A lover of the meadows and the woods,
And mountains; and of all that we behold
From this green earth; of all the mighty world
Of eye and ear, both what they half-create,
And what perceive; well pleased to recognize
In nature and the language of the sense,
The anchor of my purest thoughts, the nurse,
The guide, the guardian of my heart, and soul
Of all my moral being.[22]

To see the Sublime in all of nature did not mean that the Wordsworths were unsympathetic to the prevailing taste for the Picturesque. Thus, in her Grasmere journal Dorothy noted spending a July Sunday morning reading "Mr Knight's *Landscape*" before she and her brother "walked up to view Rydale."[23] But Dorothy never analyzed such scenery in Knight's Picturesque terms. For her, as for William, landscape and firmament were inextricably bound. Light and sky, clouds and moon, watery reflections and wave motion, the rainbow—these elements constituted the acknowledged essence of beauty as well as spiritual tokens of nature's inherent divinity.

The unselfconsciousness of the Wordsworths' Romanticism makes them all the more convincing as exponents. The pages of Dorothy's journal are filled with a mixture of notes on the weather, visiting neighbors, gardening and homemaking activities, as well as rapturous responses to the local landscape. To take one example:

> [21 June 1800] *Saturday. In the morning W. and I went to Ambleside to get his tooth drawn with very little pain—he slept till 3 o'clock. Young Mr. S. drank tea and supped with us. They fished in Rydale water and they caught 2 small fishes—W. no bite—John 3. Miss Simpson and 3 children called—I walked with them to Rydale. The evening cold and clear and frosty but the wind was falling as I returned—I staid at home about an hour and then walked up the hill to Rydale lake. Grasmere looked so beautiful that my heart was almost melted away. It was quite calm, only spotted with sparkles of light. The church visible. On our return all distant objects had faded away—all but the hills. The reflection of the light bright sky above Black Quarter was very solemn. Mr. S. did not go till 12 o'clock.*[24]

Although not a landscape designer as such, Wordsworth had definite ideas on the subject. He felt that the garden maker should respect the "*sentiment* of the place," a telling substitute for Pope's "Genius of the Place." At Rhydal Mount, the Lake District villa near Grasmere where he and Dorothy resided after he had married, acquired a family, and grown famous, he laid out gardens in the Picturesque manner. They were adorned with rustic summerhouses, rock walls encrusted with moss and covered with vines, and steps with flowers squeezing through the paving stones.

In 1806, at the request of his friends Sir George and Lady Beaumont, Wordsworth sketched a plan that would convert an abandoned quarry at their country seat, Coleorton Hall, Leicestershire, into a one-acre winter garden planted with evergreen shrubs, cypresses, and firs. A pool at the quarry's edge reflected its craggy side walls and the tall spires of the conifers. Dorothy, who wrote most of her brother's correspondence, praised the site in a letter to Lady Beaumont, noting "the hillocks and slopes and the hollow shape of the whole" and adding that "[t]he natural shelving earthy fence which

it has at present might be made perfectly beautiful."[25] Wordsworth's recommendations included encircling the garden with two rings of evergreens: an outer one of tall firs "such as were likely to grow to the most majestic height" and an inner one of "evergreen shrubs, intermingled with Cypress." Beyond this border of winter color, augmented elsewhere with bird-attracting red-berried hollies (*Ilex aquifolium*) and *Pyracantha*, one would be able to glimpse "such parts of the Cottages as would have the best effect (I mean the beautiful one with Ivy, and the other which is of a very picturesque form but very shabby surface)."[26] Justifying a less Picturesque feature in the interior part of the garden, he confessed that he was "old-fashioned enough to like in certain places even Jet d'eaux . . . [for their] diamond drops of light which they scatter round them and the Halos and Rainbows which the misty vapour shows in sunshine and the dewy freshness which it seems to spread through the air." For a garden compartment reserved for Lady Beaumont's moments of quiet contemplation, Wordsworth called for a basin containing two goldfish he called "the 'Genii' of the Pool and of the place." Here no other ornament other than "the two mute inhabitants" and "here and there a solitary wild Flower" was necessary.[27] In an adjacent section of the garden stood the quarry pool surrounded by "the rocks with their shooting plants, the evergreens upon the top, and shooting deeper than all, the naked spire of the church." Wordsworth's intention was to provide Lady Beaumont a place for sweet meditation on the joy of life in the midst of death (No. 31).

J. M. W. Turner and John Constable

Romanticism is associated perhaps most profoundly with the unceasing wonders of the sky. If no longer thought of as celestial spheres, the vast reaches of the heavens with their sunsets of roseate gold, floating clouds pierced with shafts of sunlight, mist-veiled moon, and glittering stars continue to stir the soul. Similarly, mellow light falling on fertile fields, placid water, and green vales confers a mood of peace. These responses to nature are innate and universal, but their articulation through poetry and representation in art is our legacy from the Romantics. To the same degree that Wordsworth gave voice on paper to both the dramatic sublimity and quiet beauty of nature, his contemporaries, J. M. W. Turner (1775–1851) and John Constable (1776–1837), made visible the same emotionally charged phenomena on canvas. For each of these artists, the principal subject was not merely nature but light—in Turner's case the mutable, often dramatic light over open sea and foreign land, whereas in Constable's it was the local, gentle light enlivening meadow and stream (Figs. 17 and 18). Turner's magnificent light illuminates the awesome grandeur of the mountainous Sublime in such works as *The Pass at St. Gotthard, near Faido* (1843; No. 34). His follower Francis Danby struck the same note in his fantasy landscape *The Procession of Cristna* with its beetling rock overhanging an elephant caravan and jagged mountain peaks rising in the mist (No. 35).

But Turner was less interested in the Romantic scene itself than in the expressive potential of paint. No other artist was as obsessively personal in rendering radiant light and ambiguous space. His ultimate subjects are the elements—air, earth, water, and fire—and his works have a physical intensity that is painterly in the extreme, as if he were engaged in continual combat with pigment in his effort to turn color into atmosphere.

As engaged with his medium as Turner, Constable was attracted to nature's milder guise. He found his subjects not in the Alps or on the storm-tossed seas but in his home landscape of Dedam Vale in the valley of the River Stour. His tranquil paintings of brooks and meadows, grazing cattle and workaday agriculture are imbued with a powerful sense of universal harmony, a Romantic response not shared with earlier painters who depicted the rural landscape within the conventions of the Picturesque.

Constable's deep affection for this boyhood landscape and the frequent sketching trips he made in the surrounding countryside of Suffolk provided the wellspring from which he drew inspiration throughout his career. The scenes he painted evince the same apprehension of divine presence in common beauty as we find in Wordsworth's poetry. Indeed,

Fig. 17. J. M. W. Turner, *Staffa, Fingal's Cave*, 1832, Paul Mellon Collection, Yale Center for British Art, New Haven

Fig. 18. John Constable, *The White Horse*, 1819, The Frick Collection, New York

it has been said that Constable found within the confines of his native landscape the equivalent of Wordsworth's "spots in time," past visions in nature that later acted as a source of meditative emotion and a repository of artistic capital.[28]

Constable's travels were by choice more circumscribed than Wordsworth's or Turner's. He felt no compulsion to seek his subjects in the kind of wild scenery in which Wordsworth found inspiration on his rambles in the Lake District. Yet the spiritual mood we find in Wordsworth's contemplative comparison of the respective emotions of youth and maturity in "Tintern Abbey" parallels Constable's reverential depiction of the quiet beauty of rural England. And although his numerous cloud studies are not charged with the same drama as Turner's vaporous glowing skies, light and clouds are nevertheless the principal dramatis personae in his romantically bucolic scenes.

Based in London, where his works were exhibited at the Royal Academy, Constable made frequent sketching trips in the countryside. In September 1834, he stayed with George Wyndham, 3rd Earl of Egremont, at Petworth, where Turner was also a frequent guest. In a letter dated 14 September, following a day spent sketching *View of Cathanger, near Petworth*, he wrote, "Yesterday I visited the river banks, which are lovely indeed—Claude nor Ruysdael could not do a thousandth part of what nature here presents"[29] (No. 37).

Samuel Palmer

Samuel Palmer (1805–1881) was a painter in a different vein from Constable or Turner. Strongly influenced by William Blake, his work exhibits the mystical and visionary side of Romanticism. Like Blake, he sought in his work to communicate a rapturous communion with the divine. Like Turner and Constable, he found the means of expressing emotion in his depictions of light. But unlike them he did not dramatize light so much as interiorize it, turning it into a radiance that shed "an unearthly lustre into the inmost spirits."[30] He believed that the lights of terrestrial nature—"a summer gloaming from the dusky yet bloomy east; the moon opening her golden eye, or walking in brightness among innumerable islands of light"—illumined the way to Paradise, for "After all, I doubt not but there must be the study of this creation, as well as art and vision; tho' I cannot think it other than the veil of heaven, through which her divine features are dimly smiling; the setting of the table before the feast; the symphony before the tune; the prologue of the drama, a dream of antepast and proscenium of eternity"[31] (No. 38).

For Palmer, as for other Romantic artists, drawing was a primary means of expression. In the days before photography, sketching was common among travelers and topographical artists capable of rendering landscapes with varying degrees of verisimilitude. What sets the great Romantic artists such as Constable, Turner, and Palmer apart from their contemporaries in this regard is their ability to fuse personal emotion with representation. In their hands drawings gain a life of their own. No longer simply instruments preparatory to painting, they assume a compelling presence because of their emotional immediacy. Thus, a sketch such as *Oak Tree and Beech, Lullingstone Park* exemplifies Palmer's marriage of powers of minute observation with expressionistic fervor to create a work that transcends mere documentation (Fig. 19).

Fig. 19. Samuel Palmer, *Oak Tree and Beech, Lullingstone Park*, Thaw Collection, The Morgan Library & Museum

John Ruskin

For John Ruskin (1819–1900) the pursuit of aesthetics was as much a crusade as a matter of taste. A spellbinding lecturer and mesmerizing writer, he exerted a profound influence on his Victorian contemporaries. His five-volume *Modern Painters* passionately champions nature as the moral force behind all beauty in art. Because they were studio compositions rather than landscapes painted directly from nature, the works of Claude and Poussin were, according to Ruskin, inferior to those of Turner, the modern artist he promoted with ceaseless vigor. Ruskin's admiration for Turner was based on his belief that Turner sought to capture natural phenomena through both observation and the senses. Turner thus exemplified Ruskin's notion that landscape painting should be more than topographical and should instead portray nature's *effect* upon the mind and imagination. Ruskin's own landscape sketches show an emotional responsiveness to nature that he believed to be lacking in the work of most artists of his day. His copy of Turner's *The Pass at St. Gotthard, near Faido,* which was reproduced as a steel engraving in the third volume of *Modern Painters,* shows the degree to which Romantic expressionism verges on abstraction (No. 32).

Ruskin applied Romantic principles to architecture as well as to painting. He championed the Pisan Romanesque and Venetian Gothic styles, tracing their source to organic nature. For him, industrialization was a monstrous blight on the land and the soul and mass production was the end of fine artisanship and personally expressive craft. His was a reactionary and moralizing Romanticism and as such could not withstand the gathering forces of industrial mass production or the revival of Neoclassical architecture. The Arts and Crafts movement that his teachings did so much to promote can be considered in this light as a rearguard action against what he perceived to be the mounting tide of philistinism.

John Loudon and the Gardenesque

At the same time that Ruskin was issuing his jeremiads against industrialism, England, with the botanical riches of its large empire, was in the vanguard of horticultural science, a phenomenon that encouraged the burgeoning nursery trade and led to the development of the Gardenesque style, which favored near-distance plant display over expansive stretches of naturalistic scenery. In the process, its landscape designers were led away from the Picturesque Romanticism of the late eighteenth century. Even Repton began to incorporate foreground floral display into his designs toward the end of his career.

John Claudius Loudon (1783–1843), England's most prolific and influential nineteenth-century landscape writer, originated and defined the Gardenesque style. He was also a technically minded innovator and the inventor of the wrought-iron curvilinear sash bar, which allowed conservatory panes to be angled so as to catch both morning and afternoon light while also preventing the scorching of leaves from the direct rays of the noonday sun. With this architectural development, curved-shaped, all-glass conservatories soon became commonplace Victorian status symbols.

Like Repton, Loudon realized that publication was the route to lasting reputation. Although attracting commissions, including the Derby Arboretum, England's first public park, his fame rests upon his work as an author, editor, and encyclopedist. In 1822 he brought out *An Encyclopedia of Gardening; Comprising the Theory and Practice of Horticulture, Floriculture, Arboriculture, and Landscape-Gardening,* which, over the course of fifty years, ran to several editions and revisions. Beginning at the dawn of periodical publishing, in 1826, his *Gardener's Magazine* dispensed horticultural expertise while also serving as a forum for socially progressive ideas. Among Loudon's several other books, one in particular offered guidance to a growing body of middle-class property owners regarding the principles of taste: *The Villa Gardener: Comprising the Choice of a Suburban Villa Residence; the Laying Out, Planting, and Culture of the Garden and Grounds . . . Intended . . . More Particularly for the Use of Ladies* (1850). By this time, however, the notion of what constituted taste was quite different from that put forth by the Picturesque theorists. Nevertheless, Loudon was not averse to combining Romantic elements, such as the elaborate rock formation simulating the mountains of Savoy, in the garden of Hoole House near Liverpool. In *The Villa Gardener* he explained how to construct such artificial rockworks, recommending in some instances digging a small pond at the base "which may be supposed to have existed before the spot was turned into pleasure-grounds"[32] (No. 36 and Fig. 20). He did not find any incongruity in

Fig. 20. Rockwork around a pool, illustration in J. C. Loudon, *The Villa Gardener,* second edition, London, 1850, collection of Elizabeth Barlow Rogers

placing a rustic summerhouse with flower beds in the same landscape as plantings intended to display individual specimen trees and shrubs.

Sir George Sitwell

Before the final overthrow of the Picturesque in the twentieth century, English Romantics looked once more to Italy, perceiving in its decayed villa gardens a certain kind of landscape poetry. Perhaps the most Romantic analysis of Italian villa gardens was by the early-twentieth-century English aesthete Sir George Sitwell (1860–1943), who devoted an entire chapter to its analysis in *On the Making of Gardens* (1909). Fervidly, he maintained:

> In a garden, as elsewhere, Art has the power by selection, accentuation, grouping, and the removal of defects or superfluities, to intensify and surpass the beauty of nature, thus reaching the ideal. This power, being higher than natural law, is a kind of witchcraft; . . . concerned not only with the scene but with the mind of the beholder, for more than half of what we see comes from the mind. Here then at last we have found the garden-magic of Italy, in the domain of Psychology—that occult science which deals in spells, exorcisms and bewitchments, in familiar spirits, in malign and beneficent influences and formulas of alchemy; . . . If we use the witchery that here lies ready to our hand, the garden, like the work of a great painter, may "create a mood"; may throw over the soul the spell of a persisting present, unpursued by a ravenous past, the child's illusion of an harmonious universe, free from the discords of sorrow or unkindness, from the dominion of iron Necessity or of scornful Chance; where forethought may colour the future with rainbow images of spring and hope, and memory like a fountain pool that has cast off the dark days of winter can reflect nothing but flowers and sunshine and deep blue sky.[33]

Here, in Sitwell's overwrought prose, English Romanticism appears to have run its nineteenth-century course.

ROMANTICISM IN FRANCE

It is not surprising that in a nation where rationality and intellectual rigor were traditionally prized Romanticism should have been taken up more as a fashion than as an ideology. The French *philosophes* Diderot and Voltaire drew their inspiration from the revolutionary science of Newton as much as from the Aristotelian logic and mathematical principles of their own predecessor, Descartes. For Descartes, God was intelligent design, the great artificer who set in motion all the workings of nature, the knowledge of whose principles could be more readily apprehended through the mind than the senses. Voltaire bolstered this Cartesian philosophy with inductive reasoning, the inference of general laws from particular instances.

Similarly, Georges-Louis Leclerc, Comte de Buffon, the eighteenth-century French naturalist, taxonomist, and director of the *Jardin du Roi* (later renamed the *Jardin des Plantes*), France's first botanical garden, firmly believed in the mind's capacity to comprehend nature's immutable laws and hence man's right to rule creation.

> Formed to adore his Creator, [Man] has dominion over every creature. . . . Among living beings he establishes order, subordination, and harmony. To Nature herself he even gives embellishment, cultivation, extension, and polish. He cuts down the thistle and the bramble, and he multiplies the vine and the rose. Overrun with briars, thorns, and trees which are deformed, broken, corrupted, the seeds that ought to renew and embellish the scene are choked and buried in the midst of rubbish and sterility.[34]

Buffon's strong language hardly anticipated the development of Picturesque taste. But the French did in fact adopt English innovations in landscape design. For them, however, the *jardin anglais* was understandably more a matter of ancien régime fashion than an expression of national identity. Neither their political tradition of authoritarian monarchy, which would soon be overturned, nor attachment by the nobility and landed gentry to the rural countryside, as in England, predisposed them to a Romantic view of nature. Nevertheless, their adopted son, Jean-Jacques Rousseau (1712–1788), the self-styled "citizen of Geneva," became Romanticism's (and hence democracy's) most polemical apostle.

Jean-Jacques Rousseau

Rousseau's deism was opposite the worldview of Voltaire and other *philosophes* who saw nature abstractly, a mechanistic set of universal laws merely set in motion by a divine being. For Rousseau, nature was instinct with divinity. Perceived through the senses, nature stimulated human emotion. More important was the effect nature exerted on the human mind.

The words *reverie* and *sentiment* are part of the lexicon of Rousseau's philosophy. Reverie amid scenes of nature inevitably produced rapturous sentiment.

Many people erroneously associate Rousseau with the term *noble savage*, meaning an individual living in a state of Golden Age grace and prelapsarian innocence. His Romanticism should be seen rather as a critique of civilization. He was a reformer who sought to undermine the artificiality of contemporary society with works such as *Émile* (1762), a tract on education in the guise of a novel. The curriculum he prescribed therein is based not on a belief in the superiority of the primitive but on his reformer's conviction that complete immersion in nature's simple lessons at an early age would immunize a child from the vices and artificiality of society.

Rousseau's epistolary novel, *Julie, ou la nouvelle Héloïse*, is Romantic in its plot, which revolves around the fate of two lovers, Saint-Preux and Julie (Héloïse) and in its ecstatic reveries inspired by scenes of nature (No. 40).

In a letter to Julie, Saint-Preux writes:

> *I had set out, sad with my woes, and consoled by your joy; which kept me in a certain state of languor that is not without charm for a sensible heart. I climbed slowly, and on foot, paths that were fairly rugged, led by a man I had engaged to be my guide, and in whom throughout the trip I have found rather a friend than a mercenary. I wanted to daydream, and I was always distracted from doing so by some unexpected vista. Sometimes huge cliffs hung like ruins above my head. Sometimes high and thundering waterfalls drenched me in their thick fog. Sometimes a perpetual mountain stream opened by my side an abyss the depth of which eyes dared not fathom. On occasion I got lost in the darkness of a dense wood. On others, on emerging from a chasm a pleasant meadow suddenly delighted my sight. A surprising mixture of wild and cultivated nature revealed throughout the hand of men, where one would have thought they had never penetrated: beside a cave one would find houses; one would see dry vine branches where only brambles would have been expected, grapevines where there had been landslides, excellent fruits among the boulders, and fields on steep inclines.*[35]

For Romantics, mountain heights are equated with the Sublime, and Saint-Preux is no exception, although his emotional response is "tranquility of soul" rather than the fearful wonder, awe, and amazement associated with Burke's definition. He

is entitled to this idiosyncratic perspective, for like Wordsworth, his view is inward; the tremendous scene is analyzed not from the dispassionate perspective of a scenic connoisseur but from the effect it has upon the human mind and soul. His letter to Julie is almost clinical in this regard.

> *... high in the mountains where the air is pure and subtle, one breathes more freely, one feels lighter in the body, more serene of mind; pleasures there are less intense, passions more moderate. Meditations there take on an indescribably grand and sublime character, in proportion with the objects that strike us, an indescribably tranquil delight that has nothing acrid or sensual about it. It seems that by rising above the habitation of men one leaves all base and earthly sentiments behind, and in proportion as one approaches ethereal spaces the soul contracts something of their inalterable purity.*[36]

In a passage in *La nouvelle Héloïse* that serves as a metaphor for Julie's virtue, Rousseau's description of her garden introduced a new paragon that in fact amounts to a treatise on landscape design. Her "Elysium," which she created on the site of an old orchard, is a locked secret garden symbolizing her chaste resolve to terminate her love affair with Saint-Preux after her marriage. Invisibly enclosed to contain birds that live joyfully in apparent freedom, it is filled with a thousand delights. Upon visiting Julie's garden, Saint-Preux rhapsodizes:

> *I followed tortuous and irregular alleys bordered by these flowered woods, covered with a thousand garlands of Judean vine, creeper, hops, bindweed, Bryony, clematis, and other plants of that sort, among which honeysuckle and jasmine saw fit to mingle. These garlands seem to have been casually cast from tree to tree, as I had sometimes seen in forests, and formed something like draperies above us which protected us from the sun, while we had under foot a soft, comfortable, and dry path on a fine moss without sand, grass, or rough shoots. . . . All these little walkways were bordered and crossed by clear, crystalline water, sometimes circulating through the grass and flowers in nearly imperceptible rivulets; sometimes in larger streams running over pure and dappled pebbles which made the water more sparkling. . . . And so the soil thus constantly refreshed and moistened yielded forth new flowers and kept the grass always verdant and lovely.*[37]

Julie says that a dozen days of work each year from her gardener and two or three of her servants suffice to maintain her Elysium. According to Rousseau, creating a naturalistic landscape is virtually effortless: nature collaborates with art, and with a little imagination, one can create a personal Eden that will grow spontaneously at practically no cost. As anyone who has ever made a wild garden will attest, this is not so. Julie's garden, however, is not meant to be understood in practical terms; rather it makes the case for the charms of natural simplicity and rustic taste. As such, it was extremely influential in transforming the style of landscape design in France.

The Marquis de Girardin

Nowhere is this more evident than in the landscape Louis-René, Vicomte d'Ermenonville, Marquis de Girardin (1735–1808), made—presumably with on-site advice from Rousseau—at his estate in the north-central part of France, where he sought to create a park with a high moral tone, a privileged space for solitary reverie. Rousseau's ideals as well as his landscape theories guided its creation, and during its construction he was in residence at Ermenonville, where the marquis had given him refuge in his last years and, at the end, burial on a poplar-encircled island—a temple of nature—in the lake (No. 42). There the marquis, who had already placed within the garden certain funerary features, such as broken columns and cenotaphs, consigned Rousseau's remains to an urn-topped Neoclassical monument. In 1780 a marble sarcophagus designed by artist and sometime garden designer Hubert Robert and inscribed with the words *Here rests the man of Nature and Truth* was substituted for it. Although Rousseau's remains were later transferred to the Panthéon in Paris, the sarcophagus on the small island in the lake at Ermenonville can still be seen today.

It would be hard to exaggerate the influence that Rousseau's tomb on its poplar-surrounded island had in stimulating the practice of secular burial and the Romantic attitude toward death. As a dissenter, the Deist philosopher would have been denied a church funeral in any case, but the importance of the garden site for his interment lay not only in the legitimatization it gave to burial on unconsecrated ground but also in the stimulus it provided to the cult of sweet melancholy and the practice of secular

burial in the so-called rural cemetery, an important landscape type that will be discussed later.

Ermenonville became celebrated as Rousseau's posthumous fame soared. His tomb was an important pilgrimage site for French republicans who revered him as their patron saint. Even after his disinterment, Rousseau's tomb served as a monument to the Romantic belief in the importance of memorials as prompts to reverence and sweet melancholy. Indeed, it had not been placed on the island merely for expedience because the great *philosophe* happened to die at Ermenonville but rather as a part of the garden's itinerary of Romantic features. In addition to the elegiac monuments, there were memorial busts honoring great men of ancient times—Lycurgus, Socrates, Homer, and Epaminondas—and a brick pyramid dedicated to Theocritus and Virgil along with the contemporary poet James Thomson. The Temple of Philosophy, intentionally incomplete, stood as a memorial to Montaigne, and the Altar of Dreams commemorated a poem on the importance of love by Voltaire. Girardin supplied an especially Romantic touch when he created the Tomb of the Stranger to mark the last resting place of a mysterious visitor who took his life on this scenic spot without leaving any trace of his identity or explanation of his motives. Although this may be an extreme example of the trend, the marquis was not alone in conflating the funerary and the Picturesque. The creators of other late-eighteenth-century gardens throughout Europe expressed a similar strain of Romantic sentimentalism with the building of pyramids, temples, and commemorative monuments. In addition, replicas of Roussesau's poplar-encircled island became a familiar trope in landscape design.

Girardin translated his own treatise on landscape gardening, *De la composition des paysages* (1777) into English; it was published in London 1783. In it the marquis (sounding very much like Knight, Price, or Gilpin) maintained:

> *It is only by considering the effect of [nature] as a picture, that one can dispose pleasing objects to advantage; for the picturesque effect depends entirely upon the choice of the most agreeable forms, the elegance of outline, and keeping the distances; it consists in managing a happy contrast of light and shadow, in giving projection and relief to*

the objects, and producing the charm of variety, by showing them in different lights, in different shapes, and under different points of view; also in the beautiful assemblage of colours, and above all, in that happy negligence which is the peculiar characteristic of grace and nature. . . . It is not then as an architect or a gardener, but as a poet and a painter, that landscape must be composed, so as at once to please the understanding and the eye.[38]

In a practical vein, he advised the landowner who wished to create such a landscape to engage a painter. In order for the painter to achieve the proper perspective, he was to be taken up to the top of the house, from which vantage point he could, after considering foreground and background, begin to sketch in simple strokes of the pencil "the great outlines of the principal objects, and the general disposition of the large masses."[39] Then the sketch was to be shown to "people of taste, and always with the intention to seize the most natural and simple ideas," after which the painter would render it in color. Although he received assistance from the landscape designer and engineer Jean-Marie Morel and the Scottish botanist and landscape gardener Thomas Blaikie, the artist who conceived the scenery of Ermenonville was probably Hubert Robert.

Both the north and south views from the château were composed in the manner of paintings. The view to the north was a quiet rural view of a flat field with a gently curving stream winding through it; the southern perspective was framed by a grotto and cascade (Fig. 21). Elsewhere the garden was a textbook illustration of the precepts of Rousseau, who believed in the primacy of images in stimulating reverie (Figs. 22 and 23). Reverie, for him, was the foundation for the empire of the imagination in which instructive contemplation gave birth not to idle fantasy but rather to thoughts that put one in harmony with the true order of things.

Ermenonville was thus explicitly a garden of moral sentiment, and the structures and markers with inscriptions that are depicted in *Promenade, ou Itinéraire des jardins d'Ermenonville* (1788) and in Alexandré Laborde's *Description des nouveaux jardins de la France et de ses anciens châteaux* (1808), a handsome folio-size book of text and copperplate engravings, are testaments to Rousseau's philosophy (No. 47).

Fig. 21. J. Mérigot fils, *Vue du coté du nord*, illustration in *Promenade, ou itinéraire des jardins d'Ermenonville*, Paris, 1788, The Morgan Library & Museum

Fig. 22. J. Mérigot fils, *Monuments des anciennes amours*, illustration in *Promenade, ou itinéraire des jardins d'Ermenonville*, Paris, 1788, The Morgan Library & Museum

Fig. 23. J. Mérigot fils, *La brasserie*, illustration in *Promenade, ou itinéraire des jardins d'Ermenonville*, Paris, 1788, The Morgan Library & Museum

The Jardin Anglais *and the* Jardin Anglo-Chinois

In his liberal philosophy and patronage of Rousseau, the Marquis de Girardin stood apart from his ancien régime contemporaries for whom the garden was essentially a theatrical arrangement of exotic and rustic *fabriques* or follies—grottoes, hermit's huts,

Gothic chapels, Moorish pavilions, Chinese teahouses, Turkish tents, sham ruins—a landscape designed primarily for aristocratic entertainment rather than for solitary reflection. The Rococo playfulness of this type of garden had its origins in the *genre pittoresque,* a style perfected by such eighteenth-century French painters as François Boucher, Jean-Honoré Fragonard, and Hubert Robert. Boucher's scenes sentimentalizing the rusticity of peasant life, Fragonard's depictions of neglected, overgrown seventeenth-century gardens in which lovers amorously disport themselves, and Robert's ruins are typical subjects that find their counterparts in designed landscapes of the period (Figs. 24–26).

Many French artists went to Rome, where they appropriated picturesque decay as their subject matter. The Romantic sensibility they brought to their work corresponded with that of garden designers. As mentioned above, Robert was both a painter and a garden designer, and his representations of actual and imaginary Roman ruins were undoubtedly a source of inspiration for the faux ruins he created and recorded at Méreville and other gardens. The rural countryside was a further influence, as seen in his collaboration with the landscape designer Morel at Ermenonville and with the architect Richard Mique at the Petit Trianon at Versailles, site of the *petit hameau,* or "pretend hamlet," created for Marie-Antoinette. Boucher's rustic cottages in the *style champêtre* served as prototypes for *hameaux* elsewhere. Fragonard's series of paintings in the Frick Collection on *The Progress of Love* is set in what

Fig. 25. Jean-Honoré Fragonard, *The Progress of Love: The Meeting,* 1771–73, The Frick Collection, New York

Fig. 24. François Boucher, *Thatched Mill Cottage and Shed with Two Trees at the Edge of a Stream,* The Morgan Library & Museum

Fig. 26. Hubert Robert, *The Return of the Cattle,* The Metropolitan Museum of Art, New York

may be interpreted as an imaginary version of one of the romantically derelict formal gardens of Louis XIV. Thus, elegiac nostalgia prompted by ruins; a taste for things old, rustic, and rural; the attraction of the abandoned park as a setting for amorous sport—such are the sentiments with which landscapes are imbued in the elegant twilight of the ancien régime.

In terms of landscape theory, François Paul Latapie's translation into French of Whately's *Observations on Modern Gardening* in 1771, the year after it was published in English, had a singular impact on European garden design. The subsequent publication in 1775 of the dual-language version of Walpole's *Essay on Modern Gardening; Essai sur l'art des jardins modernes* (No. 15) and in 1788 of *Le jardin anglois, poëme en quatre chants,* a translation of the four-book didactic poem on the English Garden by William Mason (1725–1797), were similarly influential. Many aristocrats soon destroyed the fine parterres and bosquets of the old geometrically arranged gardens of their ancestors, replacing their straight allées with winding paths and their sculptures of classical deities with replications of classical ruins, hermitages, and faux hamlets. The inclusion of four highly Romantic aquatint illustrations of Prunay, a rebuilt garden near Marly, in the prose translation of Mason's poem (the original English edition has no illustra-

Fig. 27. *Conduisez-moi, vite à mon berceau de chevrefeuil,* illustration in William Mason, *Le jardin anglois: poëme en quatre chants,* Paris, 1788, collection of Elizabeth Barlow Rogers

tions) exemplifies the trend (Fig. 27). In several cases the *jardin anglais* did not replace a historic garden but was built as an annex to it, notably at Versailles and Chantilly in France, Sanssoucci in Prussia, and Drottningholm in Sweden (No. 45).

Perhaps the most bizarre appropriation of the *jardin anglais* in France was the one that court architect Emmanuel Héré de Corny (1705–1763) created at Lunéville, where the twice-deposed pretender to the Polish throne, Stanislas Leszczynski, was installed as the last Duke of Lorraine (r. 1737–66). Its famous *rocher,* depicted in Héré de Corny's *Recueil des plans élévations et coupes, tant géométrales qu'en perspective des châteaux, jardins, et dépendances que le roy de Pologne occupe en Lorraine,* was constructed by clock maker François Richard over several years begin-

Fig. 28. *Veue et perspective du rocher,* illustration in Emmanuel Héré de Corny, *Recueil des plans . . . des châteaux, jardins, et dépendances que le roy de Pologne occupe en Lorraine,* Paris, 1753–56, collection of Elizabeth Barlow Rogers

ning in 1742 and completed by the architect Richard Mique (Fig. 28). This elaborate creation introduced artificial rusticity into the architectural fabric of a palatial château of French Baroque design. Within an artificial rockery created beneath a raised terrace on two sides of the courtyard, Héré de Corny installed eighty-six life-sized automata portraying peasants, animals, and a hermit. Their mechanical movements, cries, and music—along with the grotto-dwelling hermit's beating of his chest—constituted a Rococo representation of rural life similar to that found in less architecturally compressed garden settings.

The taste for *chinoiserie,* an important facet of Rococo design, owed no small debt to William Chambers's *Designs of Chinese Buildings, Furniture, Dresses, Machines and Utensils.* It is fair to say that its French edition, published simultaneously with the English one in 1757, made Chambers the doyen of structures and decorative arts in the Chinese taste in France. In his translation of Whately, Latapie had taken great pains in his introduction to quote Chambers at length and to suggest that the Chinese garden was, in fact, a source for much of the vaunted English landscape innovation. This led to the French coinage of the term *jardin anglo-chinois,* which in fact aptly described the hybrid design form that sought to ornament the English-style garden with *chinoiserie* features—pagodas, teahouses, Chinese bridges, and the like.

The Désert de Retz, built on the edge of the Forêt de Marly by François Nicolas Henri Racine de Monville (1734–1797) is a conspicuous example of the *jardin pittoresque,* as is Parc Monceau, the 46-acre pleasure garden Louis de Carmontelle (1717–1806) designed for the anglophile Philippe d'Orleans, duc de Chartres, later called Philippe Egalité, now a pleasant park in the sixteenth arrondisement of Paris (Figs. 29–31). The numerous exotic features seen in a large folio published by Carmontelle in 1779 bear the stamp of Chambers's influence. In his prospectus for the garden, Carmontelle, who also served as a playwright, set designer, and master of ceremonies for the duke, stated that he wished to create a garden "based on fantasy, . . . the extraordinary, and the amusing, and

Fig. 29. Louis Claude Legand after Louis de Carmontelle, *Vüe de la tente tartare,* illustration in *Jardin de Monceau,* Paris, 1779, collection of Elizabeth Barlow Rogers

Fig. 30. Pierre L'Épine after Louis de Carmontelle, *Vüe des ruines du temple de Mars,* illustration in *Jardin de Monceau,* Paris, 1779, collection of Elizabeth Barlow Rogers

Fig. 31. Louis Le Sueur after Louis de Carmontelle, *Vüe du bois des tombeaux,* illustration in *Jardin de Monceau,* Paris, 1779, collection of Elizabeth Barlow Rogers

not on the desire to imitate Nature."[40] Since the duc de Chartres was a Masonic Grand Master of the Grand Orient of France, some of the *fabriques* of the Parc Monceau displayed Masonic symbolism; others such as the rustic pyramid, false ruins inspired by the paintings of Robert, and a secluded *bois des tombeaux* were in keeping with the now fashionable alliance of the garden with the cult of elegaic emotion. Basically, however, Parc Monceau was intended as an elaborate entertainment facility, a magical place evoking other lands and other periods in history like a theme park of today.

The explanation for the differences we perceive between those French gardens that lean more toward Rococo taste and those with a more sober didactic motive lies perhaps in the revolutionary character of Romanticism. Aristocrats of the old order wanted to inflect the art of the Baroque into a more playful vein with exoticism and faux rusticity as its essential modes of expression within the landscape. Their notion of the garden can be viewed perhaps as a form of escapism. In contrast, for the Marquis de Giradin, an aristocrat with liberal sympathies, a sober didacticism governed the landscape program, and the visitor making the prescribed circuit of Ermenonville was provided with seating at certain points along the route in order to contemplate various features that were intended to impart specific moral lessons.

Père Lachaise, the First Rural Cemetery

Rousseau's tomb was not the only precedent for secular burial. In several English parks, landscapes were adorned with memorials and monuments intended to stimulate national pride and a poetical attitude toward death. At Stowe, the Temple of British Worthies, along with the rostral column commemorating Captain Thomas Grenville and the pyramidal monument to William Congreve, come to mind. There the naming of Kent's meadow-embraced valley the Elysian Fields and the stream flowing through it the River Styx evoked the ancients' notion of the afterlife. Architect Nicholas Hawksmoor's pyramid and massive mausoleum at Castle Howard (1728), the resting place of the 3rd Earl of Carlisle, is an early example of the association of landscape design with death and the use of a garden as the locus of interment. Wordsworth was of the decided view that being laid to rest amid scenes of rural nature was vastly preferable to urban churchyard burial. But the extramural cemetery as a communal burial garden was a French invention, one that grew out of a combination of post-Revolutionary anti-

clericalism, public health issues, and the notion that a garden offered the most desirable setting in which to indulge the sentiment of sweet melancholy as a form of mourning.

There were, furthermore, practical reasons for expanding cities to consider extramural burial grounds. The charnel stench and unsanitary conditions of churchyards in these increasingly populous urban centers called for reform, and the purchase of individual lots offered a solution to this problem while also according the dead the dignity denied them by common-pit burial and the subsequent disturbance of their remains as new corpses were added to the jumble of old. For those who could not afford this means of permanent repose, cemetery leaseholds would ensure that descendants could visit the grave sites of their forebears for a period of time.

The design demonstration of the French initiative in burial reform began in 1799 with Jacques Molinos's *Champs de repos*, which the project's sponsor, Jacques Cambray, an administrator of the Department of the Seine, proposed for the site of the Montmartre quarries. Molinos, Paris's architect and inspector of civil buildings, devised a circular plan in which a Picturesque landscape was traversed by serpentine paths leading to a monumental funerary pyramid that was intended to serve as a crematory and columbarium or, alternatively, as a repository for urns. Although this project was never realized, in 1801 the French legislature set forth the guidelines for communes to purchase land outside their boundaries for the purpose of creating cemeteries. The prefect of Paris, unable to acquire Parc Monceau, bought an estate called Mont Louis on the eastern edge of the city, a site of picturesquely varied topography on a high escarpment with views of the Panthéon and other prominent landmarks. The Neoclassical architect Alexandre-Théodore Brongniart (1739–1813) was appointed to draw up a plan. At Père Lachaise—as the Cemetery of the East was renamed in honor of the former Jesuit proprietor—Brongniart, using some elements of the original design, combined a formal chestnut-lined *tapis vert* with straight and winding poplar-bordered carriage drives and acacia-shaded

Fig. 32. Léon Jean-Baptiste Sabatier and Adolphe Jean Baptiste Bayot, *Cimetière du Père Lachaise,* illustration in *Paris dans sa splendeur: monuments, vues, scènes historiques, descriptions et histoire,* Paris, 1861–63, The Morgan Library & Museum

footpaths. Weeping willows and cypresses provided the appropriate funerary symbols (Fig. 32).

It took several years for Père Lachaise to become fashionable. Indeed, in the beginning, the construction of false tombs was necessary to create its prestige. An amalgam of twelfth-century Gothic fragments covering the purported remains of Abélard and Héloïse was transferred from the Museum of French Monuments, and mausoleum-like cenotaphs commemorating La Fontaine and Molière were placed over the alleged bones of these literary lions who had in reality been buried in common pits. But by the middle of the nineteenth century, the French bourgeoisie had made Père Lachaise the postmortem address of choice, and denizens of the fashionable world sought the services of the funerary architects, stonecutters, iron-fence makers, and florists who had set up shop nearby.

An 1852 guide, *Le Père Lachaise historique, monumental et biographique,* written and published by A. Henry, has a foldout plan showing numerous impressive mausoleums and obelisks as well as an area reserved for the cross-marked graves of the five- and ten-year leaseholds (No. 51). The key constitutes a who's who of the prosperous and the great, including the composers Chopin, Rossini, and Bellini; the painters Géricault and David; and the poet Delille. This legend contains the names of the 288 deceased persons buried on the parklike high ground as well as the names of 439 individuals occupying leased plots lower down. The notion of permanent burial—perpetual rest—was, of course, an important consideration in popularizing Père Lachaise and the rural cemeteries that would come later, a practice that would have been incomprehensible before Romanticism altered attitudes toward death.

Although many mausoleums and monuments were marked with Christian crosses, an additional nonreligious vocabulary of memorial design was essential to a secular cemetery. It was to antiquity, therefore, that the creators of Père Lachaise and the so-called rural cemeteries that were its successors looked for a sculptural and architectural vocabulary of commemoration. They turned to Greece, Rome, and Egypt. In late fifth-century B.C.E. Athens, large-scale, carved stone versions of *lekythoi*—small, slender, ceramic urns—became popular grave markers, along with memorial altars, inscribed stelae, and sculptures of lions. In the Kerameikos cemetery outside the Dipylon—the double gateway that formed the principal entrance to the city—the practice of commemorating the deceased members of noble families with costly bas-relief sculptures prevailed until the fourth century B.C.E., when the law decreed an end to such ostentation. After that the Athenians honored their dead with simple round columns.

The mausoleums that became the final homes of the distinguished deceased at Père Lachaise and later rural cemeteries also found precedent in those that lined Rome's Appian Way. As was the case in eighteenth- and nineteenth-century English gardens and parks and their Continental cousins,

Greek and Roman temples provided architectural models for cemetery structures. In addition, the Napoleonic wars familiarized the French with the cult of the dead that had been the most prominent aspect of ancient Egyptian culture, and the scaled-down versions of obelisks and pyramids that had already found their way into the *jardin anglais* became popular cemetery monuments.

Along with the practice of laying the dead to rest in an extramural natural setting furnished with an eclectic array of urns, stelae, columns, pyramids, obelisks, and temples, the ancients conferred as their legacy the observance of the rites of mourning, family visitation, and floral offerings. This did not mean, however, that the forms expressing Christian belief had vanished. Gothic chapels and monuments surmounted by crosses, angels, and other Christian symbols found their place in the new cemeteries as well. Overall, however, it was the perennial beauty of nature that served as the rural cemetery's principal emblem and primary source of consolation. The opening up of royal gardens, such as the Tuileries and the Luxembourg, and the creation of public landscapes without a funerary function within Paris and other cities was the necessary next step in recognizing access to nature as an entitlement of the population at large.

Baron Haussmann, Charles-Adolphe Alphand, and the Parks of Paris

In 1853 Emperor Napoleon III appointed Baron Georges-Eugène Haussmann (1809–1891) prefect of the Department of the Seine. With superb administrative skills and financial acumen, Haussmann quickly set about fulfilling the emperor's dream of transforming Paris into the world's first modern city. His primary consideration was a series of infrastructure projects—notably the laying out of water and sewer lines and a system of straight boulevards that would connect the center of the city with the newly constructed train stations on its perimeter. Incising the medieval tangle of streets and lanes with this modern system of circulation was also presumed to provide the forces of

law and order a tactical advantage against attempts to build barricades in times of insurrection. In addition to enabling transurban circulation by carriages, pedestrians, and mounted gendarmes, Haussmann's boulevards with their wide sidewalks gave birth to the *flâneur*, the stroller whose pastime was looking at the wares displayed in the new plate-glass shop windows and eyeing the passing parade of the beau monde. Paris was justly dubbed the City of Light after the installation of gaslit street lamps along the new thoroughfares. It might equally have been called the City of Trees because of the miles of trees that lined these broad avenues (Fig. 33).

Haussmann's plan, with its axial, tree-bordered boulevards radiating from rond-points was nothing less than a version of André Le Nôtre's plan for Versailles on a metropolitan scale. The only difference between the new Paris and the garden of the Sun King and its attendant town was the termination of its long axes in monuments of classical grandeur, such as the Opéra and the Madeleine. Included in the plan for the new Paris were several parks, and these, interestingly, departed from rest of the urban design paradigm. Executed by Jean-Charles-Adolphe Alphand (1817–1891), the landscape designer Haussmann put in charge of constructing new parks, promenades, and city squares, these might justly be termed *romantique à la mode*.

Fig. 33. Jean-Joseph Sulpis after Emile Hochereau and Louis-Emile Dardoize, *Profils de voies publiques*, illustration in Jean-Charles-Adolphe Alphand, *Les promenades de Paris*, Paris, 1867–73, collection of Elizabeth Barlow Rogers

Alphand redesigned the Bois de Boulogne, formerly a royal hunting park on the western edge of the city, as an elegant pleasure ground with passages of Picturesque scenery interspersed with a racetrack and restaurants. While developed in the *jardin anglais* manner, with a serpentine lake and undulating paths replacing all but two of the old hunting park's straight allées, it remains primarily a collection of heterogeneous landscape features and popular dining and recreational facilities.

Although the Bois de Boulogne was conceived as a fashionable resort of the affluent—equestrians, owners of carriages, and well-dressed promenaders—rather than as a means of providing a public park for the masses, Haussmann's efforts encompassed the entire population. At the opposite end of Paris, next to the eastern working-class district, he directed Alphand to convert the Bois de Vincennes from a hunting preserve for French kings into a pleasure ground designed in the same *jardin anglais* manner as the Bois de Boulogne (Fig. 34). At the city's northwestern edge, his plan for creating modern Paris called for transforming Parc Monceau, Carmontelle's eclectic creation for the Duc de Chartres, into a public park while retaining several of its remaining *folies*.

In terms of Romanticism, Alphand's *chef d'oeuvre* is Parc des Buttes-Chaumont in Paris's northeastern quadrant. Here he converted an abandoned, vermin-infested rock quarry-turned-garbage-dump into a 55-acre piece of Picturesque scenography. At twice the cost of redesigning the much larger Bois de Boulogne, he added huge quantities of artificial rockwork to the existing old quarry faces, thereby creating a pseudomountainous landscape rising out of an artificial lake. The park also contains two streams, one originating in a waterfall that spills dramatically from on high into a grotto with artificial stalactites and stalagmites. Crowning the promontory that forms the park's central feature, a circular temple serves as a belvedere with panoramic views of Paris. The visitor can attain the steep elevation of this former quarry crag by means of a high suspended bridge named with Romantic melodrama the Bridge of Suicides; sinuous paths provide an alternate, somewhat longer, means of ascent. This scene was meant to induce a *grand frisson*, or "thrill of amazement," something quite different from the contemplative mood and poetic reverie advanced by Rousseau and, later, by the American landscape architect Frederick Law Olmsted.

Olmsted had the opportunity to note this difference in 1859 when he went to see the Paris parks under construction and to meet with Alphand. His firsthand observation seconds the previously remarked upon theatricality of French eighteenth- and nineteenth-century landscape design: "The principal rock-work is much more like an operatic

Fig. 34. Theodor Alexander Weber, *Bois de Vincennes—Rotonde et grotte de l'île de Reuilly,* illustration in Jean-Charles-Adolphe Alphand, *Les promenades de Paris,* Paris, 1867–73, collection of Elizabeth Barlow Rogers

fairy scene than any thing in nature; and as its great size prevents it from being regarded as puerile or grotesque, like Chinese garden scenes, it may be considered to have been conceived in an original style to which the term romantic may be rightly applied."[41] More bluntly caustic in his assessment, the Irish-born garden writer and editor William Robinson (1838–1935) wrote: "In the plans of the best French landscape-gardeners it is quite ridiculous to see the way the walks wind about in symmetrical twirlings, and, when they have entwined themselves through every sweep of turf in the place, seem to long for more spaces to writhe about in"[42] (Fig. 35).

The parks of Paris are well-maintained and much-appreciated amenities for residents and tourists alike. Delightful to stroll in, they present themselves as additional pleasures in a city of many pleasures. But they do display, as Olmsted and Robinson noted, a significant degree of theatrical éclat and obvious artificiality. Possibly, with regard to the alignment of paths and park drives, the difference between what appears to be a mechanical drafting approach and one that allows natural topography to guide the circulation plan may be attributed to French landscape designers' use of the French curve—a drafting template with curved edges and scroll-shaped cutouts. Moreover, what is true for Alphand's parks in terms of their horizontal plans is also true in terms of their vertical sections. Although topographic surveys enabled the designers of both Central Park and the Parc des Buttes-Chaumont to accomplish the subsequent grading and filling necessary to create their desired surfaces, Alphand's manipulation of the ground plane resulted in a much more contrived terrain, the fabrication of which was intended to portray rather than disguise technological mastery of nature. It is not accidental that the park was opened on 1 April 1867, the same day as the Exposition Universelle, the largest world's fair up to that time. In addition to the display of industrial technology, the exposition was meant to showcase Napoleon III's "new Paris." Thus, Alphand's monumental two-volume *Promenades de Paris,* containing steel engravings and lithographs of all of the

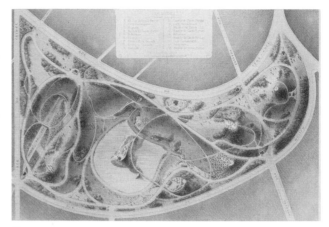

Fig. 35. Henri Durau after Emile Hochereau, *Parc des Buttes-Chaumont,* illustration in Jean-Charles-Adolphe Alphand, *Les promenades de Paris,* Paris, 1867–73, collection of Elizabeth Barlow Rogers

new infrastructure improvements—tree-lined boulevards, sewers, street furniture—as well as all of the city's new parks and squares was much more than a lavish souvenir intended for distinguished visitors and heads of state; it remains the unparalleled representation of Paris as the champion of urban modernity.

Another aspect of the dominance of art over nature in Alphand's parks can be seen in their function as showcases for ornamental plant specimens rather than as landscapes formed by a naturalistic commingling of native and exotic vegetation. By contrast, as we shall see, in Olmsted's parks all adornment—botanical, sculptural, and architectural—is subservient to a landscape composition designed to carry the visitor through romantically picturesque passages of scenery in which the overriding experience is one of movement through a continuum of connected spaces. But before discussing the work of this great American landscape architect, we must look to Germany to see how here, too, nature itself was the central Romantic theme guiding the designer's heart, mind, and hand.

ROMANTICISM IN GERMANY

In Germany Romanticism found its name and its identity as a movement, which catalyzed its spread throughout Europe.[43] Yet even as German Romantic thought was becoming universal currency, the German Romantics are characterized by a mystical dimension that sets them apart from their French and English counterparts. Romanticism in the German-speaking world is rooted in a mythic attachment to *Vaterland*. It represents an expression of national soul, a spiritual force identified with forest and folk—the German land and German people. It also represents the striving for a union of the individual with the divine as manifested in nature. This is something quite different from Rousseau's idealization of nature as the foundation for moral virtue and social harmony.

Nor is German Romanticism the same thing as English Romanticism. A collection of separate principalities, Germany premised its incipient nationalism on the bonds of blood, whereas the nationalism of England's securely established state was based on political identity. As was true of their counterparts, German Romantics were attracted to the antique classical ruins of Greece and Rome. At the same time, their zeitgeist was rooted in Nordic myth and the hoary trees of the witch-inhabited forest found in German fairy tales. The source of their Romantic identity was the primeval woods, *Urwald*, and the term *Heimat*, or "homeland," is synonymous with nature.

This does not mean, however, that German culture was immune to the currents of Romanticism springing from England and France. The Enlightenment philosopher Immanuel Kant had in his study a picture of Rousseau. His *Beobachtungen über das Gefühl des Schönen und Erhabenen* (Observations on the Feeling of the Beautiful and Sublime), written in 1763, draws the same distinctions between the two aesthetic categories as Burke's *Philosophical Treatise*, adding the dimension of time to that of space. He maintained, "A long duration is sublime. If it is of time past, then it is noble. If it is projected into an incalculable future, then it has something of the fearsome in it. A building of the remotest antiquity is venerable . . . [whereas] the coming eternity stimulates a mild horror, and of the past, transfixed wonder."[44]

Christian Hirschfeld

As was mentioned earlier, a designed landscape cannot represent the same degree of sublimity as a painting. This, however, does not necessarily diminish the ability of certain landscapes to reflect Romantic cultural values. In this regard, Christian Cajus Lorenz Hirschfeld's (1742–1792) influential aesthetic treatise, *Theorie der Gartenkunst* (Theory of Garden Art), promotes the garden as a moral force. This five-volume work is neither a suggestive guide for gardeners nor a beautifully illustrated album for landscape lovers but rather a case for landscape as an important—in his opinion *the* most important—branch of aesthetics. Hirschfeld maintains as a fundamental principle that "a garden can move the imagination and senses powerfully, more powerfully than can an area whose beauty comes from nature alone."[45] Blending nature and art, the Hirschfeldian garden is a romantically enhanced landscape, a place meant to stimulate the senses and imagination, stir the spirit, instruct the mind, and impart moral precepts.[46]

To lead the reader to his way of thinking about gardens, Hirschfeld offers a concise history of landscape design. It is an opinionated one, with a recurring nationalistic bent. He abhors imitation of other countries' landscape styles and is especially eager to correct "Gallomania, a particular malady of our nation." He dismisses the gardens of Le Nôtre as "exaggerated, affected, and in part poorly executed. There may be feeling there, but it was false; genius, but it was wasted for lack of direction."[47] For Hirschfeld, suppleness is always a more pleasing approach to design than anxious calculation and meticulousness. Admiring the English for their taste and character in spite of their faults, he sees in the liberty they bequeath to the plant world a social metaphor for the benevolent ruler who allows his subjects a just amount of freedom. He asserts that Germans, being lovers of nature, are tasteful by nature as well as possessed of strong moral character.

Hirschfeld's affinity for the tropes of religious virtue and his country's historical greatness is evident in his recommendation that a garden include "Gothic ruins and ancient oaks; rustic grottoes declaring a simple piety; monuments honoring the warrior spirit; inscriptions praising heroic virtues;

a reverence for the Germanic past."[48] A man of social conscience, he favored public access to landscape experience, advocating the creation of the *Volksgärten*, or "people's garden." The Englischer Garten in Munich, designed by Friedrich Ludwig von Sckell (1750–1823) and Benjamin Thompson (1753–1814) in 1808, and Berlin's Tiergarten, designed by Peter Joseph Lenné (1789–1866) in 1833, are realizations of this ideal. Hirschfeld saw a popular educational purpose and the opportunity to engender patriotic sentiment in such public gardens by placing in them monuments and statues commemorating great national heroes, "men to whom we owe enlightenment, freedom, prosperity, pleasure." By now sculptural programs that glorified monarchs with an array of emblematic mythological figures were a things of the past. Similarly, it was appropriate, in Hirschfeld's opinion, for landowners to situate cemeteries or memorials in a section of a park or wood, thereby creating "a place that encourages proper sentiments,"[49] an idea that Goethe was to incorporate into the plot of his *Elective Affinities*. In this regard he signals out Rousseau's resting place at Ermenonville, an object of reverence bringing to mind the man whose "spirit rises above this scene and wanders through finer pastures."[50] Given the growing international influence of Rousseau's writings, it is not surprising that, contemporary with Hirschfeld's endorsement, imitations of Ermenonville's poplar-encircled island with its simple funerary urn were incorporated as sentimental elements in European garden design, a prominent example being that of Wörlitz in Dessau (No. 54 and Fig. 36).

Although Hirschfeld uses the term *romantisch* several times in his *Theory*, he was not, strictly speaking, a Romantic. A judicious mediation between art and nature constitutes his proposed "middle way," a manner of designing that "forsakes the old style but does not become entirely lost in the new, one that, while occasionally veering down a path already cleared, still more often follows its own direction."[51] He argues for an architecture of restraint and modesty in country residences, maintaining that "Pomp is not

Fig. 36. Christian Gottlieb Geyser after Christian Friedrich Schuricht, *Haller,* illustration in Christian Cay Lorenz Hirschfeld, *Théorie de l'art des jardins,* Leipzig, 1779–85, collection of Elizabeth Barlow Rogers

dignity, and sumptuousness not beauty." Small classical buildings, especially round temples such as those that now adorn so many eighteenth- and nineteenth-century parks and gardens, were an ideal complement to natural settings, providing them with an appropriate Arcadian imagery. He stresses moderation in the use of garden ornament and is charitable with regard to surviving gardens of a previous age when he argues against completely forsaking the old style for the new at a time when the Continental fashion for the *jardin anglais* was motivating many landowners to destroy their ancestral gardens.

Hirschfeld is particularly eloquent in discussing landscape design as one of the fine arts, one moreover that surpasses landscape painting. In his opinion, its supremacy as an art form derives from its encompassing the flow and sound of water, the growth of plants and their swaying in the breeze, the changeability of light with different times of day and year, and the variableness of weather. Such continual alteration creates movement of a sensory, temporal, and seasonal sort. A more immediately obvious form of movement is that which is physical: passage through a landscape that is sufficiently expansive to provide a variety of scenes perceived from multiple vantage points. Such being the case, temples, gazebos, hermitages, and other Picturesque elements are merely decorative features, incidental accents within various sequences of naturalistic scenery. These in turn are parts of an overall landscape that can never be apprehended all at once in its entirety. This kind of symphonic orchestration of views through movement can be said to be the hallmark of mature Romantic landscape design.

Hirschfeld stands on the cusp of this form of Romanticism. He does not employ the fervent language that would characterize Romantics of the next generation. Still, the Romantic notion of something never completely resolved and always becoming is inherent in his theory. Above all, Hirschfeld anticipates the highest achievement of Romantic landscape design in his notion that nature itself should be its necessary central motif. His advocacy of landscape design in the public interest, his belief that architectural and monumental features conducive to sentimental reflection should be few and subservient to broad vistas and the general spatial layout of parks and estate grounds, the importance he gives to movement as the viewer passes through a series of varied scenes, and his fundamental principle of nature as the designer's highest source of inspiration anticipated the creations of Prince Pückler-Muskau, Frederick Law Olmsted, and other nineteenth-century designers to be discussed later. But first we must consider the genius of the age, who, while giving the initial impetus to the Romantic movement, retreated from its excesses in order to redress the balance between a practical, responsible conduct of human affairs and an unfettered personal freedom that often led to rabid radicalism and sometimes harmful and even tragic consequences.

Johann Wolfgang von Goethe

Johann Wolfgang von Goethe (1749–1832), the great polymath, had as his philosophical mentor Johann Gottfried von Herder (1744–1832). Herder, who advocated intuition over rationality, prompted the young Goethe's interest in Pietism and primeval legends, including the purported Gaelic poems of Ossian, "translated" by James Macpherson. Goethe's Romantic proclivities gained further strength from German Gothicism, the epic power of Homer, and the raw grandeur of Shakespeare. His novel *Die Leiden des jungen Werthers* (The Sorrows of Young Werther; 1774) was revolutionary. The license Goethe gave to romantic passion in his work ushered in the Sturm und Drang movement. The novel's tragic ending, to say nothing of the youthful suicides it stimulated, subsequently became an embarrassment to Goethe. In the end, the notion that feeling was more important than reason was antithetical to his mature intellectual powers. His status as a hero of Romanticism was tempered by a countervailing classicism nourished by his extended sojourn in Italy as well as by the art-historical writing of Johann Joachim Winckelmann (1717–1768), the originator of art history as an intellectual discipline in which classical ruins became subjects for serious period study rather than mere prompts for elegiac sentiment. Goethe's scientific curiosity, as evidenced by his attempt to develop a botanical system of classification, also counteracted the premium Romantics put on unfettered intuition.

Nevertheless, Goethe's interest in landscape design followed the developing Romantic taste. He even advised on the creation of an actual garden when he was employed as a counselor at the court of Duke Karl August Saxe-Weimar-Eisenach in 1775. There he performed various political and administrative duties, chaired commissions, wrote and directed plays, composed poetry, and accompanied the duke on military forays and diplomatic errands while also pursuing his studies of the natural sciences. In May 1778 he visited Wörlitz with Karl August in order to see the 150-square-kilometer (58-square-mile) *Gartenreich*, or garden kingdom, Prince Leopold III, Friedrich Franz of Anhalt-Dessau, had begun constructing a few years earlier. Inspired by a visit to England five years earlier, this progressive prince combined the principles of William Shenstone's *ferme ornée* at Leasowes with the placement in the landscape of temples, sham ruins, and inscribed monuments in the manner of Stowe.

On a second trip to Wörlitz in 1794 Goethe was able to see the landscape in its mature form. By this time the garden boasted a miniature Vesuvius that simulated eruption when fire and smoke were pumped out of a crater as water was being poured over the lip of the cone into which were set pieces of illuminated red-tinted glass. This feature accorded with the contemporary interest in volcanism as inspired by a fascination with the eruptions of Vesuvius and the recent discovery of Pompeii.

Even though Goethe had largely admired Wörlitz, by this time he had rejected the excesses of Early Romanticism that he had once espoused and was highly critical of the garden created by Duke Karl August's intimates Count Moritz Brühl with his wife Christina in the Seifersdorf valley near Dresden. Here all the tropes of *Empfindsamkeit*, or "sensibility," could be found. These included temples, statues, a chapel, an obelisk, grottoes, ruins, a Rousseau-inspired poplar island, and monuments to prominent men of letters, including Goethe himself. Probably because of its plethora of rustic features and monuments as well as its focus on sentimental tropes rather than spatial composition, he found this kind of Romanticism distasteful. Indeed, in a letter to Schiller, he called the garden an "*Unwesen*," an abomination (Fig. 37). At home in Weimar he advised on the design of a park along the Ilm River, a landscape that eschewed such theatrical effects in favor of a more tranquil aesthetic. A comfortable but ordinary garden house along its banks was his home and the center of his protean literary output.

By 1809 when Goethe published *Die Wahlverwandtschaften*, or *Elective Affinities*, his philosophy had moved away from what he now considered to be the disproportionate sentimentality of *The Sorrows of Young Werther*. The title *Elective Affinities* was derived from a chemical process discovered by the Swedish scientist Torbern Bergmann. It signifies the series of dissolutions and recombinations of chemical components comparable to the shifting emotional relationships of Goethe's four protagonists. The story mostly takes place in a garden informed by the author's knowledge of Wörlitz and Hirschfeld's principles of landscape design. Because Goethe, unlike Rousseau, had genuine experience of laying out a park, the garden in *Elective Affinities* is not so much a metaphorical construct as a realistic setting that propels the elegantly constructed plot and, in a sense, acts as a fifth protagonist. Unlike Rousseau's imaginary garden, this one becomes the locus of tragedy rather than redeeming reverie (No. 53).

The building of the garden is central to the plot of *Elective Affinities*, and Goethe approached the subject from both a poetical and a practical perspective. His text is more descriptive of what a Romantic landscape might consist of than was Rousseau's account of Julie's Elysium. For Goethe,

Fig. 37. Johann Adolf Darnstedt, *Youngs Kindern, Philander und Narcissa gewidmet*, illustration in Wilhelm Gottlieb Becker, *Das Seifersdorfer Thal*, Leipzig, 1792, collection of Elizabeth Barlow Rogers

landscape design did not mean a collection of charming, evocative features arranged in a naturalistic setting. As the story moves forward, it becomes apparent that the original concept of the garden as a pretty wildwood adorned with rustic features is too ingratiatingly Picturesque to be fully Romantic; something grander in scale encompassing the larger landscape of the entire estate is needed.

The opening scene takes place in the newly finished moss hut that Charlotte, the mistress of a large estate near Weimar, has designed. Here she greets her husband, Eduard, and has him sit "in such a position that he could at a single glance view the different aspects of the landscape through the door and windows as though they were pictures in a frame."[52] When another protagonist, the Captain, Eduard's boyhood friend and an experienced engineer, comes to live with them, it becomes apparent that an overall plan encompassing the entire property should be made, with consideration of the views not just of Charlotte's garden but of the entire estate and its surrounding scenery. The Captain sets to work, and "The topographical map was soon finished. It represented, to a fairly large scale, the estate and its environs made palpable in their characteristic outlines by pen and paint and fixed by trigonometrical measurements the Captain had been making."[53]

Eager to mitigate the slight Charlotte was feeling because her plans for the garden were being superseded, the men decide to "take out the English books giving descriptions of parks with copper-plates." The books, which we might assume were those of Humphry Repton, "presented an outline of each region and a view of the landscape in its original condition, then on other pages the changes art had made upon it so as to take advantage of and enhance every existing good feature. From this it was very simple to pass over to their own property, to their own environs, and to what might be made of them."[54] (Practical Charlotte frequently reminds the men of the costs entailed by the new plan.)

The shift in the nature of garden design from the *Empfindsamkeit* sentimentality of the Seifersdorf garden of Count Brühl and his wife (and Charlotte's initial garden) toward the mature Romantic style as expressed in the construction of the garden encompassing the entire estate in *Elective Affinities* is indicative of an important alteration in the nature and scope of landscape design. Now, with space displacing Picturesque tropes as the designer's primary consideration, the layout of paths for the best views to be achieved as one moved through the landscape was of critical importance. In this regard, the fourth principal character, Charlotte's beautiful ward, Ottilie, plays a role: "Putting her finger on the highest part of the rise, she says: 'I would build the summer house here. You wouldn't see the manor from there, of course, since it would be hidden by the clump of trees; instead, you would be in a new and different world, with the village and all the houses hidden from sight. The view of the lakes, toward the mill, the hills, mountains and countryside, is extraordinarily beautiful; I noticed it as we went past.'"[55]

In *Elective Affinities*, Goethe took up cemetery design, a landscape genre then gaining importance. During the time she had been busy transforming the estate into a picturesque composition, Charlotte had all the gravestones in the cemetery moved and set up against a wall of the church. She then had the ground leveled and "sown with various kinds of clover, which provided a fine green and flowery expanse."[56] Understandably, this provokes debate over the merits of a unified lawnlike landscape with a few monuments, perhaps with elegiac inscriptions, versus a heterogeneous mélange of parishioners' gravestones. Goethe's representative of the opposition, a young solicitor whose clients are suing for the revocation of a bequest they have promised the church, declares:

> You will understand that all persons, the highest and the humblest, are concerned to mark the place in which their loved ones lie. To the poorest peasant burying one of his children it is a kind of comfort and consolation to set upon its grave a feeble wooden cross, and to decorate it with a wreath, so that he may preserve the memory of that child for at any rate as long as his sorrow for it endures, even though such a memorial must, like that grief itself, at last be wiped away by time.[57]

The rebuttal is voiced by Charlotte's architect, who is standing by:

To the architect's suggestion that there should be "well-conceived, well-executed monuments, not scattered about all over the place but erected on a spot where they can expect to remain," Charlotte replies, "If artists are as rich in ideas as that, tell me why we can never get away from the form of a petty obelisk, a truncated column or a funeral urn."[59] In this way Goethe confirms the commemorative forms now widely adopted for secular burial, the same ones that would soon ornament Père Lachaise and the American rural cemeteries discussed below.

While it stands as an important literary work, *Elective Affinities* can also be read as a landscape treatise. It puts forth a comprehensive plan that retains some Picturesque structures while opening the garden up to broad views of the countryside, partially hiding a village from view while integrating it into the overall scheme. Though disregarded, there is an understanding of the high costs involved in executing such a large-scale Reptonian project. There is also awareness that the scenery sequentially revealed by movement through the landscape is the primary component of large-scale park design, thereby making road and path alignment extremely important. Finally, it puts forth a new approach to the design of cemeteries. It is clear that Goethe must have read Hirschfeld's *Theory of Garden Art* when he wrote *Elective Affinities*. Because of his Hirschfeldian belief that monuments, hermitages, grottoes, and other sentiment-prompting features should remain subservient to unadorned nature, Goethe may be said to have anticipated the principles underlying the mature phase of Romantic landscape design. Indeed, one could say that in *Elective Affinities*, he had formulated the theory that would receive its actual expression in the great park designs of Prince Pückler-Muskau in Germany and Frederick Law Olmsted in America.

Caspar David Friedrich

In terms of painting, the work of Caspar David Friedrich (1774–1840) epitomizes Romanticism's alliance with the Sublime more than that of any other artist. In Friedrich's work we sense a mystical and religious communion with nature. Guided by German transcendentalist philosophy, he infused his paintings with intimations of nature's divinity. This takes the form of scenes charged with drama: nocturnal landscapes illuminated by moonlight as well as sunset and dawn panoramas. Such tropes as the solitary figure dwarfed by towering peaks or gazing with awe into the distance while standing on a vertiginous precipice, a ruined chapel in the snow, or a cross planted in enigmatic isolation in a wild landscape are indicative of the relocation of religious piety from Catholic doctrine to Protestant pantheism (Fig. 38). The German-American painter Albert Bierstadt (1830–1902) was probably influenced by Friedrich's example in his use of similar Romantic metaphors in his grand Andean and other exotic landscapes, which, like Friedrich's, are dramatically lit by alpenglow (Fig. 39).

One explanation for the heightened sublimity found in Friedrich's work may lie in the fact that he painted in an age of waning faith. His infinite spaces viewed from a dizzying height symbolize the substitution of the unfathomable for the certainty of a God-ordained universe. Yet his works assert that, even in the face of the void, nature projects the power of divine creation and opens the way for ecstasy. Solitary communion with the sacralized wild landscape rather than institutionalized worship brings intimations of immortality. For Friedrich and other Romantics, such as Wordsworth, the tokens of God's presence were the ethereal light of the moon and the prismatic colors of the rainbow.

Carl Gustav Carus

Friedrich's friend Carl Gustav Carus (1789–1869), who was both a physician and a painter as well as an aesthetic theorist, could have been describing a Freidrich painting when he wrote:

Climb to the topmost mountain peak, gaze out across long chains of hills, and observe the rivers in their courses and

Fig. 38. Caspar David Friedrich, *Two Men Contemplating the Moon*, ca. 1825–30, The Metropolitan Museum of Art, New York

Fig. 39. Albert Bierstadt, *Sunrise on the Matterhorn*, after 1875, The Metropolitan Museum of Art, New York

all the magnificence that offers itself to your eye—what feeling takes hold of you? There is a silent reverence within you; you lose yourself in infinite space; silently, your whole being is purified and cleansed; your ego disappears. You are nothing; God is all.[60]

Like Ruskin, Carus believed that the study of nature was not an end in itself but rather a means of portraying the artist's subjective feelings. Like Constable, he made numerous cloud studies in order to match natural atmospherics with human emotion. In his *Nine Letters on Landscape Painting,* which serves as an illuminating aesthetic treatise on Romanticism in art, Carus proclaimed that inasmuch as "our own feelings are inherently founded on an aspiration toward the infinite, so the sky, as its image, profoundly and powerfully sets the mood of the whole landscape over which it arches, and indeed establishes itself as the most glorious, the most indispensable component of landscape itself"[61] (No. 65).

Now, at the full tide of the Romantic movement, Burke's categories of Beautiful and Sublime seem irrelevant. For Carus, the two are conflated into a single overpowering sensation that is deeply religious. "Beauty," he said, "is what makes us feel the divine essence in nature" (i.e., in the world of sensory phenomena).[62] But what of the manifestly grotesque? Writing a quarter of a century before the publication of Darwin's *Origin of Species,* Carus could assert that the apparent ugliness of some forms of life (he suggested mollusks, worms, spiders, lumpfish, flatfish, toads) is due to the fact that they are only transitional, "the expression of imperfect evolution, of thwarted aspiration toward higher form."[63] It is perception of the unity of all nature that fosters feelings of transcendental harmony, for "Nature as such is necessarily and entirely beautiful, and is recognized as beautiful in the degree to which its inwardness, the divinity of its essence, manifests itself."[64]

Prince Pückler von Muskau

Hermann Ludwig Heinrich, Prince of Pückler-Muskau (1785–1871)—known as Germany's garden prince—was the exceptional and original landscape designer who combined his own ideas with Hirschfeld and Goethe's prescriptions to achieve one of the most Romantic landscapes in Germany. From 1816 until 1846 he dedicated himself to the transformation of his 1,350-acre (546-hectare) ancestral estate straddling the River Neisse into an idyllic landscape that unified castle, town, and park with the surrounding region both functionally and aesthetically.

Eager to indulge his self-confessed "parkomanie" and love of natural scenery, he took an extensive carriage tour through England and Ireland in 1828–29. The travelogue version of his letters to his wife, published in translation in 1833 as *Tour in England, Ireland, and France in the Years 1828 and 1829 in a Series of Letters by a German Prince,* provides a lively account of English scenery and manners combined with penetrating social insights and detailed descriptions of the places he visited. His observations on London's parks and numerous estates of the nobility show an informed independence of judgment colored by his own Romantic ideas. He considered Stowe "another specimen of English grandeur and magnificence" with grounds "in many respects beautiful, and remarkable for fine lofty trees." However, he found them "so overloaded with temples and buildings of all sorts, that the greatest possible improvement to the place would be the pulling down ten or a dozen of them."[65] He also visited Studley Royal, where the great attraction was the ruins of Fountains Abbey, which he extolled as "the largest and most beautiful in England" (see Fig. 4). Yet he complained about the pleasure ground, which, like Stowe, was "rather encumbered with a multitude of old-fashioned summer-houses, temples, and worthless leaden statues." In spite of his unqualified admiration of the architecture of the ruined monastery, he disliked the fact that it was framed by a smooth-mown carpet of grass. "Were this poetic structure mine," he declared, "I would immediately set about creating a little more artificial wildness about it; for the whole ought to partake of that air of half-decayed grandeur which has the greatest power over the imagination."[66]

Although completely confident in his own

judgment as a landscape designer, Pückler considered Repton his exemplar. He gained ideas and technical advice from his writings and even sought to hire him to come to Muskau as a consultant. Moreover, he adopted Repton's manner of illustrating his books with large-format, before-and-after colored plates in his 1834 treatise, *Andeutungen über Landschaftsgärtnerei* (Hints on Landscape Gardening; Nos. 56–63).

Pückler began the *Andeutungen* by announcing his fundamental theory: "One principle should, above all, underlie the art of park design; namely, the creation, from the material at hand, out of the place as it stands, of a concentrated picture having Nature as its poetical ideal; the same principle which, embodied in all other spheres of art, makes of the true work of art a microcosm, a perfect, self-contained world in little."[67] Divided into two parts, the first half of the book attests to how much technical expertise he had amassed. Its concise and informative chapters concern the overall layout of parks and, within them, the disposition and design of lawns, meadows, and pleasure gardens. They also deal with the grouping of buildings, trees, and shrubs as well as with water, islands, rocks, earthworks, and esplanades. There is an important chapter on roads and paths, and unlike most previous garden writers, Pückler concluded with a chapter on perhaps the most critical factor in the continuing life of a designed landscape—maintenance. The second part of the book is a description of the park in Muskau and its origins.

While Pückler was romantically passionate in his advocacy of using nature as the designer's template, he, like Repton, was interested in the practical application of his theories to the actual landscape. Always ready to speak from his position as a member of the privileged class, he began his chapter on trees and shrubs with these words: "Fortunate the man to whom his forbears have bequeathed lofty woods of old oaks, beeches, and lindens, these proud giants of our Northern clime, standing still untouched by the woodman's murderous axe. . . . May an ancient tree be to you, kind reader, who love Nature, a holy thing. And yet, here

also, the individual tree must be sacrificed, if need be, to the general group."[68]

He would forgo, albeit reluctantly, the venerable oak for the well-composed view, choosing vistas of varied scenery with alternating patterns of light and shade over the display of uniform specimen groupings. Pückler thus maintained, "There is nothing more beautiful and more in accordance with untrammeled Nature than a luxurious mixed forest where the sun dances among the many hues of green, and nothing more monotonous and dismal than a district where one passes now a clump of firs, then a long stretch of larches, here a patch of birches, and in another place a collection of poplars or oaks, and a thousand paces on the same tedious rows beginning again."[69]

He believed that for a designer, as for a painter, light was a primary consideration. Indeed, he approached landscape design as if he were a painter: "If the lights and shadows are arranged in due proportion in the picture, the grouping as a whole will be successful. Grassplots, water, and fields, which do not themselves throw any shadow, but only receive it from other objects, are lights in the hands of the landscape artist, while trees, forests, and houses (and rocks where they can be used) must serve as shadows."[70] In this way he sought to reproduce within the natural limitations of the site the same effects the Romantic painter could achieve with greater freedom on canvas.

Pückler's meadows were to him "the canvas of Nature-painting, the playground where the sun disports an element of brightness which set out the whole landscape."[71] Here, as elsewhere, his prescriptions are informed by practical experience and ecological understanding. As an example, in analyzing the best conditions and types of soils in which to grow certain varieties of grass he wrote, "In wet ground the greater part should be timothy *(Phleum pratense)*; for heavy soil, rye grass *(Lolium perenne)*; for loam, yellow clover *(Medicago lupulina)* and French rye grass *(Arrhenatherum elatius)*; for light soil, honey or velvet grass *(Holcus lanatus)*; for high ground, white clover *(Trifolium repens)*, etc."[72] One can guess that much of the credit

Fig. 40. August Wilhelm Schirmer, *Cottage in the Garden of the Hunting Lodge,* illustration in Hermann Fürst von Pückler-Muskau, *Andeutungen über Landschaftsgärtnerei,* Stuttgart, 1834, Stiftung Fürst-Pückler-Park Bad Muskau

for this and other forms of horticultural expertise as well as sound maintenance practices is due to good advice from his head gardener, Jacob Rehde. But however he came by his considerable knowledge, Pückler's clear instructions in the *Hints* are still of benefit to landscape designers and the owners of country places.

Like Repton, Pückler was concerned with the laws of perspective and the relative scale of objects, which change in appearance as one moves closer to them. He criticized English landscapes, particularly Brown's, as boring because of their enclosing belts of trees, which obstructed views into the surrounding countryside. He argued that artful screening of some areas outside the park, while opening up other portions of its borders to create views of surrounding fields and distant forests, would enhance the impression of its extent and prevent what he considered to be the monotonous character of the tree-circumscribed boundaries of English parks. This hide-and-reveal strategy would provide many pleasant surprises for those touring the park as, after riding through a forested area, they would find a beautiful view opening up before their eyes. He criticized English estates for being exclusionary and recommended that other German landowners follow his example and open their parks to visitors.

Pückler felt that "Buildings should never stand freely exposed, lest they appear as spots, uncon-nected with the natural surroundings."[73] He also believed that they should not be merely ornamental but have a positive purpose. He preferred Picturesque irregularity in park buildings and partial concealment, for "the eye frequently finds more pleasure in a single chimney in the distance, with its spiral of gray smoke curling upward against a background of trees, than in a bare palace exposed to view on all sides, which Nature has not yet lovingly approached and embraced"[74] (Fig. 40). He opposed ornamental temples and inscriptions except "where they are occasionally necessary, as on the finger-post at a crossroad." While he approved of preserving historic buildings, he opposed designing new buildings in an old style, saying that "a dallying with things Gothic is as silly as a man in second childhood." In a similarly practical vein, he allowed that "a park must have the character of untrammeled Nature," but that it betrays "a lack of taste to ignore the human element altogether, and, in order to keep the illusion of wild Nature, to have to wade through the tall grass and tear one's self on thorns in the woods, and come upon a bench for the weary without a rest for the back, although Rousseau recommends all this."[75]

Traversing a landscape in the same manner that one listens to a piece of music—rather than moving along the prescribed course of a didactic itinerary as at Ermenonville—is, as noted above,

a fundamental characteristic of the mature Romantic landscape. The placing of monuments and Picturesque features within it is no longer an important design objective, although such ornamental additions may still be included, if not so much for sentimental as for compositional, and sometimes practical, purposes. What is important is the pleasure—and often surprise—of experiencing alternating unfolding views, with one scenic passage harmoniously contrasting with another. In translating the compositional form of a musical theme and variations into landscape terms, Pückler believed the designer should follow the dictates of the natural topography and landforms in laying out his paths and drives, keeping in mind that they "should never make a turn without the requisite obstacle that necessitates it." There are plates in the *Andeutungen* that demonstrate the correct, as well as the incorrect, way to align a path (Fig. 41).

Since the sensory pleasure of movement itself is an important ingredient of the Romantic landscape experience, smooth carriage drives are essential to the enjoyment of the various views of turf, wood, and water offered by a large park, and paths are necessary for its further exploration. Macadam—pavement made of layers of compacted broken stone according to a formula developed by John McAdam—was a recent improvement in road construction and one that made Pückler's carriage rides in England more agreeable than elsewhere.

Speaking again in a practical vein, he boasted of building his park roads according to a better formula than that used for macadamized roads, "which consist entirely of broken granite, are comfortable only after considerable travel has smoothed them down, being at first very hard on horses and foot travelers."[76] He then provided his recipe of road fines and carriage-drive building instructions.

In discussing water, Pückler claimed that "Though not so indispensable to landscape as a rich vegetation, fresh and clear water, whether stream or lake, greatly increases its charm." He went on to point out the backwardness of English landscape designers in this matter, saying, "Even the ornamental waters of Repton, their best landscape artist, which I have seen, failed in many respects." These comments are followed by a series of rules about how to construct banks and work with a stream's natural currents in order to avoid an artificial appearance as well as how to create lakes whose outlines are not visible in a single glance: "partly by means of islands, partly by very deep bays, the limits of which are mostly concealed in shrubbery." Here, as elsewhere, he thought it essential to consider the effects of light and shadow in a painterly fashion so that "open, grassy banks, single high trees, woods, and thickets should vary the effect with broad spots where the sunlight can have full entry, in order not to deprive the water of its transparency and brilliance by concealment." He also gave instructions on how to create naturalistic islands, for "a lonely spot in a well-wooded island, or the distant view of a mass of arching foliage swimming on the crystal surface of the water is more attractive to many than all the charms obtainable on dry land."[77] Streams could be made Picturesque if rocks appeared to be "driven together by floods." To make this point, he provided an illustration of a stream at Muskau in which a low dam is covered with stones that have been set "in a slanting direction, as if they had been forced up in that manner,"[78] making the dam over which the water spills invisible while the stones animate the current (Fig. 42).

Pückler's remarks on maintenance strike at the essential drawback—and perhaps asset—of landscape design as an art form: "It is impossible to create a finished, permanent work of art in landscape gardening, such as a painter, sculptor, and architect are able to produce, because our material is not inanimate, but living." A landscape is always in a state of becoming. For this reason, "a skillful guiding hand" must remain active over the entire life of a park so that "beauties are continually being added without losing or sacrificing those already in existence." He added, "The chief tool which we use—that is, our brush and chisel—is the spade for *construction;* the chief tool for *maintenance* and *improvement* is the axe."[79] Being a private landowner, Pückler could prune and thin his trees and shrubs and open up vistas as he chose without the vociferous opposition encountered by public park managers.

In sum, Pückler understood spatial composition, as seen in his broad meadows and controlled views of the rural countryside beyond the park, in the primacy given native vegetation and natural landscape forms in the development of his design, in letting topography and existing landscape features dictate the alignment of roads and paths, and in his consideration of how to orchestrate the succession of scenes that unfold as one moves through the landscape (Fig. 43). With regard to these things, he happily advised other Prussian nobles who sought his assistance in laying out the grounds of their estates, but, unlike Repton, he was an aristocrat and not a professional landscape gardener who worked for clients. When financial ruin forced him to sell Muskau to Prince Frederick of the Netherlands, he turned his creative energies to Branitz, his second seat and final resting place. The massive pyramidal earthwork that Pückler had built as his memorial and tomb there is, like Rousseau's tomb at Ermenonville,

Fig. 42. August Wilhelm Schirmer, *Design of Weirs,* illustration in Hermann Fürst von Pückler-Muskau, *Andeutungen über Landschaftsgärtnerei,* Stuttgart, 1834, Stiftung Fürst-Pückler-Park Bad Muskau

Fig. 43. August Wilhelm Schirmer, *View over the Plain Toward the Riesengebirge,* illustration in Hermann Fürst von Pückler-Muskau, *Andeutungen über Landschaftsgärtnerei,* Stuttgart, 1834, Stiftung Fürst-Pückler-Park Bad Muskau

situated on an island in a lake. It is much grander in scale than the masonry pyramids that served as *fabriques* in eighteenth-century French gardens and strikes the visitor as something of an anomaly within the context of the otherwise naturalistic composition of Branitz, where the park's meadows and ancient trees are wedded to pleasant views of the surrounding rural fields.

Prince Pückler created the parks at Muskau and Branitz in the knowledge that he lived at the twilight of the power and privileges of his class. In the face of the rise of bourgeois capitalism and the demise of the old aristocratic way of life, he had this to say:

Many ultra-liberals will perhaps smile at such a thought, but every form of human development is worthy of honor, and just because that of which I speak is perhaps nearing its end, it assumes a universal, poetic, and romantic interest, which so far cannot be extracted from factories, machines, or even constitutions, suum cuique. *Yours is now money and power—leave to the poor, worn-out nobility its poetry, the sole thing which is left to it. Honor the weak old age, ye Spartans![80]*

Park Jurjavés

Although his work was confined to his estates at Muskau and Branitz and the advice he gave to others, as in the laying out of Park Babelsberg in Potsdam, Pückler's influence, especially after the publication of the *Andeutungen* in 1834, was considerable. In the 1840s, Park Jurjavés, a particularly fine and little-known 700-acre (283-hectare) Romantic park in Croatia was created by Archbishop Juraj Haulik de Varallya on the lands of his wealthy diocese stretching from Zagreb Mountain to the Sava plain. Opened in 1843, it was the first public park to be built in this part of Europe. Now called Maksimir after its original progenitor, Bishop Maksimilijan von Vrhovac, its design by Archbishop Haulik owes a considerable debt to Pückler. In following Pückler's prescriptions, the archbishop and Michael Sebastian Riedl, the park's director, created a landscape of sweeping lawns and distant vistas. Other elements in line with Pückler's theories were the inclusion of views of orchards, vineyards, and agrarian scenery, the elimination of Gothic and Chinese follies, faux ruins, and hackneyed inscriptions in favor of more natural features associated with the character of the locale and climate, and the reliance on the beauty of indigenous plant material rather than exotic specimens.

To describe and portray the park in a large folio album in the manner of Pückler's *Andeutungen*, Bishop Haulik commissioned the Viennese artist Ivan Zasche to paint several views, which were lithographed and published as the *Park Jurjavés* in 1853. The description accompanying the eleven hand-colored plates speaks of the park's seeming boundlessness, praising the site as "so favorable that the entire surrounding countryside, viewed from different points, seems to merge into nature and the whole visible horizon gives the impression of an immense English park"[81] (No. 55). Beyond the realm of Romantic aesthetics, the park had agronomy as part of its program. Archbishop Haulik was the first chairman of the Croatian Slavonic Agricultural Society, formed in 1841, and he intended the farmstead portion of the park to demonstrate the latest technical improvements and farming principles. The album describes a creamery, hop kiln, brewery, mill, sawmill, poultry coop, silkworm farm, and apiary as well as a large orchard and flower garden.

Park Jurjavés may be considered Romantic for the degree to which Archbishop Haulik used natural scenery as the chief design motif. Like Pückler, he placed ornamental flowerbeds on the grounds immediately adjacent to his summer residence in order to display the many horticultural specimens newly available to nineteenth-century gardeners. This kind of feature, however, was an anomaly within the context of the park's overall naturalistic design.

In summary, the European Romantic park in its fully developed stage, as seen at Muskau and Jurjavés, implies the primacy of nature in guiding the designer's plan and providing the landscape's predominant motif. Inherent in the concept of the mature Romantic park is the notion of unbounded space created by an absence of visible boundaries and the selective incorporation of the agricultural environs as an important scenic element. The egalitarianism implicit in Romanticism was a necessary philosophical underpinning of Hirschfeld's concept of the *Volksgarten*, or "people's park." Even in advance of the movement to create public parks in municipalities, the spirit of the times caused aristocrats, such as Pückler and Archbishop Haulik, to paternalistically make their landscape creations accessible to nearby townspeople. Although the Englischer Garten in Munich was designed as a public park in 1789 by Friedrich Ludwig von Sckell and Liverpool's Birkenhead Park was created in 1847 by Sir Joseph Paxton, to see the fullest expression of the purpose-built people's park as a lasting municipal institution we must turn to the nation in which democracy was the founding form of government.

ROMANTICISM IN AMERICA

American Romanticism is not a single cultural attitude but rather one pole of an ambivalent, multifaceted dialectic. For most Americans, civilization was equated with the conquest of wilderness for economic gain. This motive for settling the frontier was tempered by the twin ideals of Deism—the belief that God resides in Creation rather than in institutionalized religion and can be apprehended directly by the individual through His glorious handiwork—and Transcendentalism—the belief in the all-pervading spirit of the universe—a philosophy epitomized in Emerson's manifesto declaring that "Nature always wears the colors of the spirit"[82] and is the proper school in which to instruct the soul in ways that lead to an apprehension of the divine.

Later, following the disappearance of the American frontier, the dichotomy persisted. There was on one hand a desire to showcase wilderness on the part of those who believed in exploiting the wonders of nature for tourist recreation and, on the other, an impulse toward preserving it by those who wished to see government set aside certain large tracts of scenic wilderness as a precious residue of the beauty and sublimity of pristine nature before the continent's settlement. Both impulses were tied up with an assertion of national identity. Europe had its architectural glories and poetical ruins, but chauvinistic Americans believed that its splendid wonders—Niagara Falls, the Yellowstone geysers, the Grand Canyon, and cordilleras of forested mountains—were sources of even greater pride and that exceptional parts of the national scenery should remain in the public domain for all to enjoy. The creation of American municipal parks is a further demonstration of the Romantic belief that the experience of nature is a common right and a particular virtue of democracy.

Jonathan Edwards

Because of the initial dangers and abundance of the American wilderness, the American attitude toward nature was an evolving one, flipping from terror and wary exploitation to reverence and greed. With a tenuous hold on the land, the seventeenth-century Puritans viewed the vast forest with its towering, centuries-old trees as a wilderness to be subdued in accordance with the biblical injunction to take dominion over the earth. The eighteenth-century Calvinist theologian Jonathan Edwards (1703–1758), however, was sufficiently attracted to Newton's theory—that the phenomena of nature were grounded in eternal law—to take the daring step of reinterpreting scriptural doctrine to embrace the concept of God's revelation and grace in Nature. In his autobiographical narrative, Edwards described an epiphany he experienced while taking a solitary walk of contemplation, "looking upon the sky and clouds." There came over him "so sweet a sense of the glorious *majesty* and *grace* of God, as I know not how to express." With a fervor that sounds very much like Romanticism, he described how he saw "God's excellency, his wisdom, his purity and love . . . in the sun, moon, and stars; in the clouds and blue sky; in the grass, flowers, trees; in the water and all nature." Articulating a personal version of the Sublime, he went on to say, "I used to sit and view the moon for a long time; and in the day, spent much time in viewing the clouds and sky, to behold the sweet glory of God in these things. . . . And scarce any thing, among all the works of nature, was so sweet to me as thunder and lightning."[83] Clearly Edwards's notion of Sublime nature did not accord with Burke's aesthetic category so much as it prefigured Wordsworth's rapturous personal response to nature.

Thomas Jefferson

Thomas Jefferson (1743–1825), a Deist and Enlightenment intellectual, set his architectural masterpiece, Monticello, upon an eminence with spectacular views of forested mountain ridges growing blue in the distance. Rhetorically, he queried, "where has nature spread so rich a mantle under the eye? mountains, forests, rocks, rivers. With what majesty do we there ride above the storms! How sublime to look down into the workhouse of nature, to see her clouds, hail, snow, rain, thunder, all fabricated at our feet! And the glorious Sun, when rising as if out of a distant water, just gilding the tops of the mountains, and giving life to all nature!"[84]

However Romantic in extolling the stupendous scene, Jefferson saw this grand continental vista as a bounty for future generations of Americans—fulfilling in reality the antique myth of a pastoral Golden Age by turning the immense and potentially fruitful continent into independently owned farms. The means he sought to achieve this end did not envision a settlement pattern that discriminated between scenery to protect and land to exploit. Following the Louisiana Purchase of 1803, Jefferson extended the Land Ordinance of 1785, superimposing upon the natural landscape of the states and yet-to-be-settled territories a mile-square surveyor's grid. This enabled the disposition of the vast federal land holdings into sale parcels of 640-acre sections and ultimately into quarter sections of 160 acres (395 hectares). From the air today one can see how road alignments following the national grid have etched a pattern resembling a giant piece of graph paper onto the country west of the Ohio River.

The same dichotomous view of nature in mathematical terms on the one hand and Romantic terms on the other is nowhere better illustrated than in Jefferson's description of the chasm beneath the Natural Bridge in *Notes on Virginia:*

> *The fissure, just at the bridge, is, by some admeasurements, 270 feet deep, by others only 205. It is about 45 feet wide at the bottom and 90 feet at the top.... Its breadth in the middle is about 60 feet, but more at the ends, and the thickness of the mass, at the summit of the arch, about 40 feet.... Though the sides of this bridge are provided in some parts with a parapet of fixed rocks, yet few men have resolution to walk to them, and look into the abyss. You involuntarily fall on your hands and feet, creep to the parapet, and peep over it.... If the view from the top be painful and intolerable, that from below is delightful in an equal extreme. It is impossible for the emotions arising from the sublime to be felt beyond what they are here; so beautiful an arch, so elevated, so light, and springing as it were up to heaven, the rapture of the spectator is really indescribable!*[85]

Jefferson's simultaneous embrace of the rational and the romantic is evident in the respective layouts of the Poplar Forest—the farm that served as his retreat from his incessant stream of visitors—and Monticello. Poplar Forest's plan is firmly geometrical. It consists of a tree-defined perfect circle within which two identical circular mounds sym-

THE NATURAL BRIDGE, VIRGINIA.

WITH ILLUSTRATIONS BY HARRY FENN.

THE Falls of Niagara and the Natural Bridge are justly esteemed the most remarkable curiosities in North America. So exceptional is the beauty, mingled with sublimity, of these famous scenes, that thoughtless persons have characterized them as "freaks of Nature." But in Nature—great, beneficent, and doing all things in order—there are no freaks. She shows her power in the grand

Fig. 44. Harry Fenn, *The Natural Bridge, Virginia,* illustration in William Cullen Bryant, ed., *Picturesque America,* New York, 1872–74, The Morgan Library & Museum

metrically flank an octagonal villa. Monticello, on the other hand, was conceived as a *ferme ornée*—a farm with occasional ornamental features adorning a pleasing rural landscape.

In 1771 he went so far in the direction of Romanticism as to fantasize a design for "a Burying place [in] some unfrequented vale in the park . . . among antient and venerable oaks." Here he planned to erect "a small Gothic temple of antique appearance," into which would be admitted "very little light, perhaps none at all, save only the feeble ray of an half extinguished lamp."[86] He also envisioned channeling a stream into a cistern, which might serve as a pool for bathing. At the mouth of the spring he would carve a grotto that was to be decorated with translucent pebbles and beautiful shells and in which a sculpture of a sleeping nymph would rest on a couch of moss. These projects, however, inevitably took a back seat to his more pragmatic horticultural interests. No temple ever rose at Monticello, no grotto was built to adorn a spring, and instead of the Romantic burial ground, a simple square graveyard enclosed by a fence was laid out in 1773.

Ralph Waldo Emerson

Born in the year of President Jefferson's Louisiana Purchase, the essayist and poet Ralph Waldo

Emerson (1803–1882) became the leader of the Transcendentalist movement in America. In 1836, having absorbed the tenets of Transcendental philosophy espoused by Novalis—the pseudonym of Georg Philip Friedrich Freiherr von Hardenberg (1772–1801)—and other German thinkers, he wrote his famous essay *Nature*. Like them, he was capable of romanticizing the world by elevating the most humble aspects of life to reverence and did not need to seek the Sublime in wild nature in order to experience religious awe. For him, as for Constable, it could be readily found close to home. Thus, Emerson apprehended divinity in "the charming landscape which I saw this morning," a scene made up of some twenty or thirty farms, each owned but yet not owned by any farmer because "There is a property in the horizon which no man has but he whose eye can integrate all the parts, that is, the poet."[87] The poetry Emerson had in mind was not necessarily literary, the province of the actual poet. It was instead a system of metaphysics accessible to all who were able to comprehend the meaning of the beauty spread all around them in every season and every time of day.

Beauty for Emerson was not an end in itself, a subject of aesthetics in the manner of Burke and Gilpin. Rather than characterize scenery as Picturesque or Sublime, he maintained, "The shows of day, the dewy morning, the rainbow, mountains, orchards in blossom, stars, moonlight, shadows in still water, and the like, if too eagerly hunted become shows merely, and mock us with their unreality. . . . The presence of a higher, namely, of the spiritual elemental is essential to its perfection."[88] Beauty could be embodied in art, for "This love of beauty is Taste. . . . But beauty in nature is not ultimate. It is the herald of inward and eternal beauty, and is not alone a solid and satisfactory good. It must stand as a part, and not as yet the last or highest expression of the final cause of Nature."[89] That cause was God. With the oratorical skills honed during his brief tenure as a Unitarian minister, Emerson exhorted men to "see the miraculous in the common" and "kindle science with the fire of the holiest affections."[90]

William Cullen Bryant

It would be hard to underestimate the pervasiveness of Transcendentalism and its influence on nineteenth-century American Romantic ideals. Emerson's contemporary William Cullen Bryant (1794–1878) took up the theme of nature as a moral force. Bryant's boyhood in the Berkshires had imbued him with a Romantic enjoyment of natural scenery, and as a young man practicing law in Great Barrington, he wrote to a friend saying that he congratulated himself "on being a resident of so picturesque a region."[91] But his appreciation of his native locale went deeper than this. As a precocious youth, Bryant had indulged his voracious appetite for classical literature and poetry in his father's ample library while nourishing his love of natural science outdoors. He was, in his own words, a "passionate botanist," and some of his youthful poems such as "The Yellow Violet" and "To the Fringed Gentian" marry his extensive and careful observation of plant life with an ecstatic love of nature. As a Romantic nature poet, he felt a strong kinship with Wordsworth, and on an 1845 trip to England he made a point of calling on the great man at Rydal Mount. Nevertheless Bryant was thoroughly and consciously a poet of his own country. The Berkshire countryside of his boyhood was his Lake Country, and he sought to write in an unfettered native idiom on themes related to a distinctly American landscape.

Bryant's poem "Thanatopsis" (1811), written when he was only seventeen, enjoins us to "Go forth, under the open sky, and list / To Nature's teachings, while from all around— / Earth and her waters, and the depths of air— / Comes a still voice—" For Bryant, the still voice was that of God, and primeval nature had a solemn grandeur unmatched by the most magnificent architectural works of humankind. America's old-growth forest, which had not yet been cleared, represented the Golden Age sanctuaries when the world was young. Here was a most worthy place of worship to which he sang this paean in "A Forest Hymn."

> The groves were God's first temples. Ere man learned
> To hew the shaft, and lay the architrave,

And spread the roof above them—ere he framed
The lofty vault, to gather and roll back
The sound of anthems; in the darkling wood,
Amid the cool and silence, he knelt down,
And offered to the Mightiest solemn thanks
And supplication. For his simple heart
Might not resist the sacred influences
Which, from the stilly twilight of the place,
And from the gray old trunks that high in heaven
Mingled their mossy boughs, and from the sound
Of the invisible breath that swayed at once
All their green tops, stole over him, and bowed
His spirit with the thought of boundless power
And inaccessible majesty. Ah, why
Should we, in the world's riper years, neglect
God's ancient sanctuaries, and adore
Only among the crowd, and under roofs
That our frail hands have raised? Let me, at least,
Here, in the shadow of this aged wood,
Offer one hymn—thrice happy, if it find
Acceptance in His ear.[92]

This meditation on nature as spiritual succor and the healer of grief over death is philosophically in tune with the arguments that were soon to be advanced for the creation of rural cemeteries.

Whether as the reluctant young New England lawyer or, a few years later, as the distinguished editor of New York's *Evening Post*—his pulpit for many liberal and nationalistic causes, such as resisting the expansion of slavery and championing the creation of a Central Park—Bryant cherished the hours spent in rural rambles as a respite from urban toil. And like Wordsworth laying out his garden at Rhydal Mount, Bryant took a keen interest in the landscape of his summer residence of Cedarmere on Long Island. Here he and his wife, Frances, spent happy hours planning and planting their garden and orchard, and in time Cedarmere became a renowned horticultural showplace.[93]

Although a nationalistic champion of American scenery, Bryant's Romantic curiosity and appetite for adventure found an outlet in foreign travel. Thanks to the generosity of a wealthy young friend, Charles Leupp, Bryant was able to go abroad as Leupp's traveling companion to England and Europe, to the Orkney and Shetland Islands, and to Egypt and the Holy Land. On these occasions the absentee editor was able to act as his own travel correspondent for the *Evening Post* and, more importantly, to further his thinking about an emerging American national culture from a foreign vantage point.

Unlike the artist Thomas Cole, Bryant found little inspiration in Old World landscapes, but the exoticism of the Middle East was another matter. During his passage to Alexandria in 1852 he had several illuminating conversations with the renowned British botanist Robert Fortune, whose previous expeditions to collect specimens for the Royal Horticultural Society and the British East India Company had taken him to China and India. In Egypt he was overcome at the sight of the great temples at Luxor and Karnak, romantically proclaiming, "As I sat among the forest of gigantic columns in the great court of the temple at Karnac, it appeared to me that after such a sight no building reared by human hands could affect me with a sense of sublimity."[94] Bearded and dressed like a Bedouin as he traveled by camel caravan from Cairo to Jerusalem, he exercised his prodigious curiosity as a naturalist, avidly studying and identifying numerous species of desert flora and fauna. But the deep and colorful impressions made by his encounter with exotic lands did not deflect him from his course as a champion of the Romantic American landscape, and, like Gilpin, he was instrumental in persuading his countrymen of the pleasure to be had from touring parts of their native land, most especially the Hudson River Valley, where such establishments as the Catskill Mountain House had been built to accommodate them. Throughout this beautiful mountain-framed valley, tourists in search of the Picturesque found both nature in its Sublime guise and the newly risen mansions of the rich, such as Blithewood and others built by the architect Alexander Jackson Davis, many of which had Picturesque grounds laid out according to the advice of Andrew Jackson Downing (Nos. 73 and 74).

In 1872 Bryant, then age seventy-eight, agreed to serve as the nominal editor of D. Appleton and Company's publication, in a series of fascicles, of *Picturesque America . . . A Delineation by Pen and Pencil of the Mountains, Rivers, Lakes, Forests, Water-Falls, Shores, Cañons, Valleys, Cities, and Other Picturesque Features* (No. 70). By this time, the virgin groves he had reverently extolled a half century earlier were becoming destinations for tourists and amusement for armchair travelers as well as badges of national pride. *Picturesque America* was intended to serve the same purpose as Gilpin's books had in the previous century, in this instance instructing a new class of travelers by steamboat and transcontinental railroad in the niceties of scenic discrimination. Trumpeting the superiority of American scenery over that of Europe in his preface, Bryant chauvinistically asserted, "For those who would see Nature in her grandest forms of snow-clad mountain, deep valley, rocky pinnacle, precipice, and chasm, there is no longer any occasion to cross the ocean." Here he once more hailed the country's remaining hoary "trees of such prodigious height and enormous dimensions that, to attain their present bulk, we might imagine them to have sprouted from the seed at the time of the Trojan War."[95]

The watercolorist and illustrator Harry Fenn was the first artist commissioned to work on *Picturesque America*, in conjunction with other notable talents of the day, including Thomas Moran and James David Smillie (Fig. 44). Fenn's sensibilities, like theirs, inclined toward the Romantic. According to a friend, "the pursuit and the understanding of Nature and the unveiling of her beauties that others might feel and see them as he did were to Harry Fenn far more than an emotional or artistic delight; they were his religion."[96] Thus did Transcendentalism guide the artist's as well as the poet's hand.

The Hudson River School

The Romantic sensibility so evident in *Picturesque America* was an outgrowth of the now-well-established Hudson River school, of which Bryant's close friend Thomas Cole (1801–1848), America's first great landscape painter, is considered the founder. Although during a three-year sojourn in Europe, Cole was entranced by the romanticism of classical ruins and medieval castles "over which time and genius have suspended an imperishable halo," he heeded Bryant's pleas to retain a preference for native scenery and its associations with God. "American scenery . . . has features,

and glorious ones, unknown to Europe," he declared in a paper delivered in 1835 to the National Academy of Design in New York (Fig. 45). "The most distinctive, and perhaps the most impressive, characteristic of American scenery is its wildness," he continued.[97] For Cole, however, wildness and civilization were not necessarily antipodes, and in the same address he made the following prescient observation: "where the wolf roams, the plough shall glisten; on the gray crag shall rise the temple and tower—mighty deeds shall be done in the new pathless wilderness."[98]

With Cole's student Frederic Edwin Church (1826–1900), American Romantic painting reached its commercial apotheosis. Inspired by the great naturalist and geographer Alexander von Humboldt and his five-volume *Kosmos* (1845), Church set off in the explorer's footsteps to make South American flora, fauna, mountains, and volcanoes his subjects in paintings of the exotic Sublime. At a time when tropical plants were novel adornments of Victorian glasshouses, Church depicted the towering palm trees he found in the lush landscapes of South America. He was a master of light, perhaps second only to Turner in the exploitation of its dramatic potential. Sunrise and sunset were his favorite times of day, and his canvases are suffused with the pearly luminescence of morning or the roseate glow of evening (Fig. 46).

In catering to the market for representations of the exotic, Church was able to exploit an important aspect of Romantic taste. In 1859 he exhibited his most famous painting, *Heart of the Andes*, in his studio on Tenth Street in New York, charging admission for its theatrical spotlighted presentation in a room filled with South American plants. With the painting's purchase for an unprecedented $10,000 and his fame secure, Church bought a farm in Hudson, New York. On the hill above it he subsequently acquired eighteen acres with magnificent views of the river and the Catskills. On its crest, with the help of architect Calvert Vaux, he built Olana, a Victorian-cum-Persian mansion with intricate interior and exterior stenciling inspired by his travels in the Middle East. As the audience

Fig. 45. Thomas Cole, *View on the Catskill—Early Autumn*, 1836–37, The Metropolitan Museum of Art, New York

Fig. 46. Frederic Edwin Church, *El Rio de Luz* (The River of Light), 1877, National Gallery of Art, Washington, DC

Fig. 47. Shelter Proposed To Be Erected on the Carriage Concourse. Prospect Park, illustration in *Tenth Annual Report of the Commissioners of Prospect Park,* Brooklyn, 1870, collection of Elizabeth Barlow Rogers

for his heroically Romantic works waned with the changing taste of the times, Church busied himself painting small watercolors of his home and its stupendous views while also designing Olana's sloping grounds in a Picturesque manner (No. 72). Architectural evocations of the exotic, however, lived on in Moresque bandstands, Turkish kiosks, and other fanciful structures ornamenting American public parks (Fig. 47).

Thomas Moran

Other Romantic painters sought a different kind of exoticism in the landscapes of the great deserts and Rocky Mountains of the American West. In 1871 Thomas Moran (1837–1926) accompanied surveyor Ferdinand Vandiveer Hayden on a Western expedition. Moran's watercolor sketches, the basis of later oils, dramatized the strange beauty of Yellowstone's waterfalls, deep canyons, geysers, and steaming fumaroles. Moran's watercolor sketches and the photographs of William Henry Jackson, also a member of the Hayden expedition, helped convince the United States Congress to pass the 1872 bill creating the country's first national park (Figs. 48 and 49). To the delight of the railroad interests, Yellowstone, Grand Canyon, and other wonders of the West were perceived not so much as scenery to be preserved for the spiritual benefit conferred by wilderness but rather as uniquely American curiosities to be enjoyed by increasing numbers of tourists.

John Muir

In opposition to this kind of consumer Romanticism that marketed nature as a series of spectacles, John Muir (1838–1914) stands as America's great Romantic prophet of wilderness conservation. The gospel he preached in numerous essays and several best-selling books originated, like Jonathan Edwards's, in an epiphany. Soon after his arrival in California in 1868, Muir set out on foot from San Francisco for Yosemite. Transfixed by the natural beauty of its scenery, he found here his spiritual home and greatest source of happiness. The Yosemite was for Muir a landscape "that after all my wanderings still appears as the most beauti-

Fig. 48. William Henry Jackson, *Castle Geyser and Firehole Basin,* 1871, Department of the Interior, National Park Service, Yellowstone National Park

Fig. 49. Thomas Moran, *The Castle Geyser, Firehole Basin,* 1872, Gilcrease Museum, Tulsa, OK

ful I have ever beheld. . . . And after ten years of wandering and wondering in the heart of it, rejoicing in its glorious floods of light, the white beams of the morning streaming through the passes, the noonday radiance on the crystal rocks, the flush of the alpenglow, and the irised spray of countless waterfalls, it still seems above all others the Range of Light."[99] No one perhaps has ever extolled the Nature's sublimity in more truthful tones than Muir. What gives his prose its special character is its combination of fervor and fact. Description based on close observation makes credible and universal the Romantic emotions he wished to convey. The following passage from *The Yosemite* (1912) is a sample of the style in which Muir conflated Sublime depiction and reportage.

The Bridal Veil and the Upper Yosemite Falls, on account of their height and exposure, are greatly influenced by winds. The common summer winds that come up the river cañon from the plains are seldom very strong; but the north winds do some very wild work, worrying the falls and the forests, and hanging snow-banners on the comet-peaks. One wild winter morning I was awakened by a storm-wind that was playing with the falls as if they were mere wisps of mist and making the great pines bow and sing with glorious enthusiasm. The Valley had been visited a short time before by a series of fine snow-storms, and the floor and the cliffs and all the region round about were lavishly adorned with its best winter jewelry, the air was full of fine snow-dust, and pine branches, tassels and empty cones were flying in an almost continuous flock.

Soon after sunrise, when I was seeking a place safe from flying branches, I saw the Lower Yosemite Fall thrashed and pulverized from top to bottom into one glorious mass of rainbow dust; while a thousand feet above it the main Upper Fall was suspended on the face of the cliff in the form of an inverted bow, all silvery white and fringed with short wavering strips. Then, suddenly assailed by a tremendous blast, the whole mass of the fall was blown into threads and ribbons, and driven back over the brow of the cliff whence it came, as if denied admission to the Valley.[100]

Andrew Jackson Downing

If Muir was America's foremost apostle of wilderness, Andrew Jackson Downing (1815–1852) was the country's most influential apostle of taste.[101] A generation before Muir visited Yosemite, Downing tirelessly championed the rural residence, a new dwelling type enjoying the advantages of both urban proximity and immediate access to the beauties of nature. When he wrote in the mid-nineteenth century, industrializing cities were growing exponentially and rail and steamboat transportation were becoming ordinary facts of life. This fostered both the desirability and possibility of enlarging the boundaries of urban settlement. Downing's self-proclaimed mission was to instruct the emerging middle-class on how to build their homes and landscape their properties with taste. All along the Hudson River, his advice was eagerly sought by this new breed of villa owner.

The son of a nurseryman in Newburgh, New York, as a young man Downing set about educating himself thoroughly about botany and landscape gardening. In 1841, while still running the family nursery business, he published his first book, *A Treatise on the Theory and Practice of Landscape Gardening, Adapted to North America* (No. 73). Its critical and commercial success as the first book of its kind in America gained him widespread recognition as a horticultural authority and tastemaker and thus confirmed him in his pursuit of a career as a writer. *Cottage Residences* (1842), *The Fruits and Fruit Trees of America* (1845), and *The Architecture of Country Houses* (1850) followed. His own home in Newburgh and its grounds epitomized the life of rural refinement he wished for all Americans of moderate affluence.

Downing drew his landscape theories from Loudon and Repton. His knowledge of the works of Whately, Price, and Gilpin is apparent in the contrast he drew between the Beautiful and the Picturesque. In the second edition of the *Treatise* (1844), he had his engraver depict the Beautiful, or "graceful" as he alternatively called it, as a female-inhabited landscape with gently curving parts, softly rounded tree canopies, and gracious Neoclassical architectural details. By way of contrast, he had the engraver portray a Picturesque house and grounds with steeply pitched eaves, spirelike conifers, and other signs of spirited irregularity, ruggedness, and angularity that presumably accord with the masculine presence of a huntsman accompanied by his dog.

Like Loudon, Downing gained a wide audience and social influence as the editor of a periodical. Beginning in 1846 *The Horticulturist and Journal of Rural Art and Rural Taste* gave him the same kind of forum Loudon had enjoyed in England. Like Loudon, he was able within the same publication to dispense design advice and horticultural information while also advocating solutions to important social issues of the day. Thus, alongside his other columns discussing the best methods of transplanting trees, enriching soil, fertilizing orchards, growing vegetables, producing wine, constructing icehouses and greenhouses, and designing rural villas and landscaping their grounds, he proposed the creation of a metropolitan park as a boon for the residents of rapidly growing New York City. Downing's best articles in *The Horticulturist* were collected in a single volume published as *Rural Essays* in 1853, a year after his untimely death. This book provides an important perspective on the degree of attention nineteenth-century Americans gave to landscape design as a core component of urban and regional planning, a sphere that encompassed the country's first suburbs, parks, parkways, and rural cemeteries, all of which were social responses to the rapidly industrializing new metropolis.

Mount Auburn

The rural cemetery, as pioneered by Père Lachaise in Paris, is the precursor and prototype of attractively landscaped domains of the dead on the urban outskirts. In America the rural cemetery movement led to the public parks movement and can also be seen as part of the trend toward the creation of rural residences and the earliest suburbs.

In dedicating America's first rural cemetery, Mount Auburn in Cambridge, Massachusetts, on 24 September 1831, U.S. Supreme Court Associate Justice Joseph Story made a persuasive case for the nondenominational rural cemetery as the ideal burial ground for Christians. In biblical cadences and with unabashed sentimentality and strong emotion, Judge Story, recently bereaved, proclaimed Mount Auburn to be the consolation of the mourner as well as an instructive reminder to the living of life's brevity and need to acquit oneself before death with deeds of goodness. "What is the grave to Us," he asked, deploying the eloquence of the bar, "but a thin barrier dividing Time and Eternity, and Earth from Heaven?" He extolled the superiority of the rural cemetery over the church crypt and the urban burial ground, arguing his case in Romantic terms. He cited as precedents the cemeteries of the ancient Greeks, which were placed "in shady groves, in the neighborhood of murmuring streams and mossy fountains, close by the favorite resorts of those, who were engaged in the study of philosophy and nature"; the practice of the Romans, who "erected the monuments to the dead in the suburbs of the eternal city . . . on the sides of their spacious roads, in the midst

of trees and ornamental walks, and ever-varying flowers"; and the Moslem "burying-grounds in rural retreats [in which] the cypress is planted at the head and foot of every grave, and waves with a mournful solemnity over it." He went on to exhort his listeners, "Why should not Christians imitate such examples? They have far nobler motives to cultivate moral sentiments and sensibilities; to make cheerful the pathways to the grave; to combine with deep meditations on human mortality the sublime consolations of religion." The rural cemetery alone could provide the setting for this kind of elegiac reflection, for it "seems to combine in itself all the advantages, which can be proposed to gratify human feelings, or tranquillize human fears; to secure the best religious influences, and to cherish all those associations, which cast a cheerful light over the darkness of the grave."[102]

Turning to the occasion of the day, Story praised Mount Auburn.

> *There are around us all the varied features of her [nature's] beauty and grandeur—the forest-crowned height; the abrupt acclivity; the sheltered valley; the deep glen; the grassy glade; and the silent grove. Here are the lofty oak, the beech . . . the rustling pine, and the drooping willow;— the tree that sheds its pale leaves with every autumn, a fit emblem of our own transitory bloom; and the evergreen, with its perennial shoots, instructing us, that 'the wintry blast of death kills not the buds of virtue.' Here is the thick shrubbery to protect and conceal the new-made grave; and there is the wild-flower creeping along the narrow path, and planting its seeds in the upturned earth. All around us there breathes a solemn calm, as if we were in the bosom of a wilderness, broken only by the breeze as it murmurs through the tops of the forest, or by the notes of the warbler pouring forth hiss matin or his evening song.[103]*

James Smillie's 1847 engravings of Mount Auburn, where the dead would not be disinterred but rest alongside their kin within a beautiful landscape, show strolling figures enjoying sweetly melancholy moments as they contemplate the pillars and pedestals surmounted by urns and the sarcophagi (some resembling Rousseau's tomb) that served as marble accents within shady groves and sun-streaked glades (No. 76). Several of these images portray parents with children in tow, testifying to Judge Story's hope that Mount Auburn

Fig. 50. Owen G. Hanks after James Smillie, *Revd. Dr. Channing's Monument*, illustration in Cornelia W. Walter, *Mount Auburn Illustrated*, New York, 1851, collection of Elizabeth Barlow Rogers

would serve as a moral teaching ground (Fig. 50). Conflating ancient and Christian, the imposing obelisk-framed, neo-Egyptian entrance gate bore the biblical inscription: *Then shall the Dust return to the Earth as it was, and the Spirit shall return unto God who gave it.*[104]

Other American Rural Cemeteries

Mount Auburn served as the progenitor of rural cemeteries in several other American cities: Laurel Hill in Philadelphia (1836), Green-Wood in Brooklyn (1838), Spring Grove in Cincinnati (1845), and Cave Hill in Louisville (1848), to name some (No. 77). The need to build cemeteries was indeed one impetus for city planning in several Midwestern American cities. Some of the well-trained German landscape designers who had emigrated to this country in the wake of the revolutions of 1848 in Europe found ample opportunity to exercise their profession in the heartland of the country.

Among these, Adolph Strauch (1822–1883) deserves special mention. Educated as a botanist, he was employed by Pückler to work on the park at Muskau following a six-year apprenticeship in Vienna's Schönbrunn Gardens. The prince became his mentor and lifelong friend, and following his advice, Strauch traveled to the major gardens of Germany, Belgium, and the Netherlands and studied horticulture at Ghent and landscape gardening in Paris. After emigrating to the United States in 1851, he made his way to Cincinnati and in 1854 was appointed chief landscape gardener of the recently founded Spring Grove Cemetery. In this position he took charge of its complete redesign as a "pictorial union of architecture, sculpture and landscape gardening," creating what became known as the lawn cemetery, a Pückleresque landscape in which he hoped the visitor would find "cheerfulness, luxuriance of growth, shade, solitude, and repose amid scenery designed to imitate rural nature." Strauch banned the kind of cast-iron fencing enclosing burial lots found at Mount Auburn and Green-Wood, authorizing only low markers beside family monuments. In addition to designing an uninterrupted, sculpturally ornamented, flowing greensward, Strauch made Spring Grove even more parklike with meandering lakes stocked with exotic waterfowl. Beyond this, he introduced plant material from all over the world, thereby giving the cemetery unofficial status as a botanical garden. The high acclaim Spring Grove enjoyed brought Strauch numerous other cemetery design commissions: Oakwoods in Chicago, Crown Hill in Indianapolis, Forest Lawn in Buffalo, Woodmere in Detroit, and Lake View in Cleveland. In addition, he was called in as a consultant at Cave Hill in Louisville; Oak Ridge in Springfield, Illinois; Woodlawn in the Bronx; and West Laurel Hill in Philadelphia.

Jacob Weidenmann (1829–1893), a Swiss immigrant trained in architecture and engineering, became a successful park designer, working for a time in partnership with Frederick Law Olmsted, who, after Strauch's death, spoke of him as the country's foremost authority on the subject of cemetery design—a high compliment in a period when cemetery building was a preoccupation among American city fathers. After a brief stint as superintendent of Mount Hope Cemetery in Chicago, Weidenmann wrote several essays on the subject in which he propounded the merits of the lawn-cemetery plan. They were subsequently collected and published in book form in 1888 as *Modern Cemeteries*.[105]

From the beginning of the rural cemetery movement in the 1840s—well before the development of the lawn plan downplaying funerary elements—those who frequented cemeteries did not necessarily go to experience the Romantic sweetness of melancholy emotion. For many they were simply pleasant retreats for a Sunday outing. The evident enjoyment of Brooklyn's Green-Wood Cemetery as a pleasure ground as well as a place of interment caused William Cullen Bryant and other civic-minded New Yorkers to pose the question why not a people's park devoid of reminders of mortality? In one of his essays in *The Horticulturist,* Andrew Jackson Downing had argued, "Does not this general interest, manifested in these cemeteries, prove that public gardens, established in a liberal and suitable manner, near our large cities, would be equally successful?"[106] The creation of Central Park, America's first great public landscape design work, was thus indebted to the popularity of the Romantic cemetery.

As the foremost landscape designer in the country, Downing probably would have been commissioned to design Central Park had his death in 1852 not cut short his successful career. As tragic as his untimely passing was, the hand of fate decreed a more fortunate outcome, for Downing's greatest contribution to the creation of Central Park lay not in the feature-filled design he fantasized in rosy prose but rather in the serendipity of his traveling to England in 1850 to search for an architect to assist him as his practice expanded throughout the Hudson River Valley. There he met and hired the young architect Calvert Vaux (1824–1895). Seven years later, after he had set up an architectural practice in New York City following Downing's demise, Vaux learned of the design competition for the park his former partner had proposed. By then he had met Frederick Law Olmsted (1822–1903). Sensing Olmsted's innate talent and appreciating his growing reputation as a writer and perceptive observer of scenery and social conditions, Vaux asked him to be his collaborator in the design competition, thereby launching a partnership that would imprint metropolitan landscapes all across America with a Romantic beauty that remains one of their chief assets today.

Central Park and Beyond

Neither Olmsted nor Vaux could imagine their eventual influence at the time. Olmsted still thought of himself as a man of letters, having recently published accounts of his travels in England and the American South. Economic necessity had made him seek the job of superintendent of the clearing operations necessary for the building of Central Park. Unlike Vaux, he had no training as an architect, and the profession they would establish together—landscape architecture—did not yet exist in this country. It is therefore in Olmsted's writings that we must seek clues to his unconscious preparation to become the author of a Romantic landscape design idiom for public spaces.

Although engineering technology and a working knowledge of horticultural science were essential components of Olmsted's long career as the father of American park planning, the numerous reports he wrote over the years display, in spite of their basic pragmatism, sentiments that are essentially Romantic. By his own account, his deepest religious experiences were akin to those of Wordsworth—rapt responses to nature's sublimity. Having read the works of Emerson and Ruskin, he thought of them as "familiar friends . . . [who] gave [him] the needed respect for my own constitutional tastes and an inclination to poetical refinement in the cultivation of them that afterwards determined my profession."[107] He also had read the works of the Picturesque theorists Uvedale Price and William Gilpin, "books of the last century but which I esteem so much more than any published since, as stimulating the exercise of judgment in matters of my art."[108] As his career unfolded, it was evident that he preferred their Picturesque manner of landscape design to that of his contemporary Gardenesque proponents, such as Loudon, for Olmsted was far more interested in creating naturalistic scenery than in showcasing plants.

Indeed, nothing demonstrates the mid-nineteenth-century divergence of English and American landscape design practice more than Loudon's and Olmsted's respective attitudes toward the role of flowers in parks. England's pursuit of the Gardenesque put that country on a course that emphasized horticultural interest over the Romantic appreciation of Picturesque scenery. Because of this, it is fair to say that the country most responsible for initiating the trend toward Romantic landscape design forsook it when it was coming into its fullest realization. In this regard, it is instructive to listen to Olmsted, who warmly took up the subject of distinguishing between the pleasures of looking at flowers and the enjoyment derived from Romantic scenery. In 1875, in a long and perceptive essay titled "Park" in the *American Cyclopedia*, he wrote:

> We have a greater variety of flowers [than our ancestors]; our curiosity about them is more stimulated, our science advanced, we take more interest in them from the point of view of the collector and classifier; they are matters of fashion; we use them more profusely. But there is room for doubt if they act more powerfully upon our sensibilities, and if we make on the whole a more fitting use of them. There can be no like question as to our more general susceptibility to the beauty of clouds, snowy peaks, mountain gorges, forests, meadows and brooks, as we know them in the broad combining way of scenery.[109]

Olmsted and Vaux named their Central Park design competition submission "Greensward" (No. 80). In its alteration of sweeping meadows, woodlands, and lakes, their conception of Central Park was overall a pastoral and Picturesque landscape. Employing a technique reminiscent of Repton, they presented the competition jury with paired images, one a photograph or pencil sketch and the other a small painting. By juxtaposing "Existing Conditions" and "Effect Proposed," they communicated their concept for transforming bare earth and brambles into grass and swampy ground into placid waters with lush shorelines (Nos. 81 and 82). The park's existing topography and physical features guided them. Low-lying areas were to be turned into water bodies, and the handsome outcrops of glacially polished Manhattan schist were conceived as prominent natural landmarks. Broad meadows with indistinct boundaries were always for Olmsted a primary desideratum, and the plan envisioned grading the rough and flat existing terrain into gently rolling expanses ready to be planted with grass. These meadows were intended to offer the denizens

of the rapidly expanding metropolis a therapeutic surrogate for rural scenery. The ascent to Vaux's Victorian Gothic Belvedere atop Vista Rock was made delightfully mysterious by the Ramble's circuitous paths. Once one had arrived at the Belvedere Terrace, however, this intricacy found its counterpoint in sweeping distant views of the Hudson River and Long Island Sound (No. 82).

Central Park's naturalistic appearance belies the sophistication of its underlying technical engineering. The design competition called for the creation of four transverse roads to carry ordinary east-west city traffic across town. By sinking them below the grade of the park and creating generously planted, gently rising seven-foot-high berms alongside, these busy thoroughfares would be almost completely screened from view. At the same time, the carriages on the drives bridging them would be unimpeded and their occupants unaware of the carts and draft animals moving beneath. Planting trees along the park's borders "to insure an umbrageous horizon line"[110] was another feat of landscape legerdemain the designers employed in order to occlude from view the future houses and mansions that would rise along the soon-to-be valuable lots fronting it.

On 28 April 1858, the Central Park Board of Commissioners chose Greensward as the plan for the future park, and Olmsted, assisted by Vaux, was given responsibility for overseeing its implementation. In spite of Olmsted's resignation in order to become head of the United States Sanitary Commission (the forerunner of the American Red Cross) during the Civil War, work continued. By 1873, after he had returned to New York and resumed his partnership with Vaux, the annual report to the board of commissioners indicates that the outlines of their Greensward plan—a public works project of unprecedented scale in America— had been effectively realized.

Lithographs in the early annual reports show how they carried the concept of grade separation of traffic beyond the sunken transverse roads and into the park itself. Thus pedestrians could walk beneath the carriage drives, through the stone arches, and over the bridle trails via cast-iron bridges (Figs. 51 and 52). The ornamental design of the arches and bridges was the work of Vaux, often in association with the architect Jacob Wrey Mould (1825–1886), a former apprentice of Owen Jones, author of *The Grammar of Ornament* (1856). Mould was also instrumental in the design of the carved stone panels on either side of the stairs descending to Bethesda Terrace. Their interlaced motifs of vines, flowers, fruits, birds, and animals bear out Ruskin's teachings on nature as the highest source of art. Jones's influence can be seen in the choice of the decorative polychrome Minton tiles for the Terrace Arcade ceiling.

The buildings designed by Vaux were small in scale and number and either inconspicuously sited or used to punctuate the heights of the rock outcrops, as in the case of the Belvedere and several small gazebos made of tree limbs. None of these structures were didactic tropes like the Rousseau-inspired ones at Ermenonville. They were there simply there to provide shade and shelter, modest refreshments, rustic ornament, and pleasant vantage points for scenic viewing. Thus did the Greensward plan give landscape, not architecture, the upper hand.

Olmsted's predilection for naturalistic scenery did not mean that he restricted his plant palette to indigenous vegetation. Rather he sought to achieve planting compositions reminiscent of certain faraway landscapes as well as those of a North American character. Like the artist Frederick Church, he particularly admired the lushness of the tropics. Following his term of service with the Sanitary Commission and still thinking of himself more as an administrator than as a landscape designer, he accepted a position as director of a mining venture in California. In a letter to his wife, Mary, dated 25 September 1863, when he was crossing the Isthmus of Panama en route, he tried to convey his reaction to the lush tropical vegetation he was encountering for the first time: "I think it produces a very strong moral impression through an enlarged sense of the bounteousness of Nature. I could not help asking whether the idea I had of producing some such effect about the island in the park was preposterous with our Northern trees & shrubs & vines. Except

Fig. 51. Calvert Vaux and E. C. Miller, *Archway Under Carriage Drive*, illustration in *Third Annual Report of the Board of Commissioners of the Central Park*, New York, 1860, collection of Elizabeth Barlow Rogers

Fig. 52. Calvert Vaux and E. C. Miller, *Archway Under Footpath*, illustration in *Third Annual Report of the Board of Commissioners of the Central Park*, New York, 1860, collection of Elizabeth Barlow Rogers

for the palm & bamboo, my conclusion was that by a careful assemblage and arrangement, all the character could be followed after, and that I had not gone wrong for a beginning in the planting or rather in my intentions"[111] (No. 84). In a letter written the following day to Ignaz Anton Pilat, Central Park's head gardener, Olmsted echoed the same Romantic sentiments regarding the effect produced by "the superabundant creative power, infinite resource, and liberality of Nature—the childish playfulness and profuse careless utterance of Nature."[112] Both on the island in the Lake in Central Park and on the one in the lake at the fairgrounds of the 1893 Columbia Exposition in Chicago, he attempted to create a tropical impression with vines, creepers, and trees with frondlike canopies suitable for the climate of northern latitudes.

During the time he spent in California as director of the Mariposa Mines, Olmsted produced certain important reports relating to scenic landscape preservation, including the "Preliminary Report upon the Yosemite and Big Tree Grove" (August 1865), written in his capacity as chairman of the commission charged with advising the California State Legislature on the scenic assets and future management of the proposed public property. Along with practical matters involving roads and maintenance budget, this document limned a Romantic portrait of the scenic grandeur of Yosemite's geology, vegetation, streams, and waterfalls. For example, he writes that the stream flowing through the valley is "such a one as Shakespeare delighted in," and "banks of heartsease and beds of cowslips and daisies are frequent, and thickets of alder, dogwood and willow often fringe the shores. . . . Beyond the lofty walls still loftier mountains rise, some crowned by forests, others in simple rounded cones of light, gray granite. . . . After midsummer a light, transparent haze generally pervades the atmosphere, giving an indescribable softness and exquisite dreamy charm to the scenery, like that produced by the Indian summer of the East."[113]

Thanks to the encouragement of Vaux, Olmsted returned to New York to resume their partnership for the purpose this time of designing Brooklyn's Prospect Park. In his capacity as landscape architect—the term he and Vaux invented to best describe their profession—he continued to write both practically and philosophically about the value of parks as crucial urban and national amenities and their purpose as a civilizing influence on the heterogeneous populations of American cities. Although less vociferous than Ruskin in expressing his opposition, he thoroughly agreed with that Romantic's bitter assessment of the excessive materialism overtaking Western culture. He saw the public park as an antidote to the pride of wealth and the social disparities of the age, and he made a strong case for its spiritually uplifting influence on the ethnically diverse populations of rapidly growing industrial cities. Under Vaux, who occupied the position of Parks Department landscape architect, and his successor and partner Samuel Parsons (1884–1923), this ideal still had its defenders. But their Romantic landscape

design proclivities were becoming increasingly out of tune with the ethos of the Gilded Age.

It is unlikely that Olmsted and Vaux were familiar with Pückler's *Andeutungen* in 1858, when they prepared the Greensward plan. In 1883, however, Olmsted was able to advise his young protégé Charles Eliot to visit the parks of Europe, especially those in Germany. Eliot traveled to Muskau where he quickly grasped the genius of the park's design. Parsons visited Muskau in 1906, and his experience made him eager to transmit Pückler's ideas to a new generation of American landscape architects. In his book, *The Art of Landscape Architecture*[114] Parsons, who was overseeing an English translation of the *Andeutungen* (Hints on Landscape Architecture) at the time, quotes large sections of Pückler's text. More than a quarter of his book's forty-eight illustrations are of Muskau, comprising photographs by Thomas W. Sears, drawings made from old prints, and diagrams and perspectives reproduced from the *Andeutungen*. Confirming Parsons's reliance on the prince as one of his profession's preeminent authorities, his chapters parallel Pückler's exactly, often with the same titles and in the same order. Indeed, his book is essentially a compendium of quotations drawn from Pückler and should be considered more or less an Americanization of the prince's design theories.

One can only speculate as to why Parsons held up Pückler rather than Olmsted as the principal exemplar in a book instructing American landscape architects. As Vaux's friend and partner, he was no doubt unhappy that Olmsted's greater fame as Central Park's codesigner and his later reputation as America's preeminent landscape architect appeared to have eclipsed Vaux's rightful professional recognition. This may account for his devoting such a large portion of his text to Pückler while only mentioning Olmsted briefly. In any case, his discovery in Germany of a predecessor whose work demonstrated such a strong correspondence to Olmsted's design philosophy helped perpetuate the Romantic ideals of the Greensward era even as the newly institutionalized profession of landscape architecture was moving in another direction.

Parsons's textbook for landscape architects

represents the twilight of the Romantic park era. Both Pückler and Olmsted, the profession's founder, whose long career left its imprint on many American cities, campuses, and country places, carried this tradition to a more expansive vision of parkmaking than had any previous designer. They both embraced prevailing technology to create circulation systems that enabled movement through scenery where nature was enhanced by the art of landscape design. By the time Parsons wrote his textbook based on Pückler's theories and practice, both American architects and landscape architects were being trained at the École des Beaux-Arts in Paris and at the newly founded American Academy in Rome. They were designing French Renaissance and Italianate mansions and formal gardens for Gilded Age plutocrats. Even Frederick Law Olmsted, Jr., who had inherited his father's practice and become one of the founders of the American Society of Landscape Architecture, was willing to combine the turn-of-the-twentieth-century Neoclassical urban design vocabulary with the naturalistic nineteenth-century park landscape tradition to which he was heir. This melding of the Beaux-Arts and the romantically Picturesque styles in twentieth-century parks and gardens continued until the 1940s, when modernist landscape architects made a determined break with both of these influences.

During the first decades of the twentieth century, Italy, which had served as the fount of inspiration for so much artistic poeticizing of classical ruins, had one last Romantic card to play. Renewed interest in Renaissance art and architecture at the end of the nineteenth century became a countervailing force to Ruskin's medievalism and virulent antipathy to the Renaissance. For English and American expatriates especially, Italy's sixteenth- and early-seventeenth-century villa gardens held

Fig. 53. Garden, Villa Medici, Rome, Charles A. Platt Albumen Print Collection, Century Association Archives Foundation, New York

a peculiar charm. Writers such as Edith Wharton spoke of their "garden magic" as an elusive yet definable quality, a mood induced by their age and partial neglect. By the time Wharton wrote *Italian Villas and Their Gardens* (1904), the multiple encoded meanings found in their original designers' elaborate symbolical programs were of very little significance. In a series of photographs, the American artist and architect Charles Platt attempted to capture the poetic beauty of these partially decayed Italian villa gardens, which he published in a book, *Italian Gardens* (1894; Fig. 53).

But the American love affair with Renaissance Italy yielded something other than Romantic sensation. The graduates of the École des Beaux-Arts and those like Platt who received fellowships to study at American Academy in Rome were instrumental in fostering the Italianate style in America. Thus did twentieth-century American patrons of Gilded Age architecture and Country Era estates seek to replicate Renaissance classical forms in their landscapes in much the same way that eighteenth-century English lords had appropriated ancient Greek and Roman classical forms into theirs. In this way Classicism, Romanticism's opposite, served as both an early and a late strand in the great Romantic tapestry woven over two centuries.

CONCLUSION

Like all movements in history, Romanticism is an expression of human values. These values, which together constitute an ethos, are inevitably governed by notions of time and space that find their terrestrial reality in the cultures of period and place. They are portrayed in art and inscribed on the ground by landscape design.

In the seventeenth century, the Renaissance project of retrieving the culture of the ancients evolved into a confident, forward-looking, humanistic worldview. Concomitantly, belief in an Earth-centered cosmos was overthrown by Copernicus's discovery of the universe's heliocentric principle. Following this line of knowledge, Descartes saw space as infinitely extensible. Versailles, with its vast array of mythological deities, including the symbolically all-important sun god Apollo and its principal axial allées disappearing into the seemingly illimitable distance, stands on the cusp of the old and new meanings of humanism. But the arrogance that allowed monarchs, princes, and nobility to conflate humanistic ideals with individual glory could not be sustained. It was left to space itself, not iconography, therefore, to be the chief compositional component bequeathed by the seventeenth century to the subsequent era of landscape design.

The beginning of the eighteenth century saw the origins of Romanticism. Deists, such as Voltaire and other Enlightenment philosophers, found it impossible to square the teachings of the Church with the continued disclosures of Newtonian science and the corresponding understanding of humanity's place within the universe. An appreciation of nature's complexity and grandeur—fostered by Locke's earlier insights leading to a new human psychology that valued the senses along with the need to nourish the spirit with a sustenance that traditional Christianity could no longer offer—constituted the soil in which Romanticism flourished.

The fact that space and time are unbounded and infinite is still difficult for the human mind to comprehend. Romanticism can therefore be seen as the search for the divine in the boundlessness of the firmament and belief in nature as eternal and

God-ordained, a bulwark against despair over the darkness-bracketed transience of life. Wordsworth confirms this Romantic aspiration toward the union of Mind, God, and Nature in "The Ascent of Snowdon" at the conclusion of *The Prelude*:

> *A meditation rose in me that night*
> *Upon the lonely Mountain when the scene*
> *Had pass'd away, and it appear'd to me*
> *The perfect image of a mighty Mind,*
> *Of one that feeds upon infinity,*
> *That is exalted by an underpresence,*
> *The sense of God, or whatsoe'er is dim*
> *Or vast in its own being . . .* [115]

In Romantic painting the landscape itself became the subject, not merely the background or the setting. The works of Turner, Friedrich, and Church bespeak the sublimity of sky and distant horizon. By such means Romantic art elevates the mind and heart to something approaching joy, peace, and an intuitive apprehension of the divine in the face of the unfathomable immensity and mystery of the universe.

Nature as both place and space is the medium and the compass of Romantic landscape design. Revealing the "genius of place" accords nature particularity and personality. The eighteenth-century Romantic designers did not treat space as a tabula rasa, a neutral ground plane on which to plant vegetation in geometrical shapes and alignments, as was the case in the seventeenth century. Because of its more practical objectives and domestic sphere of activity, landscape design, unlike painting and poetry, cannot incorporate rugged peaks, vertiginous deeps, or crashing waterfalls—hallmarks of the Sublime. Nevertheless, landscape design is Romantic in its mood-evoking treatment of space, allying itself with nature, obscuring boundaries, and reaching for what lies beyond. We can therefore appreciate Central Park's seemingly unbounded acres of green spaciousness not only as playing fields but also, as Olmsted intended, an illusion of unrestricted nature fostering a state of relaxed dreaminess and democratic sociability.

Romanticism's relationship to time is one of emotionally tying the historical past to the present day. Memorializing important events and admired personages is essentially a Romantic impulse that did not exist to any great degree before the eighteenth century. The decorative romanticizing of the antique past with temples and ruins is also part of the Romantic concept of time. The rural cemetery as a means of softening sorrow over life's brevity and death's destruction with elegiac melancholy is another example of Romanticism's consciousness of temporality.

Besides the cosmological concepts of time and space, other aspects inform the Romantic garden. In the *jardins anglo-chinois* of the ancien régime, we noted how playful exoticism constitutes one phrase in the lexicon of the Romantic landscape. In the opposite vein, Rousseau's *Julie, ou la nouvelle Héloïse* (Julie, or the New Eloise) and Goethe's *Wahlverwandtschaften* (Elective Affinities) present the garden as the locus of thwarted romantic passion and tragedy. The construction of faux farmsteads, rude huts, and gazebos, bridges, and railings made from tree branches are part of a Romantic impulse to place value on the humble, rural, and rustic. The pastoral scenery in Constable's paintings has its counterpart in the grazing herds that served, like the flock on Central Park's Sheep Meadow, as bucolic accents in real Romantic landscapes.

In the last analysis, we may conclude that Romanticism is above all a transaction between the human mind and nature in which no universal, but many diverse meanings, elicit a range of personal responses, among which are rapture, delight, pleasurable fear, sweet melancholy, and philosophical contemplation. Although this incomplete list of emotions may sound quaint, the perception of nature as a sublime miracle is a residue of Romanticism still capable of offering spiritual sustenance and heightened self-awareness.

NOTES

1. In 1798 Wilhelm Friedrich Schlegel (1772–1829), editor of the journal *Athenaeum*, wrote an article in which he articulated the principles of Romanticism as a distinct movement. In 1846 Charles Pierre Baudelaire (1821–1867), the French poet of modern urban life, wrote an influential Salon review in which he argued that, while many excellent contemporary artists, such as Delacroix, still painted admirable works within the aesthetic framework of Romanticism, Realism had in effect superseded it and that French art should now be seen primarily as a reflection of everyday bourgeois life. Thus, Romanticism may be said, strictly speaking, to have run its course between 1798 and 1846. Placing it within such a precise time frame, however, fails to include its roots in the early eighteenth century and its continuing influence well beyond the middle of the nineteenth.

2. Shaftsbury's use of this phrase prefigures Alexander Pope's advice to Lord Burlington (and all gardeners) to "Consult the Genius of the Place in all . . . " (see p. 16).

3. As anthologized in Hunt and Willis 1988, p. 142.

4. Addison's *ferme ornée* prescription of designing in partnership with nature, along with a similar recommendation in *Theorie der Gartenkunst* by Christian Lorenz Hirschfeld (1742–1792), underlies the "garden kingdoms" of Prince Leopold III Friedrich Franz of Anhalt-Dessau (1740–1817) at Wörlitz and Prince Hermann Ludwig Heinrich von Pückler-Muskau (1785–1871).

5. Hunt and Willis 1988, p. 142.

6. Thomson 1730, pp. 173–74.

7. Thomson 1730, pp. 191–92.

8. Torrance 1998, p. 996.

9. Pope 1961, pp. 141–43.

10. Castell 1728, pp. 116–17.

11. Walpole 1785, p. 11.

12. Walpole 1785, pp. 55–57.

13. Walpole 1785, pp. 57–61.

14. As quoted in Manwaring 1925, p. 170.

15. Hunt and Willis 1988, p. 284.

16. Hunt and Willis 1988, p. 321.

17. Hunt and Willis 1988, p. 321.

18. In 1759, a certain P. Decker (possibly a fictitious name) published *Chinese Architecture, Civil and Ornamental. Being a Large Collection of the Most Elegant and Useful Designs . . . to adorn Gardens, Parks, Forests, Woods, Canals, &c. . . . From Real Designs Drawn in China*, a compendium of illustrations based on a 1754 pattern book. Chambers irately dismissed this and other efforts to popularize chinoiserie as "extravagancies that daily appear under the name of Chinese."

19. These include *Observations on the River Wye, and Several Parts of South Wales . . . Made in the Summer of the Year 1770* (1782); *Observations, Relative Chiefly to Picturesque Beauty, Made in the Year 1772, on Several Parts of England, Particularly the Mountains, and Lakes of Cumberland, and Westmoreland* (1786); *Observations, Relative Chiefly to Picturesque Beauty, Made in the Year 1776, on Several Parts of Great Britain, Particularly the High-Lands of Scotland* (1789); and *Remarks on Forest Scenery and Other Woodland Views, (Relative Chiefly to Picturesque Beauty), Illustrated by the Scenes of New-Forest in Hampshire* (1791).

20. Gilpin 1789, p. 186.

21. Austen 1818, vol. 1, pp. 260–64.

22. Wordsworth and Coleridge 1798, pp. 206–8.

23. Wordsworth 1986, pp. 53–54.

24. Wordsworth 1986, p. 44.

25. Wordsworth 1967–93, pp. 99–100.

26. Wordsworth 1967–93, p. 112.

27. Wordsworth 1967–93, p. 116.

28. See Honour 1979, p. 89.

29. Constable 1962–68, vol. 5, pp. 18–19.

30. Honour 1979, p. 86.

31. Honour 1979, p. 86.

32. Loudon 1850, p. 188.

33. Sitwell 1909, p. 48.

34. From *Of Nature: First View* as excerpted in Torrance 1998, p. 1135.

35. Rousseau 1997, p. 63.

36. Rousseau 1997, p. 64.

37. Rousseau 1997, pp. 387–90.

38. Girardin 1783, pp. 14–15.

39. Girardin 1783, p. 25.

40. Wiebenson 1978, p. 57.

41. "Essay on Parks at Home and Abroad" (1861); see Olmsted 1977, vol. 3, p. 349.

42. Robinson 1869, p. 64.

43. See note 1.

44. Kant 1960, pp. 48–49.

45. See Hirschfeld 2001, p. 148.

46. Hirschfeld takes pains at the outset of his treatise to instruct the reader as to exactly what he means by the term *garden art:* "Here *art* means uniting those things that are agreeable and interesting in nature in exactly the same way and by exactly the same means as she herself does, and knowing how to collect in a single place the beauties that she scatters throughout her landscapes." See Hirschfeld 2001, p. 138.

47. Hirschfeld 2001, p. 85.

48. Hirschfeld 2001, p. 36.

49. Hirschfeld 2001, p. 223.

50. Hirschfeld 2001, p. 223.

51. Hirschfeld 2001, p. 137.

52. Goethe 1971, p. 20.

53. Goethe 1971, p. 46.

54. Goethe 1971, pp. 68–69.

55. Goethe 1971, p. 76.

56. Goethe 1971, p. 156.

57. Goethe 1971, p. 157.

58. Goethe 1971, p. 158.

59. Goethe 1971, pp. 156–59.

60. Carus 2002, p. 87.

61. Carus 2002, p. 94.

62. Carus 2002, p. 96.

63. Carus 2002, p. 97.

64. Carus 2002, p. 98.

65. Pückler 1833, p. 110.

66. Pückler 1833, pp. 233–34.

67. Pückler 1917, p. 13, note.

68. Pückler 1917, p. 58.

69. Pückler 1917, p. 67.

70. Pückler 1917, p. 31.

71. Pückler 1917, p. 48.

72. Pückler 1917, p. 49.

73. Pückler 1917, pp. 31–32.

74. Pückler 1917, p. 32.

75. Pückler 1917, pp. 39–40.

76. Pückler 1917, p. 87.

77. Pückler 1917, pp. 90–96.

78. Pückler 1917, pp. 100–101.

79. Pückler 1917, pp. 105–6.

80. Pückler 1917, p. 131.

81. Maruševski and Jurković 1993, p. 36.

82. Emerson 1983, p. 11.

83. Torrance 1998, p. 1175.

84. Letter to Maria Cosway, 12 October 1786, in Jefferson 1950, vol. 10, p. 447.

85. Torrance 1998, p. 1177.

86. See Beiswanger 1983.

87. Emerson 1983, p. 9.

88. Emerson 1983, p. 16.

89. Emerson 1983, pp. 18–19.

90. Emerson 1983, p. 47.

91. Muller 2008, p. 25.

92. Bryant 1875, p. 79.

93. Muller 2008, p. 181.

94. Muller 2008, p. 228.

95. Rainey 1994, p. 311.

96. "Harry Fenn: An Appreciation: by a Friend," *Harper's Weekly*, 13 May 1911, p. 10, as quoted in Rainey 1994, p. 45.

97. Thomas Cole, "Essay on American Scenery," *Atlantic Monthly Magazine* 1, 1836, pp. 4–5, as quoted in Nash 1982, pp. 80–81.

98. Nash 1982, p. 9.

99. Muir 1912, pp. 5–6.

100. Muir 1912, pp. 51–52.

101. See Schuyler 1996.

102. Story 1831, p. 16.

103. Story 1831, pp. 16–17.

104. Walter 1851, p. 18.

105. See Linden 2006 for further discussion of Strauch, Weidenmann, and other nineteenth-century German-speaking landscape designers working in America.

106. Downing 1856, p. 157.

107. Frederick Law Olmsted to Elizabeth Baldwin Whitney, 16 December 1890, Frederick Law Olmsted Papers, Manuscript Division, Library of Congress, Washington, DC. Transcription courtesy of Charles E. Beveridge.

108. Ibid.

109. Olmsted 1977, supplementary series, vol. 1, p. 344.

110. Frederick Law Olmsted and Calvert Vaux, *Description of a Plan for the Improvement of Central Park: "Greensward"* in Fein 1967, p. 71.

111. Olmsted 1977, vol. 5, p. 80.

112. Olmsted 1977, vol. 5, p. 85.

113. Olmsted 1977, vol. 5, pp. 490–91.

114. *The Art of Landscape Architecture*, New York and London, 1915, was reprinted in 2009 by the University of Massachusetts Press in association with the Library of American Landscape History with an illuminating introduction by Francis R. Kowsky, author of *Country, Park, & City: The Architecture and Life of Calvert Vaux*, New York, 1998.

115. Wordsworth 1991, vol. 1, p. 315.

The Romantic
Ethos

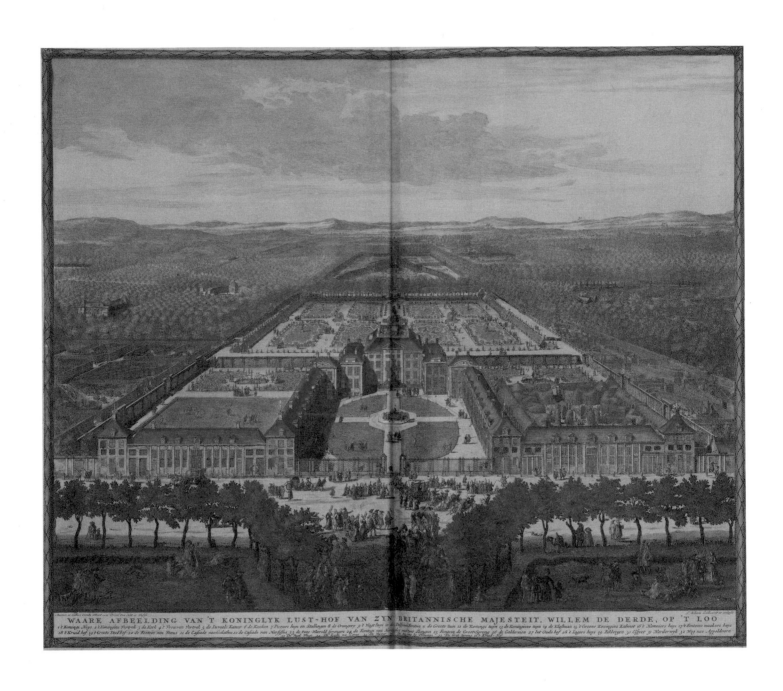

WAARE AFBEELDING VAN 'T KONINGLYK LUST-HOF VAN ZYN BRITANNISCHE MAJESTEIT, WILLEM DE DERDE, OP 'T LOO

LAURENS SCHERM (active ca. 1689–1704)

1 ✎ *Waare afbeelding van 't koninglyk lust-hof van zyn britannische majesteit, Willem de derde, op 't Loo*

Hand-colored etching, published in Amsterdam by Carel Allard, ca. 1700.

Collection of Elizabeth Barlow Rogers

In the decades preceding the emergence of the more naturalistic landscape garden, magnificent formal gardens were often published as a medium of propaganda extolling the splendor of an ambitious sovereign and the well-ordered prosperity of his domain. After William of Orange became king of England in 1689, his palace at Het Loo expanded to reflect his heightened status and enlarged entourage. Amsterdam printmakers developed a particularly impressive style of rendering bird's-eye views of gardens related to his court. This view of Het Loo exemplifies the type, with its high vantage point centered on an axis integrating a symmetrical complex of palace and gardens extending to a remote natural landscape—an ideal portrait of a perfected place, the dazzling abode of power. ESE

MATTEO RIPA (1682–1746)

2 ✎ Etched view of a pavilion by a lake at Jehol

[Jehol, China: s.n., 1713?].

Gift of Paul Mellon, 1980; PML 76758

LITERATURE: *Pelliot 1923; Gray 1960; Wittkower 1969; Sirén 1990; Maggs cat. 1212, item 88; Yu 2008.*

By the emperor's command, the missionary Matteo Ripa and two Chinese assistants etched on copper thirty-six views of the palaces and gardens in the imperial summer resort at Jehol. These views are among the first intaglio prints ever made in that part of the world. Ripa returned to Europe in 1724 and stopped off in England, where he sold or gave a set of the Jehol prints to the art patron Lord Burlington. Quite possibly they influenced the innovative redesign of Burlington's pleasure ground at Chiswick, one of the first English gardens in the naturalistic style.

Now in the British Museum, Burlington's set of these etchings contains captions in Ripa's hand and the bookplate of Chiswick House, strong evidence of a direct connection. Here, one might like to say, Western technology helped to transmit Eastern aesthetics—but the Chinese origins of the English style are not so readily apparent. They could be traced back to 1685, when Sir William Temple praised the pleasing irregularity of Chinese gardens in contrast to the prevailing English penchant for strict "symmetries, or uniformities."[1] They could have been derived from even earlier Dutch publications about China, most notably Johan Nieuhof's copiously illustrated and frequently reprinted 1665 account of an embassy to Beijing, which included descriptions of cascades in gardens and artificial rockwork. Prints based on Nieuhof's illustrations circulated widely and may have influenced English designs. Horace Walpole and other English garden historians rejected claims of oriental influence and objected to the term *jardin anglo-chinois*, which the French appear to have coined partly as a chauvinistic means of deflecting credit due to a rival nation.

Ripa admired the landscaping projects he had seen in China and thought that Europeans had a lot to learn from them. He noted that they were designed in a completely different style than that of Western formal gardens, which by comparison, could be seen as arrogant, overbearing, and intrusive:

> whereas we seek to exclude nature by art, levelling hills, drying up lakes, felling trees, bringing paths into a straight line, constructing fountains at a great expense, and raising flowers in rows, the Chinese on the contrary, by means of art, endeavour to imitate nature.[2]

Whether Ripa actually met with Burlington and discussed gardening aesthetics with him and others in his circle remains a matter of conjecture. Nonetheless, Burlington was not the only one to obtain a set of the Jehol prints when they first became available in England. The Morgan set is in a red morocco Harleian-style binding, quite possibly executed during the 1720s, judging from the design and the tools, which are to be found in a nearly identical binding on a 1719 English imprint. An English collector commissioned the Morgan binding at a time when Ripa was all the rage in English high society. Ripa conversed with the king, met with the directors of the East India Company, and dined out in the company of gentlemen curious about Chinese customs; perhaps one of them persuaded him to part with this set of prints. JB

PIERRE FOURDRINIER (active 1720–1760) after ROBERT CASTELL (d. 1728)

3 ✕ *Tuscum*

Folding engraved plate in Castell's *The Villas of the Ancients Illustrated.* London: Printed for the author, 1728.

Collection of Elizabeth Barlow Rogers

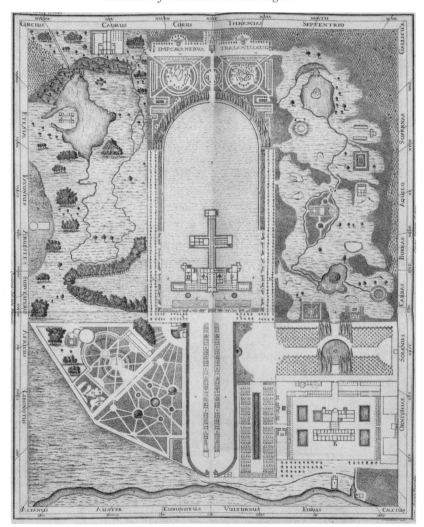

LITERATURE: *Harris and Savage 1990, pp. 149–54, no. 108; RIBA Early Printed Books, vol. 1, no. 581; Millard 1993–2000, vol. 2, pp. 64–66, no. 11; Du Prey 1994, pp. 131–42.*

Following Father Ripa's visit to England in 1724, the idea of irregular Chinese gardens inspired the innovative circle around Lord Burlington, which included William Kent and Alexander Pope. The Chinese style even infiltrated the first English translation and illustration of two villas described in first-century Roman letters by Pliny the Younger, the only surviving Latin texts to record the arrangement of imperial Roman gardens. Castell dedicated this work to Burlington, principal English patron of the classical and Palladian revival, who owned a set of Ripa's prints.

Searching for universal rules of design based on classical authority,[1] Castell defined three types of garden: the rough improvement of land with a watered selection of plants; a formal garden more elaborately laid out "by the Rule and the Line"; and a third sort, invented by the Chinese, "whose Beauty consisted in a close Imitation of Nature; where, tho' the Parts are disposed with the greatest Art, the Irregularity is still preserved; so that their Manner may not improperly be said to be an artful Confusion, where there is no Appearance of that Skill which is made use of, their *Rocks, Cascades,* and *Trees,* bearing their natural Forms."[2]

Castell imagined Pliny's villa in Tuscany as a combination of all three varieties. He interpreted a little meadow called the Pratulum as the simplest "rough manner" of treating naturally beautiful ground. The symmetrical core of the ornamental gardens takes the shape of two hippodromes, while a more naturalistic style prevails out-side the formal area. Furthermore, after having studied ancient Roman sources, "I have presumed to add those Things omitted by *Pliny,*" such as a gamepark, poultry pens, fishponds, farmhouse, orchard, kitchen garden, apiary, and places designated for snails and dormice. Castell merged exotic, classical, and naturalistic styles with agricultural function in an ideal confluence, lending the imprimatur of civilized antiquity to wilder aspects of the emerging landscape garden.[3]   ESE

JOHN SERLE

4 ≈ *A Plan of Mr. Pope's Garden as It Was Left at His Death*

Folding engraved frontispiece in *A Plan of Mr. Pope's Garden, as It Was Left at His Death: with a Plan and Perspective View of the Grotto.* London: Printed for R. Dodsley and sold by M. Cooper, 1745.

Purchased as the gift of Grace, countess of Dudley, 1974; PML 65854

LITERATURE: *Alexander Pope, "Verses on a Grotto by the River Thames, at Twickenham, Composed of Marbles, Spars, and Minerals," written in a letter to Bolingbroke, 3 September 1740, published in* Gentleman's Magazine, *January 1741 and again in October 1743, reprinted in Pope 1745; Bracher 1949; Mack 1965; Martin 1976; Brownell 1982; Willson 1998; Batey 1999.*

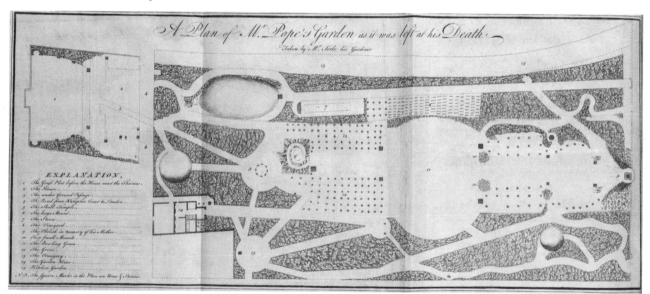

In 1719 the poet Alexander Pope (1688–1744) expanded a cottage on the Thames River at Twickenham into a classical villa, "a Mixture of Beauty and Ruin," in his words. His basement became an artificial grotto with waterfalls and a bath, providing access to his garden through a passage under a public highway. Part of the garden was a "wilderness" with cockleshell paths "in the natural Taste" and a rustic temple covered in shells.[1] Grottoes were already regarded as quintessentially romantic spots. As early as 1654, John Evelyn had described an artificial cave as "a squalid den made in the rock, croun'd yet with venerable Oakes, & respecting a goodly streame, so as were it improv'd as it might, 'twere capable of being render'd one of the most romantique & pleasant places imaginable."[2] Evelyn also described a natural grotto at Cliveden: "a romantic object, & the place alltogether answers the most poetical description that can be made of a solitude."[3]

In 1711 Joseph Addison wrote of Leonora, whose reading of romances had "given her a very particular

Turn of Thinking," leading her to create "a kind of Wilderness" around her country house. "The Rocks about her are shaped into Artificial Grottoes covered with Woodbines and Jessamines. The Woods are cut into shady Walks, twisted into Bowers, and filled with Cages of Turtles."[4]

Pope, who described himself as romantic,[5] admired the landscape garden at Sherborne accordingly: "those views . . . are more romantick than Imagination can form them." Sherborne's attractions included "a Hill of venerable Wood overarchd by Nature . . . a natural Cascade with never-ceasing murmurs . . . a very fine fancy, a Rustick Seat of Stone, flaggd and rough, with two Urns in the same rude taste upon pedestals . . . a Bridge that crosses this Stream, built in the same ruinous taste . . . this whole Part inexpressibly awful & solemn . . . which being crost by another bridge, brings you to the Ruins, to compleat the Solemnity of the Scene."[6] He particularly associated grottoes with poetic melancholy and in 1717 wrote a Gothic romance imagining Héloïse as an anguished nun still in love with Abelard, living cloistered among "grots and caverns shagg'd with horrid thorn."[7]

In 1721 Pope and Lord Bathurst designed the first artificial garden ruin in England, a Gothic folly set in a woodland at Cirencester Park. Again at Twickenham, Pope designed the garden entrance to his grotto as a ruinous arch of rough stone, described by his gardener John Serle as "various sorts of Stones thrown promiscuously together, in imitation of an old Ruine; some full of Holes, others like Honey-combs."[8]

At first Pope decorated his grotto in a Rococo style with shells and mirrors reflecting natural and alabaster-lamp light. One admirer described the effect as magical: "Mr Pope's poetick Genius has introduced a kind of Machinery, which performs the same Part in the Grotto that supernal Powers and incorporeal Beings act in the heroick Species of Poetry."[9] After 1739 he transformed it into a geological epitome of nature, building into the walls a collection representing "all the varieties of Nature's works under ground."

Pope's fame attracted many visitors, and his "romantic grotto" (so called by the poet Thomas Warton) inspired many imitations. Serle produced this guidebook shortly after the death of the poet. Serle's plan of the garden reveals a relaxation of the old geometries in the "wilderness" near the grotto and along the side, while a central axis preserves the classicism of the design, leading to an emotive memorial obelisk commemorating Pope's mother.   ESE

PIERRE-PHILIPPE CHOFFARD (1730–1809) after NICOLAS ANDRÉ MONSIAUX (1754–1837)

5 ❧ *Approchez, contemplez ce monument pieux où pleuroit en silence un fils religieux*

Etched plate in Jacques Delille (1738–1813), *Les Jardins: poëme*. Nouvelle édition considérablement augmentée. Paris: Chez Levrault freres, 1801.

Purchased on the Gordon N. Ray Fund, 2004; PML 129580

First published in 1782, the Abbé Delille's poem extolling the landscape garden went through many editions, six of which are now in the Morgan. The augmented edition of 1801 acquired over a thousand new lines and Romantic new illustrations by Nicolas André Monsiaux.

This vision of Alexander Pope in his garden, weeping on the monument to his late mother, faces verses that describe his dying visit to his mother's tomb:

See here the secret wood, here the dim allée
Where his inspiration warmed, exhaled in beautiful verses:
Approach, contemplate this pious monument
Where wept in silence a religious son:
There rests his mother, and darker groves
On this hallowed mausoleum have redoubled their shadows.
There the favorite bard of the English Parnassus
Had himself carried, dying, to his cherished bower;
And his eye, already covered by eternal shade,
Came to salute once more the maternal tomb.[1]

Delille warned against "monotonous gaiety" in the garden, recommending the addition of tombs and urns to comfort the sensitive soul—but only to honor genuine grief. He described his own melancholy experience of the autumnal landscape with its dying leaves as an emotional union with nature.   ESE

ALEXANDER POPE (1688–1744)

6 ⚹ *Of Taste: An Epistle to the Earl of Burlington*

Autograph manuscript, 1731

Purchased by Pierpont Morgan, 1909; MA 352

LITERATURE: *Pope 1961, pp. xxvi–vii and 170–74; Brownell 1978, pp. 121, 169, and 381–83.*

One of four "moral essays" by Pope, this satirical verse epistle castigates the ignorance and vanity of aspiring art patrons who think that they can buy credentials of connoisseurs. Wealthy fools can squander riches in many different ways; none, however, displays bad taste out in the open quite so blatantly as massive landscaping projects that succeed only in satisfying a capricious whim. Pope urged proprietors of country estates to scorn expensive follies, obey the dictates of reason, and respect the "Genius of the Place," the inherent qualities of the terrain that could be enhanced with some gentle groundwork. Instead of cutting up the landscape to make a commanding prospect or grandiose parterre, they should be content with the modest virtues of the classical villa, such as Chiswick House built for Lord Burlington, the dedicatee of this poem.

While paying a compliment to his friend and patron, Pope was also imitating Horace, whose philosophical satires advocated a genteel moderation in all things and served as a stylistic model for the moral essays. Horace wrote about the delights of his Sabine farm in terms Pope would adopt to describe his rural retreat at Twickenham, where he would implement gardening principles he had learned from Burlington. The Epistle to Burlington is not a theoretical treatise on landscape design, nor is it a didactic poem on horticultural techniques. It does, however, eloquently express stylistic ideas that bridge Neoclassical concepts and a nascent Romantic sensibility. One of the revisions in the Morgan manuscript suggests that Pope did not intend to attack any particular individual's errors of taste, although some of his contemporaries assumed that he was criticizing the work of Bridgeman at Blenheim or the improvements the duke of Chandos had been making in his estate at Canons.   JB

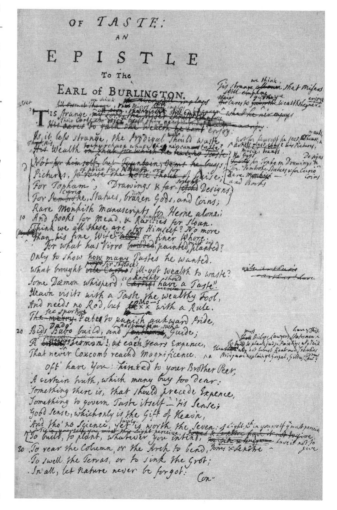

G. L. SMITH after BENTON SEELEY

7 ❧ *The Temple of British Worthies, A Gate-way by Leoni, The Cold Bath, The Grotto*

Etched plate in *Stowe: A Description of the Magnificent House and Gardens of the Right Honourable Richard Grenville Temple, Earl Temple, Viscount and Baron Cobham . . . Embellished with a General Plan of the Gardens, and also a Separate Plan of Each Building, with Perspective Views of the Same.* Revised edition. London: Printed for J. and F. Rivington; B. Seeley in Buckingham; and T. Hodgkinson . . . at Stowe, 1768.

Purchased on the Gordon N. Ray Fund, 2004; PML 128744

LITERATURE: *Clarke 1977; Harris 1968; Clarke 1992.*

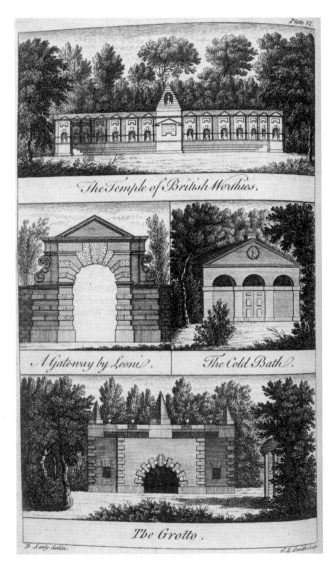

The Temple of British Worthies.

A Gateway by Leoni.

The Cold Bath.

The Grotto.

The new phenomenon of tourism at the most famous of all English landscape gardens made an unprecedented success of Benton Seeley's guidebook to Stowe, launching him from local writing master to bookseller and publisher. Numerous editions from 1744 into the 1830s reflect changes on the site. Fending off rivals with the incremental additions of an itinerary, a map, integrated pages of illustrations, and frequently updated descriptions, Seeley developed a model for the other site-specific guidebooks that would appear in England later in the century.

The grotto shown in this composite plate offers a telling case study in the eighteenth-century evolution of Romantic garden elements. Created in the late 1730s, during William Kent's era at Stowe, it originated as a symmetrical, freestanding structure decorated with flints, colored glass, and shells and accompanied by two Rococo pavilions of shells and pebbles. At first the grotto recalled a classical type of rusticated nymphaeum associated with the mythical spirits of springs, presumably informed by Kent's familiarity with similar fabrications in Italian villa gardens. A stream supplied the interior basin of a bathing Venus, then issued as an artificial river from the base of the grotto. Covered over with earth shortly after Kent's departure from Stowe, it was referred to by 1748 as a "romantic retirement."[1] The Rococo pavilions were later removed.

Continuing changes of taste inspired a new young heir, George Grenville, the future first marquis of Buckingham, to make further changes after coming into his inheritance in 1779. He buried the grotto more deeply and further rusticated its surface with tufa. New plantings of vines and evergreens also contributed to a wilder, more cavernous effect.[2]   ESE

GIOVANNI FRANCESCO VENTURINI (1650–1710)

8 ❧ *Veduta della cascata sotto l'organo nel piano del giardino*

Etching, plate 21 in Giovanni Battista Falda (1643–1678) and Giovanni Francesco Venturini, *Le fontane di Roma nelle piazze e luoghi publici della città*, vol. 4. Rome: Giovanni Giacomo de Rossi, [ca. 1680s].

Gift of Paul Mellon, 1979; PML 76264

LITERATURE: *Fowler 1961, pp. 100–101, no. 117; Berger 1974; Dernie 1996.*

EXHIBITION: *Boston 1989, pp. 202–4.*

In 1661 sculptor Gian Lorenzo Bernini altered the sixteenth-century gardens of the Villa d'Este at Tivoli to add a tumultuous cascade of water over rugged rockwork. The original gardens had been laid out according to an elaborate integrated program of iconography with the largest artificial waterfalls known in Italy up to that time, which alluded to the nearby natural falls of the Aniene River.[1] As Baroque fountains became increasingly torrential, Bernini created—in place of the classical fountain of Neptune proposed a century earlier—the most spectacular cascade of its century, erupting through the garden wall to crash down onto a stepped axis of boulders.

Venturini's etching technique effectively captured the more naturalistic style of garden design that began to emerge as early as the seventeenth century. His series of views of the Villa d'Este, published as the Grand Tour drew increasing numbers of visitors to Italy, conveys a mood of wholehearted admiration and cheerful sociability, even as the gardens entered a long period of decline. Later visitors would describe their abandonment and decay, sometimes in the language of Romanticism.   ESE

9 ⚘ *The Cascade at the Villa Aldobrandini, Frascati*

Pen and brown and black ink, brown wash, black and red chalk, heightened with white, on light brown paper, 1762

Purchased as the gift of the Fellows; 1965.18

As director of the French Academy in Rome from 1751 to 1775, Natoire upheld the requirement initiated by his predecessor, Nicolas Vleughels, that the pensioners go outdoors to draw landscapes to supplement their more conventional studio training. In a letter to the Marquis de Marigny, *Surintendant* of Buildings, Arts, Gardens, and Industries of France, he wrote, "I would very much hope that among our students, when someone is found who would not have everything it takes to accomplish history with distinction, to take on that of landscape, which is so agreeable and so necessary, because we are lacking such; but most of them, believing that they debase themselves in this department, prefer to slither along in the one than seek to distinguish themselves in the other."[1] Through assignment and example, he inspired a younger generation of French artists, including Jean-Honoré Fragonard and Hubert Robert, with enthusiasm for informal landscapes of ruins and gardens drawn on site *en plein air.*

From about 1760 onward, gardens figured prominently in Natoire's views. This drawing of the cascade at the Villa Aldobrandini at Frascati was one of a pair (now reunited in the Morgan collection) given by the artist to Marigny. It typifies the spontaneity of many of Natoire's drawings, in which varied staffage and ordinary activities deformalize the magnificence of an earlier era.   ESE

JEAN-HONORÉ FRAGONARD (1732–1806)

10 ✻ *Le Petit Parc*

Gouache on vellum, ca. 1763(?)

Gift of Mr. and Mrs. Eugene V. Thaw; 1997.85

LITERATURE: *Massengale 1993, pp. 21–31 and 70.*

EXHIBITIONS: *Baltimore and Minneapolis 1984, no. 46; Paris and New York 1988, pp. 94–96 and 153–54; New York 1990; Paris and New York 1993, pp. 164–65, no. 73; New York 1994; London 1996, no. 26.*

During the summer of 1760, while a *pensionnaire* under Natoire at the French Academy in Rome, Fragonard lived at the Villa d'Este at Tivoli with his patron, the Abbé de Saint-Non, making numerous drawings of the villa's derelict gardens and the surrounding countryside. Fragonard's sketches were noted by Natoire as "very beautiful studies which can only be very useful to him and do him much honor. He has a very keen taste for this kind of landscape into which he introduces rustic subjects that succeed for him."[1] After Fragonard's

return to Paris, Pierre-Jean Mariette would comment, "While in Rome he made a quantity of views, and above all those of the gardens of the Villa d'Este at Tivoli, which are spiritually done, and in which there reigns a great intelligence."[2]

The italianate garden in this scene is an imaginary composite[3] based on details drawn in Italy but also showing the subsequent influence of Dutch landscape studies.[4] Six versions of it have been recorded, including a painting in the Wallace Collection and an etching assigned the date 1763.[5] Fragonard rejected any emphasis on princely magnificence, preferring humble staffage, horticultural clutter, a prominent dead tree, and an impression of rampant vegetation overtaking the architectural structure of the garden.

ESE

JOHANN CHRISTIAN REINHART (1761–1847)

11 ⚓ *Arcadian Landscape with Three Figures at a Lake*

Black chalk, white gouache, on two sheets of brown paper, 1792

The Metropolitan Museum of Art, Rogers Fund; 2007.264

LITERATURE: *Schmid 1998;* Metropolitan Bulletin *2008.*

Reinhart was one of many German artists who made the pilgrimage to Rome. He arrived in 1789 and stayed there for the rest of his life, supporting himself in part by selling suites of prints through a German dealer. Many of his prints were Italian scenes on the model of Claude Lorrain and Nicolas Poussin. This highly finished drawing in the Claudian style recapitulates the theme of the *locus amoenus*, a place with a special charm and creature comforts where one might sit in solitary contemplation or engage in leisurely philosophical discourse.

The magnificent grove of trees, sacred pool, and rustic altar suggest that this is a sanctuary in the temple of nature, a retreat or a refuge from the clamorous distrac- tions of city life and the conflicting demands of civi- lized society. Here Reinhart worked toward a sense of solemnity rather than the mood of wistful melancholy expressed by his earlier Arcadian landscapes, which contain sarcophagi and other allusions to the *Et in Arcadia ego* trope made famous by Poussin and his fol- lowers. Reinhart built his reputation on work in this genre so successfully that his studio in Rome became a destination for German tourists. Among those who paid homage to the master were Prince Pückler-Muskau and August Wilhelm Schirmer, author and illustrator of the treatise on landscape design *Andeutungen über Land- schaftsgärtnerei*, Nos. 56–63 in this catalogue. JB

SAMUEL PALMER (1805–1881)

12 ❧ *Villa d'Este at Tivoli from the Cypress Avenue*

Black chalk and watercolor on blue-gray paper, 1838

Purchased as the gift of the Fellows; 1962.18

LITERATURE: *Morgan Library 1964, pp. 111–13; Malins 1968, pp. 80–85; Palmer 1974, vol. 1, pp. 236–56; Lister 1985, no. 45; Wilcox 2005, pp. 54–55, fig. 46.*

EXHIBITIONS: *New York 1998, nos. 106 and 107; London and New York 2005, p. 188, no. 110.*

In November and December 1838, during a wedding trip with his wife, Hannah, Palmer spent several weeks at Tivoli, sketching the "inexhaustible" Villa d'Este: "enchantment itself." Whereas earlier visitors invariably commented on the statuary and waterworks in these gardens, Palmer was most taken with the trees. "You must wonder at our staying so long in Tivoli, but you would not wonder if you saw it—I have got a finished study of pines and cypresses—the latter 300 years old and wonderfully fine."[1] Hannah Palmer probably referred to the present drawing (or a similar drawing at the Victoria and Albert Museum) when she took up the same theme: "We have been kept here so long by the Villa D'Este, which has yielded Mr P— a very rich drawing . . . of the Villa itself seen through these wonderful trees looking like a palace of Heaven."[2] Writing afterwards to his father-in-law, the artist John Linnell, Samuel stated, " . . . by a very abridged process [I] have learned the general characteristics of the cypress from those in the villa D'Este which are reckoned the finest in existence."[3]

In the present sketch, the intensity of color concentrates in a single cypress tree, faintly echoed in the pale wash of cypress on the flanking side of the allée. Rather than presenting an ideal specimen, Palmer chose an ancient tree that had lost its lower branches. Urns and statuary are suggested only slightly beneath the tree, and the dominant building and terraced fountains fade away in the background. Palmer moved the primary axis of a geometrically formal design to one side of his composition, relegating architecture to the pale distance while focusing our attention on the central vitality of the tree.

Palmer returned to England determined to paint "Poetic Landscape . . . to make one humble effort after deep *sentiment* and deep tone. . . ."[4] A few years later, John Ruskin would add to his third edition of *Modern Painters*

a new regard for Palmer as "deserving of the very highest place among faithful followers of nature. . . . His studies of foreign foliage especially are beyond all praise for care and fulness. I have never seen a stone-pine or a cypress drawn except by him; and his feeling is as pure and grand as his fidelity is exemplary."[5] With these observations, Ruskin expressed the tentative hope that Palmer might become "one of the probable renovators and correctors of whatever is failing or erroneous in the practice of English art."[6]

This drawing was adapted by Palmer to illustrate Charles Dickens's *Pictures from Italy* in 1846 (Fig. 1). His intermediate preparatory drawing for the illustration is also in the Morgan (1963.11).   ESE

Fig. 1. Samuel Palmer, *The Villa d'Este at Tivoli from the Cypress Avenue,* illustration in Charles Dickens, *Pictures from Italy,* London, 1846, The Morgan Library & Museum

Romanticism in
England

NICOLAS-HENRY TARDIEU (1674–1749) after WILLIAM KENT (1685–1748)

13 ⅍ *Winter*

Etched plate in James Thomson (1700–1748), *The Seasons.* London: Printed in the year 1730.

Collection of Elizabeth Barlow Rogers

Literature: Clark 1943; Brownell 1978, pp. 171–83; Hunt 1987.

Thomson's *Seasons* is a good place to look for early signs of Romanticism in nature poetry. Here are many of the characteristic traits of the genre, a sense of the Sublime, dramatic episodes, bouts of philosophical melancholy, and a display of strong emotion in response to scenic prospects viewed directly, "undisguis'd by mimic *Art.*" In his use of blank verse, Thomson looked back to Milton and ahead to Wordsworth, who adopted the same form to develop similar themes. Wordsworth was not the only poet to be influenced by *The Seasons,* an acknowledged masterpiece reprinted hundreds of times before its popularity waned at the end of the Victorian era.

This first collected edition of *The Seasons* contains engravings after William Kent, a versatile artist renowned for his architectural work, book illustrations, and landscape garden designs. He had several reasons to take a special interest in this book beyond the fame and profit he might gain from such a prestigious commission. (A luxurious quarto, it was published by subscription at a formidable price and with an impressive list of subscribers, including the queen.) He would have approved of Thomson's notions about nature and would have appreciated the passages about landscape gardening the poet inserted in this and subsequent editions. Trained as a painter and well acquainted with the European masters, Kent knew how to please contemporary taste with

his illustrations, some of which show affinities with the landscapes of Claude Lorrain. For each of the seasons, he devised an elaborate iconographical scheme with allegorical deities in the heavens, suitable scenery in the background, and figures in the foreground engaged in the characteristic occupations of that time of year.

This book also provided valuable publicity. While it was in print, Kent's services began to be increasingly in demand by proprietors of country estates who wished to reconfigure their grounds in the latest fashion. Here again his artistic training served him well. Clients no longer content with the formal gardens of the previous generation could easily admire the painterly composition of the parks he planned without resorting to the straight edge, the measuring rod and other tools of the trade. No doubt he learned something of this style from his friend Alexander Pope and his patron, the Earl of Burlington, but he gets the credit for gardening innovations at Chiswick, Stowe, Claremont, and other English estates. In the opinion of Horace Walpole, he was "painter enough to taste the charms of landscape, bold and opinionative enough to dare and to dictate, and born with a genius to strike out a great system from the twilight of imperfect essays. He leaped the fence, and saw that all nature was a garden."[1]   JB

THOMAS BOWLES, ENGRAVER

14 ⅍ *Merlins Cave in the Royal Gardens at Richmond*

Folding etched plate in Edmund Curll (1675–1747), *The Rarities of Richmond: Being Exact Descriptions of the Royal Hermitage and Merlin's Cave.* Second edition. London: Printed for E. Curll and J. Read, 1736.

Collection of Elizabeth S. Eustis

LITERATURE: *Colton 1976; Hunt 1987, pp. 62–65; Desmond 1995, pp. 6–19.*

Merlin's Cave was a "druidical" structure designed in 1735 by William Kent for Queen Caroline's gardens at Richmond. Built entirely of natural materials, including tree-trunk pillars and a thatched roof, this seminal

Gothic Revival building was supposed to manifest the indigenous natural origins of British architecture. The ancient enchanter's retreat enshrined Merlin as prophet of the dynasty along with five additional life-sized wax

figures. These were interpreted according to romances by court poets Spenser and Ariosto respectively narrating the ancient origins of the House of Hanover and the House of Este, united by the marriage of Caroline and King George II. Dual interpretations authorized the powerful regent Caroline as well as her absentee husband to rule the kingdom.[1] Opponents of Caroline and her ally, Prime Minister Sir Robert Walpole, rejected this authority by ridiculing Merlin's Cave, which nevertheless attracted many visitors and inspired a fashion for the Garden Gothic.[2]   ESE

No. 14

CHARLES GRIGNION (1717–1810)

15 ⚘ View of Strawberry Hill

Title-page vignette in Horace Walpole (1717–1797), *Essay on Modern Gardening; Essai sur l'art des jardins modernes.* [Twickenham, Middlesex]: Imprimé à Strawberry-Hill, par T. Kirgate, 1785.

Bequest of Julia P. Wightman, 1994; PML 150466
LITERATURE: *Chase 1943.*

Fourth earl of Orford and son of a prime minister, Horace Walpole is best known as a man of letters, a patron of the arts, and the presiding genius of Strawberry Hill, a country manor that he transformed into "a little Gothic castle." His home improvements mark the beginning of the Gothic Revival. On these premises he established one of the first English private presses and printed this edition of his highly opinionated, remarkably insightful history of landscape design, also a first of its kind. Walpole admired the work of William Kent, but he did not reject all the amenities of the formal garden. His estate at Strawberry Hill included a serpentine drive along the border of his property, potted plants on a terrace, a nursery, a grove of trees, an expanse of lawn, and a cleverly crafted view of the Thames. In the title-page vignette displayed here, one can see his Gothic mansion on the top of the hill and just a glimpse of the grounds. This copy belonged to the sculptor Anne Seymour Damer, one of his closest friends and a major beneficiary of his will, which gave her the right to live in Strawberry Hill.   JB

16 ⚜ *The Elevation and Plan, of an Arbour, of the Cave or Cabin Kind*

Etched plate in Thomas Wright (1711–1786), *Universal Architecture*. London: Printed for the author, 1755–58.

The New York Public Library, Astor, Lenox and Tilden Foundations
LITERATURE: *Wright 1979.*

Wright made his reputation and his living as an astronomer, although he also dabbled in rustic architecture and designed at least fifteen gardens for noble patrons. No doubt he intended to enlist additional clients with this portfolio of arbors and grottoes, containing elegantly engraved illustrations and letterpress instructions on construction techniques. This arbor was intended to be built in a secluded spot with a frame finished in rough-hewn oak so it would seem to have been "formed by the Hand of Nature." Wright could also design an arbor to serve as an aviary for attracting birds, a hermitage for solitary contemplation, or a vantage point for viewing distant prospects. Among the subscribers to this volume were the duke and duchess of Beaufort, who hired him to advise on a garden for their estate at Badminton in 1750. He proposed to build a Chinese temple, a Greek alcove, a Roman colonnade, Egyptian obelisks, and other amenities, including an arbor that must have been the origin of this design, "principally constructed for the Benefit of Shade." JB

17 ⚜ *Hermit's Cell*

Etched plate in William Wrighte, *Grotesque Architecture; or, Rural Amusement, Consisting of Plans, Elevations, and Sections, for Huts, Retreats, Summer and Winter Hermitages, Terminaries, Chinese, Gothic, and Natural Grottos, Cascades, Baths, Mosques, Moresque Pavilions, Grotesque and Rustic Seats, Green Houses, &c.* London: I. and J. Taylor, 1790.

Collection of Elizabeth Barlow Rogers
LITERATURE: *RIBA Early Printed Books, vol. 4, nos. 3722–25; Harris and Savage 1990, p. 510, nos. 952–55.*

An otherwise unknown architect called William Wrighte produced the most popular English pattern book of follies for the landscape garden, published in multiple editions from 1767 into the 1820s. Taking the *grotesque* of his title from the word *grotto*, he offered a variety of structures made of natural raw materials, including variations on the fashionable idea of the primitive hut. Some of his designs closely followed earlier inventions by William Kent and Thomas Wright.

The hermitage was a proto-Romantic novelty of the English landscape garden, sited, constructed, and planted to merge into its surroundings. Sometimes inhabited by a hired hermit, the garden hermitage more often functioned as a retreat for the proprietors. In this case, the iconography of the cross combined with skull and bones suggests a place for the contemplation of worldly vanities, death, and resurrection, curiously at odds with the sociably wide garden benches integral to this design.

Wrighte described this plate in his text:

Elevation of an hermit's cell, with rustic seats attached,

eight feet square in the inside, which should be situated in a rising wood near some running water, to be built partly of large stones and trunks of trees, set round with ivy, and lined with rushes, &c. The roof should be covered with thatch, and the floor paved with small pebble stones or cockle shells. The seats attached are intended to be composed of large irregular stones, roots of trees, &c.   ESE

18 ✣ *The Hermitage at Velserbeek*

Hand-colored engraving in Gijsbert van Laar (1767–1829), *Magazijn van Tuin-sieraaden*. Te Zalt-Bommel: Bij Johannes Noman en Zoon [1819?].

Collection of Elizabeth Barlow Rogers

Garden architect and nurseryman, van Laar is primarily remembered for his pattern book *Magazijn van Tuin-sieraaden* or *Storehouse of Garden Ornaments* (Amsterdam: J. Allart, 1802–9 and later editions). Belonging to a long-standing tradition of Dutch do-it-yourself garden print books—from Jan van der Groen, *Nederlandtsen Hovenier* (1669) to Simon Schijnvoet, *Voorbeelden van Lusthofsieraden* (ca. 1700)—this was one of the first publications specifically geared toward the middle-class property owner of limited financial means.

Containing 190 plates, this work illustrates garden plans (actual and ideal layouts), buildings (pavilions, cottages, ruins, bridges) and furniture in an eclectic assortment of Chinese, Gothic, Moresque, Rustic, and Picturesque styles. Each print is described in detail, explaining the most efficient and least expensive method of construction, which enabled dilettante gardeners to easily copy the designs in their own gardens. The accompanying description indicates how a hermitage is to be made simply of woven twigs and lime, known as wattle and daub, and how one can have a real hermit live there, or just set up a mannequin or painted figure. Van Laar advised the reader with questions about the planting of the landscape garden to consult the work of his colleague J. C. Krauss, *Afbeeldingen der fraaiste, meest uitheemsche boomen en heesters* (Illustrations of Beautiful, Mainly Exotic Trees and Shrubs), published as a companion volume to van Laar's series.

The source of many of van Laar's architectural and garden ornamental designs is J. G. Grohmann's *Ideenmagazin für Liebhaber von Gärten und englischen Anlagen* (Leipzig, 1796–1806), a contemporary German publication based in turn on a variety of foreign, primarily English, works. This particular woodland scene, however, shows the actual late-eighteenth-century landscape garden of Velserbeek at Velsen near Amsterdam, well known for its still surviving hermitage and Chinese pavilion. The Romantic-Picturesque tone of this print fits a group of similar landscapes with rustic Dutch cottages and farmsteads in his work. Van Laar's landscape garden layouts are representative of the early landscape garden style in Holland, characterized by a small size and compact inner division, which is clearly demarcated from the surrounding countryside.   VBS

P. DECKER

19 ✹ *Romantic Rocks Form'd by Art to Embellish a Prospect*

Etched plate in P. Decker, *Chinese Architecture, Civil and Ornamental. Being a Large Collection of the Most Elegant and Useful Designs of Plans and Elevations, &c. from the Imperial Retreat to the Smallest Ornamental Building in China. Likewise Their Marine Subjects. The Whole to Adorn Gardens, Parks, Forests, Woods, Canals, &c.... from Real Designs Drawn in China, Adapted to this Climate.* London: Printed for the author and sold by Henry Parker and Elirabeth Bakewell, H. Piers and partner, 1759.

Collection of Elizabeth Barlow Rogers

LITERATURE: *Harris and Savage 1990, pp. 178–79, no. 192.*

Nothing is known of the possibly fictitious "P. Decker, Architect" to whom this work is attributed, and the chinoiserie designs in this series are modified plates from *A New Book of Chinese Designs Calculated to Improve the Present Taste* by George Edwards and Matthew Darly, published in 1754 (Fig. 1). The oriental fantasy of precarious rock formations identified here as "Romantic" resembles Rococo decoration more than a practical model for garden architecture.

This kind of design infected critical reception of Romantic elements in landscape architecture with suspicions of absurdity and sometimes made the epithet *romantic* an accusation. Such follies provoked William Chambers to attempt to "put a stop to the extravagancies that daily appear under the name of Chinese, though most of them are mere inventions, the rest copies from the lame presentations found on porcelain and paperhangings."   ESE

Fig. 1. George Edwards and Matthew Darly, illustration in *A New Book of Chinese Designs,* London, 1754, Department of Printing and Graphic Arts, Houghton Library, Harvard University

EDWARD ROOKER (ca. 1712–1774) after WILLIAM MARLOW (1740–1813)

20 ✣ *A View of the Wilderness, with the Alhambra, the Pagoda and the Mosque*

Etched and engraved plate in William Chambers (1723–1796), *Plans, Elevations, Sections, and Perspective Views of the Gardens and Buildings at Kew in Surry, the Seat of Her Royal Highness, the Princess Dowager of Wales.* London: Printed by J. Haberkorn . . . for the author, and . . . A. Millar [and nine others], 1763.

Gift of Henry S. Morgan, 1962; PML 53027

LITERATURE: *Harris 1970; Harris and Savage 1990, pp. 155–64; Sirén 1990; Millard 1993–2000, vol. 2, pp. 67–70, no. 12, and pp. 77–79, no. 14.*

After traveling to Bengal and China as a merchant seaman, then studying architecture in Paris and Italy, William Chambers became the first academically trained architect to practice in England and the first to have directly observed Asian architecture. In 1757 he began to design for Augusta, Dowager Princess of Wales, new gardens at Kew with artificial ruins and a diversity of exotic architectural styles.

That same year and again in 1772, he published treatises on architecture intended to "put a stop to the extravagancies that daily appear under the name of Chinese." Correct Chinese designs would offer novelty and originality particularly appropriate to "extensive parks and gardens, where a great variety of scenes are required," or to the decoration of lesser parts of great palaces.

Included in both works were descriptions of Chinese gardens. "Their taste in that is good, and what we have for some time past been aiming at in England, though not always with success." Chambers felt that the greater success of the Chinese method was due to its similarity to composing a landscape painting, which he felt was lacking in the fashionable landscape garden style of Capability Brown. Highly influential on the Continent, Chambers' work contributed to the conflation of the *jardin anglo-chinois*, associating the English landscape garden with an older Chinese tradition of varied, irregular, and naturalistic landscape architecture.[1]

In 1757 Chambers briefly categorized Chinese gardens as pleasing, horrid, or enchanted.

Their enchanted scenes answer, in a great measure, to what we call romantic, and in these they make use of several artifices to excite surprize. Sometimes they make a rapid stream, or torrent, pass under ground, the turbulent noise of which strikes the ear of the new-comer, who is at a loss to know from whence it proceeds: at other times they dispose the rocks, buildings, and other objects that form the composition, in such a manner as that the wind pass-

ing through the different interstices and cavities, made in them for that purpose, causes strange and uncommon sounds. They introduce into these scenes all kinds of extraordinary trees, plants, and flowers, form artificial and complicated ecchoes, and let loose different sorts of monstrous birds and animals.[2]

Published in the same year as Edmund Burke's *Philosophical Enquiry into the Origin of Our Ideas of the Sublime and Beautiful*, Chambers's description of Chinese "scenes of horror" in the garden corresponds to Burke's Sublime, with "impending rocks, dark caverns and impetuous cataracts . . . [the trees] seemingly torn to pieces by the violence of tempests . . . the buildings are some in ruins, others half-consumed by fire."[3] In 1772, far removed from his voyage to China, he elaborated at fanciful length on the Romantic kind of Chinese garden:

Their surprizing, or supernatural scenes, are of the romantic kind, and abound in the marvellous; being calculated to excite in the minds of the spectators, quick successions of opposite and violent sensations. . . . Sometimes the traveller, after having wandered in the dusk of the forest, finds himself on the edge of precipices, in the glare of day-light, with cataracts falling from the mountains around, and torrents raging in the depths beneath him; or at the foot of impending rocks, in gloomy vallies, overhung with woods, on the banks of dull moving rivers, whose shores are covered with sepulchral monuments, under the shade of willows, laurels, and other plants, sacred to Manchew, the genius of sorrow.

His way now lies through dark passages cut in the rocks, on the side of which are recesses, filled with colossal figures of dragons, infernal fiends, and other horrid forms, which hold in their monstrous talons, mysterious cabalistical sentences, inscribed on tables of brass; with preparations that yield a constant flame; serving at once to guide and to astonish the passenger: from time to time he is surprized with repeated shocks of electrical impulse, with showers of artificial rain, or sudden violent gusts of wind, and instantaneous explosions of fire; the earth trembles under him, by the power of confined air; and his

ears are successively struck with many different sounds, produced by the same means; some resembling the cries of men in torment; others the roaring of bulls, and howl of ferocious animals, with the yell of hounds, and the voices of hunters; others are like the mixed croaking of ravenous birds; and others imitate thunder, the raging of the sea, the explosion of cannon, the sound of trumpets, and all the noise of war. . . . sometimes, in this romantic excursion, the passenger finds himself in extensive recesses, surrounded with arbors of jessamine, vine and roses, where beauteous Tartarean damsels, in loose transparent robes, that flutter in the air, present him with rich wines, mangostans, ananas, and fruits of Quangsi; crown him with garlands of flowers, and invite him to taste the sweets of retirement, on Persian carpets, and beds of camusath skin [corrected to camusathkin in errata] down.

These enchanted scenes always abound with waterworks, so contrived as to produce many surprizing effects; and many splendid pieces of scenery. Air is likewise employed with great success, on different occasions . . . all which are calculated to embarrass, to surprize, or to terrify the passenger in his progress.

All sorts of optical deceptions are also made use of . . . The Chinese Artists introduce into these enchanted scenes, all kinds of sensitive, and other extraordinary trees, plants and flowers. They keep in them a surprizing variety of monstrous birds, reptiles, and animals, which they import from distant countries, or obtain by crossing the breeds. These are tamed by art; and guarded by enormous dogs of Tibet, and African giants, in the habits of magicians.[4]

Although he was ridiculed for these excesses, Chambers's typology of Chinese gardens heightened the idea of provoking powerful emotional responses through selected effects in landscape design: "the spectator is to be amused . . . his curiosity excited, and his mind agitated by a great variety of opposite passions."[5] To this end, "Gardeners, like poets, should give a loose to their imagination."[6]   ESE

JOHN MARTIN (1789–1854)

21 ✒ *View of the Temple of Suryah and Fountain of Maha Dao, with a Distant View of North Side of Mansion House*

Etching with aquatint added by Frederick Christian Lewis (1779–1856), in Martin's series of views of Sezincote, ca. 1818

Bequest of Gordon N. Ray, 1987; PML 143240

LITERATURE: *Betjeman 1931; Balston 1947; Colvin 1954, entry on Samuel Pepys Cockerell, pp. 262–64; Sutton 1954; Weinhardt 1958; Norton 1963; Malins 1980; Peake 2004.*

EXHIBITIONS: *Williamstown, Lawrence, and Oberlin 1986; York 1992.*

Influenced by views of Indian buildings, and in particular by the Mausoleum of Hyder Ali Khan at Lal Bagh, architect Samuel Pepys Cockerell (1754–1827) designed the house at Sezincote about 1805 for his brother Charles, a "nabob" made wealthy by thirty years in India. Charles Cockerell consulted Humphry Repton on plans for the grounds, but to transform the countryside of the Cotswolds into an exotic landscape, he turned to the artist Thomas Daniell (1749–1840), whom he had met in India. Following a ten-year tour sketching the scenery and architecture of the Subcontinent, Thomas and his nephew William Daniell had returned to London and published, from 1795 to 1807, their monumental compendium of aquatints called *Oriental Scenery.*

In 1811 Thomas Daniell designed the Thornery garden at Sezincote as a dream of India, with subtropical plants and a shrine to the Hindu sun god beside a lotus-shaped pool with sacral fountain. The temple housed a figure of Surya carved in Coade & Seeley's Patent Imitation Stone.

Before achieving fame as a Romantic painter and printmaker of sublime mezzotints, John Martin etched ten views of Sezincote, a series of great rarity privately printed for Sir Charles Cockerell about 1818. Martin would later insert occasional details from the Sezincote gardens and from the Daniells' architectural studies into his dramatic pictorial landscapes, from a cataclysmic Babylon to Paradise.   ESE

WILLIAM GILPIN (1724–1804)

22 ❧ *River-Views, Bays, and Sea Coasts*

Album, pen and brown ink, brown and gray-brown wash, over preliminary indications in graphite, on paper washed with ochre, 1781

Purchased as the gift of Mrs. Enid A. Haupt; 1978.39

LITERATURE: *Templeman 1939; Barbier 1963.*

EXHIBITION: *Brussels 1994, p. 86, no. 43.*

The Reverend William Gilpin invented the picturesque travel book based on his own series of tours beginning in 1768. Recording his first impressions in notebooks and rough sketches while he traveled, he later wrote polished text and finished views that provided "general ideas" rather than "exact portraits" to illustrate principles of correct landscape composition. He often structured these final drawings with three pronounced planes of dark foreground, middle ground, and light background, as in this river scene with a promontory looming over diminutive figures.

Gilpin pasted many of his drawings into albums. Until 1785 these were given to members of his family.[1] A published aquatint corresponding to this drawing has not been identified. ESE

23 ✣ View of Goodrich Castle

Aquatint in William Gilpin (1724–1804), *Observations on the River Wye, and Several Parts of South Wales, &c. Relative Chiefly to Picturesque Beauty, Made in the Summer of the Year 1770.* London: Printed for R. Blamire, sold by B. Law and R. Faulder, 1782.

Collection of Elizabeth Barlow Rogers

LITERATURE: *Templeman 1939; Hipple 1957; Barbier 1963; Boudreau 1973; Andrews 1989; Orestano 2003.*

Gilpin's tour along the River Wye, initially published in 1782, was the first guidebook to popularize the idea of Picturesque travel, a process of judicious appreciation of landscape views from sequential vantage points. Although his sought-after observations were circulating in manuscript by 1774, publication was delayed by the difficulties of discovering and mastering the closely guarded new printmaking technique of aquatint.

Before Gilpin, garden-tour itineraries similarly conducted the visitor from one viewpoint to another. Gilpin's first published work was a point-to-point description of Stowe and the first English book to critique the pictorial values of scenic landscape.[1] With his Picturesque guidebooks, he transposed a connoisseur's method of critical viewing from the artifact of the garden to the relatively natural countryside.

In a rare concession to the artistic competence of nature, Gilpin called the setting of ruined Goodrich Castle seen here "correctly picturesque."

> *This view, which is one of the grandest on the river, I should not scruple to call correctly picturesque; which is seldom the character of a purely natural scene.*
>> *Nature . . . works on a vast scale; and, no doubt harmoniously, if her schemes could be comprehended. The artist, in the mean time, is confined to a span. He lays down his little rules therefore, which he calls the principles of picturesque beauty, merely to adapt such diminutive parts of nature's surfaces to his own eye, as come within its scope.*[2]

Gilpin attempted to define picturesque beauty as a purely visual phenomenon, a rough kind of beauty that is not only suitable for a picture, but also independent of the moral value otherwise considered essential to beauty. This definition did not hold. Henry David Thoreau, for example, reversed his initial admiration of Gilpin's approach: "Nature was so shallow all at once I did not know what had attracted me all my life. . . . The perception of beauty is a moral test."[3]

Gilpin occasionally called a particularly thrilling landscape romantic rather than picturesque to indicate that it conjures up a more imaginative response beyond the appreciation of well-composed appearance. On the River Wye, for example, the landscape garden at Persfield [Piercefield] and its views cannot be called picturesque: "They are either presented from too high a point; or they have little to mark them as characteristic; or they do not fall into such composition, as would appear to advantage on canvas. But they are extremely romantic; and give a loose to the most pleasing riot of imagination."[4]　　　　ESE

JOHN HEAVISIDE CLARK (ca. 1770–1836)

24 ❧ *Lightning*

Aquatint, plate 13 in Clark's *A Practical Illustration of Gilpin's Day, Representing the Various Effects on Landscape Scenery from Morning to Night in 30 Designs from Nature.* Second edition. London: Priestley and Weale, etc., 1824.

Bequest of Gordon N. Ray, 1987; GNR 5625

LITERATURE: *Bermingham 2000, pp. 119–21; Orestano 2003.*

Scottish artist John Heaviside Clark added color to an unauthorized posthumous publication of Gilpin's monochrome drawings of the times of day, accompanied by instructions to amateur artists on selecting color for specific effects. Apparently inspired by the presence of a gibbet, Clark transformed Gilpin's midday landscape into the more sensational nocturnal scene *Lightning:* "The sudden burst of vivid light, and tremulous flashings of the electric fluid, present a scene in nature, awful and sublime."

The heightened emotional resonance of this adaptation signals a shift from Gilpin's more analytical and strictly visual eighteenth-century Picturesque. Years later, John Ruskin would mistake these plates as a first work published by J. M. W. Turner and consider them "already as pathetic in feeling as any work he ever did to the end of life" and "of intense moral interest, showing already all his sadness of disposition."[1]　　　　ESE

THOMAS ROWLANDSON (1756–1827)

25 ❧ *The Doctor Sketching the Lake*

Pen and watercolor drawing for "The Schoolmaster's Tour" in *The Poetical Magazine* (May 1810) with text by William Combe; reprinted in book form as *The Tour of Doctor Syntax in Search of the Picturesque.* London: Published by R. Ackermann, 1812.

Purchased by Pierpont Morgan before 1913; 2006.24: 2
LITERATURE: *Paulson 1972; Savory 1997.*

Gilpin's success in popularizing the Picturesque inspired this parody by Rowlandson working in collaboration with the enterprising publisher Rudolph Ackermann and the hack writer William Combe. Following Gilpin's example, the curate-schoolmaster Dr. Syntax visits picturesque locales in hopes of making his fortune by publishing a book about his artistic adventures. He views fashionable attractions, such as a country churchyard and a Gothic ruin, but the hapless pedant overlooks the true beauty of his surroundings and instead blunders into a series of comic predicaments and ridiculous situations. This pratfall in the Lake District is a typical example of the accidents he endures, sketchbook in hand.

Rowlandson's drawing displays the picturesque features of this scene more prominently than the aquatints in the published versions, in which the mist shrouding the hills on the opposite shore has been allowed to dissipate and the hills have become rounded rather than rugged. Inevitably some details were lost in the course of the many reprints of *The Tour of Doctor Syntax*, one of Ackermann's most ingenious and profitable publishing ventures. It sold so well that he commissioned

Rowlandson and Combe to produce two sequels and a spinoff, *The History of Johnny Quae Genus, the Little Foundling of the Late Doctor Syntax* (1822). The demand for Syntax was so strong that rival publishers issued imitations of the tours, theatrical impresarios put the doctor on the stage, and his immediately recognizable features appeared in figurines, dinnerware, and other merchandise designed to capitalize on this popular sensation. The Syntax series also enhanced the sales and prestige of other publications by Ackermann, who specialized in color-plate books, including several lavishly illustrated topographical works written by Combe and illustrated by Rowlandson. While making a parody of them, he was building up a thriving trade in books of Picturesque tourism and even offered a line of watercolor paints and artists' supplies for amateurs who would have liked to try their hand at landscape painting in the manner of William Gilpin. His attack on the genre was actually a clever cross-marketing scheme intended to promote it along with related publications and consumer products he had for sale at his bookstore, the Repository of Arts.   JB

BENJAMIN THOMAS POUNCY (d. 1799) after THOMAS HEARNE (1744–1817)

26 ✸ *Beautiful* and *Picturesque*

Etchings, folding plates in Richard Payne Knight (1751–1824), *The Landscape: A Didactic Poem. In Three Books. Addressed to Uvedale Price, Esq.* London: Printed by W. Bulmer and Co. and sold by G. Nicol, 1794.

Collection of Elizabeth Barlow Rogers
LITERATURE: *Hipple 1957, pp. 247–83; Clarke and Penny 1982, pp. 47 and 156–58, nos. 114–15; Ballantyne 1997.*

"Beautiful"

"Picturesque"

Richard Payne Knight rejected the rules and servile repetition of any garden style; he insisted instead on landscape design as the apparently spontaneous expression of genuine inspiration fulfilling the natural vitality of a site. His "didactic poem" agreed with promoters of Picturesque design, notably Uvedale Price, that the prevailing formula for beautiful grounds developed by Capability Brown—gently undulating terrain, serpentine lines, open meadows surrounding the house, clumps of trees—should be condemned in favor of a more naturalistic effect. He argued that the achievements of the great landscape painters, especially Claude Lorrain, should inform the visual effects of a designed landscape. (Knight possessed an important collection of works by Claude.)

The artist Thomas Hearne illustrated *The Landscape* with two contrasting treatments of a single scene.[1] One of these images represents the monotonous and "insipid" style of Capability Brown and his followers. Knight summed up his rejection of Brown's dull constraints in verse:

See yon fantastic band,
With charts, pedometers, and rules in hand,
Advance triumphant, and alike lay waste
The forms of nature, and the works of taste!
T'improve, adorn, and polish, they profess;
But shave the goddess, whom they come to dress;
Level each broken bank and shaggy mound,
And fashion all to one unvaried round;
One even round, that ever gently flows,
Nor forms abrupt, nor broken colours knows;
But wrapt all o'er in everlasting green,
Makes one dull, vapid, smooth, and tranquil scene.

(I. 261–72)

Hearne's alternate view represents a Picturesque approach to the same place, replacing the classicized villa with an irregular mansion, the Chinese bridge with a rustic one, and tidy clumps of trees in a meadow with a wilder style of rampant planting.

Departing from the position of Price and other champions of the Picturesque, Knight would eventually insist that pictorial values, because they are merely sensual, do not suffice in the creation of a landscape garden that can "captivate the soul." Banal beauty must be seasoned with associations conveying the power and passion of poetry. Before Romanticism was recognized as a movement, Knight broke through superficial preoccupation with Picturesque appearances to connect the individual immersed in a designed landscape with primal and transcendent powers of nature. ESE

HUMPHRY REPTON (1752–1818)

27 *A Romantic Bridge*

Pen and brown ink and watercolor on paper, in Repton's Red Book of Ferney Hall; Album, 1789

Collection of Mrs. J. P. Morgan, Jr., Gift of Junius S. Morgan and Henry S. Morgan; 1954.17

LITERATURE: *Morgan Library 1955, pp. 76–78; Daniels 1999.*

EXHIBITION: *New York 1998, no. 132.*

In one of his earliest Red Books, Repton proposed renovations of the landscape at Ferney Hall, Hertfordshire, for barrister Samuel Phipps. This original manuscript reveals a close study of the Reverend William Gilpin's works on Picturesque landscape, especially in this rotund sepia view, which imitates the style of Gilpin's illustrations. It also reflects the influence of Repton's meetings in Hertfordshire with the other leading advocates of the Picturesque, Richard Payne Knight and Uvedale Price, both neighbors of Ferney Hall.

At this early stage of his career, Repton envisioned a "Romantic" response to a woodland that he described in the language of the Sublime as:

> . . . that awful Scene of shatterd Rocks, where the vestiges of some great Convulsion of Nature arrest the attention with wonderous but delightful horror.

> When I look'd at this unexpected Scene, my imagination presented a rude but not neglected path, traversing the magic chasm in various directions, now passing betwixt the divided rocks which project like the shatterd walls of some ruin'd Castle, then crossing from one to the other by a Romantic bridge thrown dreadfully across the Chasm, & then again creeping through an arched cavern bored thro' the rugged mass, where some chosen fragments of the fossil shels with which it abounds [are] placed conspicuously . . . all this I have supposed within the magic Circle mark'd in the Map Enchanted Ground, such a circular fence will be necessary to secure this uncommon Scenery from the mischievous depredations of the idle natives.

Years later, Repton recalled the response of Phipps, who formatively urged him to restrain his "exuberant imagination" and place the comfort of his client before self-indulgent vanity. ESE

HUMPHRY REPTON (1752–1818)

28 ✕ *Hatchlands in Surry a Seat of George Holme Sumner Esqr.*

Pen and brown ink and watercolor on paper, in Repton's Red Book of Hatchlands; Album, 1800

> Collection of Mrs. J. P. Morgan, Jr., Gift of Junius S. Morgan and Henry S. Morgan; 1954.16
> LITERATURE: *Morgan Library 1955, pp. 76–78.*
>
> EXHIBITIONS: *Brussels 1994, p. 129; New York 1998, no. 131.*

Repton proposed to change Hatchlands from "a large red house by the side of a high road, to a Gentleman-like residence in the midst of a Park." In order to do so, he would paint it the color of stone and screen functional outbuildings from view with dense plantings. Hatchlands represents Repton's least Romantic side—his practical professional aspect that drew fire from grand advocates of the Picturesque. This is a smaller scale project in which he had to negotiate with the owner to add a lawn and remove a few trees for better light. ESE

JOSEPH CONSTANTINE STADLER (active 1780–1812)
after HUMPHRY REPTON (1752–1818)

29 ✒ *The General View from the Pavillon*

Folding acquatint in Humphry Repton (1752–1818), *Designs for the Pavillon at Brighton*. London: Printed for
J. C. Stadler and sold by Boydell and Co., etc., 1808

Bequest of Julia P. Wightman, 1994; PML *152316*

LITERATURE: *Conner 1978; Dinkel 1983, pp. 39–45; Daniels 1999, pp. 191–205; Jones 2005, pp. 56–70; Repton 2005, pp. 145–56.*

EXHIBITION: *Norwich and London 1982, pp. 85–88 and 107.*

Overlays down

Overlays up

Fig. 1. Thomas Daniell, *Hindoo Temples at Bindrabund on the River Jumna,* illustration in *Oriental Scenery,* London, 1795–1807, The Morgan Library & Museum

tal Scenery. This apparently whimsical appropriation of style for a pleasure-loving prince occurred shortly after English colonization of the Mughal Empire was fully achieved with the occupation of Delhi in 1803.[1]

In this general view of the Western Lawn at Brighton, the conical aviary revealed on the left re-creates one of Daniell's *Hindoo Temples at Bindrabund on the River Jumna* (Fig. 1) as a transparent confection. Because the prince intended to make Brighton his permanent residence, Repton advised that these gardens should be planted for perpetual bloom. He would have enclosed them with a continuous range of conservatories, screening out the town and forming a gallery with removable windows that could become an open covered walk in summer.

With the Brighton project for the chronically indebted prince at a standstill, Repton published his proposal in partnership with printmaker J. C. Stadler, who etched the aquatints. Years later, to Repton's chagrin, Brighton Pavilion was finally completed by his former assistant, architect John Nash. ESE

Immediately following his experience at Sezincote, Repton was summoned to Brighton by the Prince of Wales. In 1806 he proposed the most boldly exotic designs of his career, a conversion of Brighton Pavilion into a fantasy of Indian design, borrowing from examples published in Thomas and William Daniell's *Orien-*

WILLIAM WORDSWORTH (1770–1850) and SAMUEL TAYLOR COLERIDGE (1772–1834)

30 ❧ *Lyrical Ballads, with a Few Other Poems*

London: Printed for J. & A. Arch, 1798

Gift of Samuel C. Chew, 1960; PML *50898*

This slender volume marks a turning point in English literature and a starting place of English Romanticism. Coleridge's "Rime of the Ancyent Marinere" and Wordsworth's "Tintern Abbey" appeared here for the first time. In the second edition, of 1800, they were accompanied by a preface by Wordsworth that contains a theoretical rationale for his innovations in theme and diction. Literary critics are still exploring Romantic themes in "Tintern Abbey," which can be interpreted in many ways, but most effectively as a nature poem, or rather, a philosophical inquiry into the perception of beauty in nature.

Once in 1793 and again in 1798, while preparing the *Lyrical Ballads,* Wordsworth visited the ruined abbey and walked through the Wye Valley, already a destination for tourists after the publication of William Gilpin's *Observa-*

```
                    201

                  LINES

         WRITTEN A FEW MILES ABOVE
             TINTERN ABBEY,
  ON REVISITING THE BANKS OF THE WYE DURING
                  A TOUR,
              July 13, 1798.

         ══════════════

Five years have passed ; five summers, with the length
Of five long winters ! and again I hear
These waters, rolling from their mountain-springs
With a sweet inland murmur.*—Once again
Do I behold these steep and lofty cliffs,
Which on a wild secluded scene impress
Thoughts of more deep seclusion ; and connect

    * The river is not affected by the tides a few miles
above Tintern.
```

tions on the River Wye (No. 23). He owned a copy of Gilpin's guidebook and may have even brought it with him on his return trip in 1798. But to Wordsworth, Gilpin's guidance was less important than the ability to observe landscape as a direct emotional experience unmediated by the intellect or any preconceptions about the picturesque qualities of a particular locale. That was how he first saw the Wye as an impetuous youth, when nature could inspire "aching joys" and "dizzy raptures." Older and wiser, he viewed the same scenery with less elation but with a "sober pleasure" and a greater understanding of its potential to inspire "lofty thoughts." As much as he regretted the loss of emotional immediacy, he could find ample recompense in a mature outlook seasoned by experience and tempered by powers of reflection revealing a divine purpose, a moral basis, and a spiritual comfort in nature.   JB

WILLIAM WORDSWORTH (1770–1850)

31 ❧ Plan for a winter garden at Coleorton Hall, Leicestershire, seat of Sir George Beaumont

In an autograph letter of Dorothy Wordsworth to Lady Beaumont, 23 December 1806

Gift of the Fellows, 1954; MA 1581.20

LITERATURE: *Knight 1887, vol. 1, pp. 210–12; Wordsworth 1967–93, vol. 2, pp. 112–31; Buchanan 2001, pp. 89–111.*

In 1806 Wordsworth received an invitation to design a winter garden for the wife of his patron Sir George Beaumont, proprietor of Coleorton Hall in Leicestershire. This project fired the imagination of the poet, who proposed to create a cheerful, comfortable, and secluded place where one could meditate on the change of seasons and cherish hopes of spring. His sketch shows how Lady Beaumont might stroll through the grounds, which would be protected from the rigors of winter weather by a double bulwark: a line of evergreens, and a border of majestic firs.

Inside this enclosure would be a series of "compartments," each with a different vista or feature, such as an alley of trees, a bed of late-blooming flowers, a bower, and a pool containing a pair of hardy gold or silver iridescent fish who would be the "Genii of the Place." Deciduous trees would be banished, lest the sight of bare branches trigger thoughts of desolation and break the spell. Instead, hollies, laurels, and yews would do their part to defeat winter with a profusion of greenery highlighted by the red berries of the hollies and the red brick of an adjacent cottage. Wordsworth so enjoyed this assignment that he made it the subject of a sonnet addressed to Lady Beaumont.

Lady! the songs of Spring were in the grove
While I was framing beds of winter flowers;
While I was planting green unfading bowers,
And shrubs to hang upon the warm alcove,
And sheltering wall; and still, as fancy wove
The dream, to time and nature's blended powers

I gave this paradise for winter hours,
A labyrinth Lady! which your feet shall rove.
Yes! when the sun of life more feebly shines,
Becoming thoughts, I trust, of solemn gloom
Or of high gladness you shall hither bring;
And these perennial bowers and murmuring pines
Be gracious as the music and the bloom
And all the mighty ravishment of Spring.[1]

JB

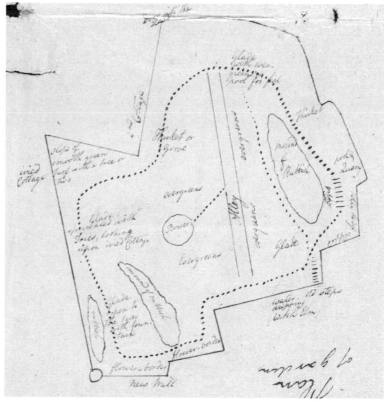

JAMES CHARLES ARMYTAGE (d. 1897) after JOHN RUSKIN (1819–1900)

32 🦢 *Lake, Land, and Cloud*

Steel-engraving. Frontispiece in vol. 3 of Ruskin's *Modern Painters: Their Superiority in the Art of Landscape Painting to All the Ancient Masters Proved by Examples of the True, the Beautiful, and the Intellectual, from the Works of Modern Artists, Especially from those of J.M.W. Turner*. London: Smith, Elder and Co., 1843–60. 5 vols.

Bequest of Gordon N. Ray, 1987; PML 133379
LITERATURE: *Illingworth 1994.*

Modern Painters began as a counterattack on critics of the landscape paintings of J. M. W. Turner but grew into a magisterial treatise on art theory and aesthetics, containing stinging social commentary as well as salient observations on literature, philosophy, and religion. Ruskin was the first to explicate the meaning of landscape as a cultural phenomenon, which could be understood just as readily by studying the poetry of Homer, Dante, and Scott as by viewing the paintings of Turner, Claude, and Constable. Ruskin's ideas greatly influenced the work of Victorian landscape garden designers, such as William Robinson and Gertrude Jekyll in England and Andrew Jackson Downing in America. They are also evident in Brantwood, his estate on the eastern shore of Coniston Water, where he cultivated native plants, devised picturesque rockwork, and built sluice gates for a cascade, landscaping projects intended to enhance the unspoiled scenery of this choice property in the Lake District. The engraved frontispiece reproduces a Ruskin drawing, an ideal landscape in the Turnerian style.   JB

JOHN RUSKIN (1819–1900)

33 ✠ "Of Modern Landscape"

Vol. 3., chapter 16, sect. 39, of *Modern Painters*. One
leaf of the autograph manuscript comprising vols. 1–5,
[1853–60].

Purchased by Pierpont Morgan, 1906; MA 393–97
LITERATURE: *Helsinger 1982, pp. 42–60; Birch 1999.*

Here Ruskin quotes a passage from Scott's *Marmion* to
illustrate a point about modern attempts to seek beauty in nature: "our delight in wild scenery" is a recent
development, quite different from the way nature was
viewed during the Renaissance, the Middle Ages, and
the Classical era. He attributed this change of heart to
fundamental flaws in Victorian society, the materialis-
tic values of industrial capitalism, the grinding ugliness
of suburban wastelands, and other modern miseries. In
his opinion, Romantic notions of pursuing beauty in
the unsullied countryside and distant past were escapist
fantasies prompted by the sordid realities of daily life.

These comments can be read as a critique of Romanticism, although Ruskin would have been the first to admit
his predilection for the Romantic Sublime in the poetry
of Wordsworth and the paintings of Turner. Ruskin remembered "the intense joy, mingled with awe" he had
experienced upon his first encounter with the scenic
splendors of the Lake District, but that did not prevent
him from censuring passages in Wordsworth and other
poets who endeavored to evoke similarly strong emotions
by attributing them to inanimate natural phenomena—
a self-indulgent practice he called the "pathetic fallacy,"
now a standard term in the canon of literary criticism.
Scott is quoted here partly because he was less likely to
commit such a fault in his nature poetry.   JB

J. M. W. TURNER (1775–1851)

34 ✠ *The Pass at St. Gotthard, near Faido*

Watercolor, point of brush, scratching out over traces of pencil, on paper, 1843

The Thaw Collection; 2006.52
LITERATURE: *Ruskin 1903–12, vol. 6, pp. 35–36; Wilton 1976.*
EXHIBITIONS: *New York 1994, nos. 59 and 62; New York 1998, no. 82; New York 2006, no. 63.*

Romantics did not always seek serenity, consolation, and
enlightenment in nature. Here Turner recounts quite a
different experience in the presence of roiling waters,
jagged rocks, distant peaks, and a lowering chasm draped
in mist, a spectacle more likely to stir the strong emotions associated with the Sublime: awe, exaltation, and a
tinge of terror. Mountains often attracted the attention
of artists who aspired to the Sublime, especially the Alps,
where they could try their hand at scenery famous for its
daunting magnificence and formidable grandeur. Turner

No. 34

made several tours of Switzerland, which inspired some of his most important landscape watercolors. This one belonged to Ruskin, who pronounced it to be "the greatest work he produced in the last period of his art."

Ruskin even went so far as to retrace Turner's steps in Switzerland to see for himself how the artist interpreted this scene. On the basis of his observations and his own sketches on site, he discussed this work at length in *Modern Painters*, where it serves as a case study of the workings of the artistic imagination. He noted that a view of the ravine would not be so prepossessing without the extra meaning it gained in conjunction with related images, the towering mountains, and turbulent river one would see on the way to this vantage point. He urged landscape artists to be aware of these ambient impressions and keep them in the mind's eye, where they would enrich the act of perception; they should strive to express the totality of the visual experience:

> *... the far higher and deeper truth of mental vision, rather than that of the physical facts, and to reach a representation which, though it may be totally useless to engineers or geographers, and, when tried by rule and measure, totally unlike the place, shall yet be capable of producing on the far-away beholder's mind precisely the impression which the reality would have produced, and putting his heart into the same state in which it would have been, had he verily descended into the valley from the gorges of Airolo.*

JB

FRANCIS DANBY (1793–1861)

35 ⚑ *The Procession of Cristna*

Watercolor and gouache, heightened with white gouache, with gum arabic, some scratching out, on vellum, ca. 1830

Purchased on the Sunny Crawford von Bülow Fund 1978; 2001.18

LITERATURE: *Adams 1973.*

EXHIBITIONS: *Bristol and London 1988, no. 99; New York 2007, no. 26.*

No. 35

Danby traveled through Norway, sketching the landscape in the summer of 1825. Afterward he remarked, "These kind of scenes are better in pictures than reality, and faith I own I was heartily sick of them."[1] Nevertheless the Norwegian landscape haunted him for years, informing a number of later works, including the present drawing. This Sublime fantasy has been speculatively named for *Cristna*, a lost poem by Danby that he referred to as "no more than a romance."[2] Lacking an extant narrative, the interpretation remains mysterious: Nordic rocks loom over a vaguely oriental caravan, dwarfing elephants and a faceless throng of travelers. The drawing belonged to Danby's sustaining patron John Gibbons, who regarded the artist as "a man of original genius, and in his own walk—the romantic and poetical, the visionary (in landscape) . . . unequalled."[3]   ESE

36 ⚶ *Rockwork, Lawn, and Camellia-house, at Hoole House, from the North-east*

Wood-engraved illustration in John Claudius Loudon (1783–1843), *The Villa Gardener: Comprising the Choice of a Suburban Villa Residence, the Laying Out, Planting, and Culture of the Garden and Grounds, and the Management of the Villa Farm, Including the Dairy and Poultry-Yard.* Second edition. London: Published for the editor by Wm. S. Orr & Co., 1850.

Collection of Elizabeth Barlow Rogers

As a young farmer and gardener, Loudon took courses at the University of Edinburgh before moving to London, where he began to write on gardens in 1803. Concerned throughout his life with self-improvement as well as the education of farmers and gardeners, he started an agricultural college within a few years, followed by the first gardening magazine in 1826, the first natural history magazine in 1828, and the first

No. 36

architectural magazine in 1834. Illustrations and articles from his journals were absorbed into ever-expanding editions of his numerous books. Constantly working throughout his life, he died on his feet while dictating *Self-Instruction for Young Gardeners* to his wife, Jane Webb Loudon, who later edited this edition of his volume on suburban gardening.

Among the most remarkable illustrations in any of Loudon's works are these views of the gardens at Hoole House near Chester. Surrounding a garden of circular flower beds was an early rock garden imitating the Alps at Chamonix, thirty-four feet high, with alpine plantings and marble chips suggesting snow. Romantic infatuation with the Alps converged here with a new emphasis on domestic botanical collection and display that Loudon dubbed "gardenesque."   ESE

JOHN CONSTABLE (1776–1837)

37 ✠ *View of Cathanger, near Petworth*

Pencil on two sheets of paper pasted together, 1834

> *Gift of Mr. and Mrs. Eugene Victor Thaw; 1996.146*
>
> LITERATURE: *Constable 1962–68; Honour 1979, pp. 57–72 and 87–94; Reynolds 1984, no. 34.31, pl. 938; Leslie 1995; Lambert 2005.*
>
> EXHIBITIONS: *London 1976, pp. 112–14; London 1991, pp. 479–81; London, New York, and Toronto 1994, pp. 238–39, fig. 110; London 1996, no. 55; New York 1998, no. 86; New York 2006, no. 64.*

"When I sit down to make a sketch from nature, the first thing I try to do is to forget that I have ever seen a picture."[1] Constable devoted his life to "a pure and unaffected representation of the scenes that may employ me . . . there is room enough for a natural painture."[2] His version of Romanticism rejected the dramatic Sublime in favor of an emotional response to a more familiar nature: "Painting is but another word for feeling."[3] Like Novalis, Constable romanticized the world by dwelling on ordinary wonders, studying the rural landscape as a primitive source of artistic perfection.

In 1834 Constable spent two weeks sketching at Petworth in West Sussex at the invitation of Lord Egremont. He had earlier rejected the Sussex countryside as a subject: "one of the grandest natural landscapes in the world, and consequently a scene the most unfit for a picture."[4] But now he experienced this terrain as a revelation. "I never saw such beauty in *natural landscape* before. I wish it may influence what I may do in future, for I have too much preferred the picturesque to the beautiful . . . the meadows are lovely, so is the delightfull river."[5]

This view of Cathanger Farm on the Petworth estate is the first dated drawing made during his visit. Looking out over a bend in the River Rother, Constable dwelled on the agricultural landscape of fenced meadow beneath a suggestion of vast sky, "the chief *'Organ of sentiment'* . . . the *'source of light'* in nature . . . [which] governs every thing."[6]

ESE

No. 37

SAMUEL PALMER (1805–1881)

38 ❧ *The Haunted Stream*

Pen and brown ink, brown wash, over traces of pencil, on paper, ca. 1834–35(?)

The Thaw Collection

EXHIBITIONS: *New York and Richmond 1985, no. 42; New York 1998, no. 105; Brussels 1994, p. 114, no. 68; London and New York 2005, pp. 26–27.*

Palmer broke away from the conventions of Picturesque composition to pursue a radically new and emotional vision of the landscape, first at Shoreham, Kent, from about 1826 to 1835. Palmer and his circle rejected the shallow falsities of modern life and modern art, calling themselves The Ancients and adopting the motto "Poetry and Sentiment." They were greatly influenced by William Blake, whose illustrations of Virgil Palmer

considered "the most intense gems of bucolic sentiment in the whole range of art."[1]

The seventeenth-century poetry of John Milton also inspired much of Palmer's best work. This sepia drawing of a solitary figure in the moonlight was his first to distill the mood of Milton's poem *L'Allegro*. The poet had dubiously attempted to banish melancholy and embrace a life of mirth by conjuring up a range of delightful

No. 38

fantasies, from mythic to pastoral to chivalric romance: "Such sights as youthful poets dream / On summer eves by haunted stream." Palmer's drawing dwells on the dark- ness enveloping these happy dreams, but then, departing from his text, redeems the gloom with a church spire and the reflective light of nature.   ESE

THOMAS GIRTIN (1775–1802)

39 ✲ *Melrose Abbey*

Watercolor over graphite, on paper, ca. 1796–99

> *Purchased as the gift of Paul Mellon; 1978.22*
> LITERATURE: *Girtin and Loshak 1954, no. 317; Morgan Library 1981, p. 195; Smith 2002.*
> EXHIBITIONS: *New York 1992, fig. 12; New York 1998, no. 74.*

For tourists in the Romantic era, Melrose Abbey had many of the same charms as Tintern Abbey as well as the additional allure of its scenic location in the Scottish Border Country. Sir Walter Scott advised visitors to view by moonlight the "broken arches" of the abbey, which provided local color in his wildly popular Border ballad *The Lay of the Last Minstrel.* Ruined abbeys fre-

quently figure in the watercolors of Girtin, who made several sketching tours in this region. Although he was trained as a topographical artist, Girtin was not so much interested in architectural detail as in the spirit of the place, atmospheric effects, and interpretative touches that might evoke emotion or set a mood.

Girtin's first major patron was a wealthy antiquarian who hoped to record and preserve the "monastic remains" of England, Wales, and Scotland. Many of his earliest surviving watercolors are dramatic views of Gothic monuments after the purely topographical pencil sketches of his patron. Patriotic sentiments were running high while England was at war against revolutionary France and spurred a renewed interest in these antiquarian pursuits along with a greater appreciation of the nation's artistic achievements during the Middle Ages. These ruins also inspired moralizing reflections on the ravages of time and the mutability of fortune, just as Piranesi prints brought to mind the transitory glories of an empire reduced to rubble. But a view of the Roman Forum, once a bustling center of politics and business, has quite a different meaning than a watercolor of a medieval monastery, a house of prayer, a religious retreat, and a refuge from worldly concerns. Girtin could celebrate the bygone magnificence of Melrose Abbey while suggesting that some of its spiritual power remained on site, still a suitable locale for solitary contemplation. (Scott told his readers to "go alone" when they visited Melrose.) Here the ancient edifice is actually becoming part of the landscape, its crumbling masonry crowned with foliage that, left unchecked, could complete its destruction and return it to a state of nature. JB

Romanticism in France

au dedans que la porte étant masquée par des aulnes et des coudriers qui ne laissent que deux étroits passages sur les côtés, je ne vis plus en me retournant par où j'étois entré, et n'appercevant point de porte, je me trouvai comme tombé des nües.

En entrant dans ce prétendu verger, je fus frappé d'une agréable sensation de fraicheur que d'épais ombrages, une verdure animée et vive, des fleurs éparses de tous côtés, un gazouillement d'eaux courantes et le chant de mille oiseaux portèrent à mon imagination du moins autant qu'à mes sens; mais en même tems je crus voir le lieu le plus sauvage, le plus solitaire de la nature, et il me sembloit d'être le premier mortel qui jamais eut pénétré dans ce desert. Surpris, saisi, transporté d'un spectacle si peu prévu, je restai un moment immobile, et m'écriai dans un enthousiasme involontaire: Ô Tinian! ô Juan Fernandes! Julie, le bout du monde est à vôtre porte! — Beaucoup de gens le trouvent ici comme vous, dit-elle avec un sourire; mais vingt pas de plus les ramènent bien vîte à Clarens: voyons si le charme tiendra plus longtems chez vous. C'est ici le même verger où vous vous êtes promené autrefois, et où vous vous batiez avec ma Cousine à coups de pêches. Vous savez que l'herbe y étoit assés aride, les arbres assés clair-semés, donnant assés peu d'ombre, et qu'il

* Isles désertes de la mer du Sud, célèbres dans le voyage de l'amiral Anson.

n'y avoit point d'eau. Le voilà maintenant frais, verd, habillé, paré, fleuri, arrosé: que pensez-vous qu'il m'en a coûté pour le mettre dans l'état où il est? car il est bon de vous dire que j'en suis l'unique maitresse, et que mon mari m'en laisse l'entière disposition. Ma foi, lui dis-je, il ne vous en a coûté que de la négligence. Ce lieu est charmant, il est vrai, mais agreste et abandonné; je n'y vois point de travail humain. Vous avez fermé la porte; l'eau est venüe je ne sais comment; la nature seule a fait tout le reste, et vous-même n'eussiez jamais su faire aussi bien qu'elle. Il est vrai, dit-elle, que la nature a tout fait, mais sous ma direction, et il n'y a rien là que je n'aye ordonné. Encore un coup, devinez. Premièrement, repris-je, je ne comprends point comment avec de la peine et de l'argent on a pu suppléer au tems. Les arbres ..... quant à cela, dit M. de Wolmar, vous remarquerez qu'il n'y en a pas beaucoup de fort grand, et ceux-là y étoient déjà. De plus, Julie a commencé ici longtems avant son mariage et presque d'abord après la mort de sa mère, qu'elle revint avec son père chercher ici la solitude. Hé bien, dis-je, puisque vous voulez que tous ces massifs, ces grands berceaux, ces touffes pendantes, ces bosquets si charmans et si négligés soient venus en six ou sept ans et que l'art les ait dirigés, j'estime que si dans une enceinte aussi vaste vous avez fait tout cela pour dix-mille francs, vous avez bien économisé. Vous ne surfaites que de dix-mille francs, dit-elle, il ne m'en a rien coûté. Comment, rien? Non, rien. A moins que vous ne comptiez une douzaine de journées

P. I 193

JEAN-JACQUES ROUSSEAU (1712–1778)

40 ❧ *Lettres de deux amans, habitans d'une petite ville aux pieds des Alpes*

Autograph manuscript of *Julie, ou la nouvelle Héloïse*, 1759–60

The Dannie and Hettie Heineman Collection, gift of the Heineman Foundation, 1977; MA 6711
LITERATURE: *Neumeyer 1947; May 1962; Willis 1972; McEachern 1989–93, vol. 1, pp. 13–145.*

Julie, her former lover, and her husband savor the noble sentiments of pure love while relishing the simple pleasures of life on a country estate, the idyllic setting of this best-selling epistolary novel *Julie, or the New Héloïse.* Not for them the brittle chatter, amorous intrigues, and enervating passions of townspeople corrupted by modern society. This letter describes Julie's garden, a scraggly orchard transformed by her modest efforts into an "artificial wilderness" resplendent with aromatic herbs, wild flowers, hanging vines, and winding paths cleverly designed to seem longer than they really were. The lush foliage was watered by rivulets diverted from a stream that also supplied water for a fountain in an old formal garden now neglected by the members of this happy household and visited only by outsiders still in thrall to conventional ideas of garden design.

Rousseau knew enough about current fashions to compare Julie's rustic retreat with the contrivances of the Chinese style and with the magnificent assortment of Picturesque attractions at Viscount Cobham's celebrated estate at Stowe. He never visited Stowe but could have easily learned about it from contemporary prints and guidebooks. In his opinion it was ingenious and impressive but that was precisely the problem with excessively clever landscaping projects, which inspired very little in the viewer except admiration for the wealth and taste of the proprietor.

This is the manuscript Rousseau copied for the printers of the six-volume first edition, published in Amsterdam in 1761. By making a fair copy, and by sending it in installments, the author allowed the printers to set the text as accurately as possible and compelled the publisher to pay for each portion of the manuscript before receiving the next one. Altogether five manuscripts of this work are known. Rousseau rewrote and corrected it with such obsessive zeal that no particular version could be considered definitive until this manuscript came to light, and even this represents only one stage in the evolution of the text. The demanding author not only inspected proofs of the six volumes while they were in press but also scrutinized the finished sheets, where he found one misprint to be so objectionable that he asked for it to be corrected by hand in all copies of the edition.

All this labor was compromised, however, by another edition expurgated by the censors, who put their version up for sale the same time as the authorized edition. Then the *Nouvelle Héloïse* became fair game in the European book trade, which produced about seventy reprints in forty years. It was one of the most popular novels of the eighteenth century, appealing to a dawning Romantic sensibility that spurned the affectations of polite society in favor of honest emotion, genuine sentiment, and rustic simplicity. Rousseau's account of Julie's carefree garden paradise greatly influenced theories of landscape design, even though he lacked the practical experience to know how much maintenance it would have really required. Likewise, his readers never knew how hard he worked at perfecting prose designed to demonstrate the virtues of doing what comes naturally. JB

NOËL LE MIRE (1724–1801) after JEAN-MICHEL MOREAU,
called MOREAU LE JEUNE (1741–1814)

41 ✒ [*Le premier baiser de l'amour*]

Engraving and etching, part of a suite of plates made for *Collection complète des oeuvres de J. J. Rousseau.* Brussels: Jean-Louis de Boubers, 1774–83.

Bequest of Gordon N. Ray, 1987; PML 140140
LITERATURE: *Cohen-De Ricci 908–9.*
EXHIBITION: *New York 1982, no. 51.*

Julie, accompanied by her "inseparable" cousin, grants a first kiss to her lover in a *bosquet* (a bower in most translations). This memorable scene was a favorite of the novel's illustrators, beginning with Gravelot, who received detailed instructions from Rousseau on how to achieve just the right combination of innocence and sensuality (Fig. 1). And yet his composition seems staid in comparison to this version by Moreau le Jeune, who admired Rousseau's works and had studied them closely. Moreau understood what kind of bower the author had in mind, not the neatly trimmed trellis imagined by Gravelot but rather a grand arch and a balustrade overgrown by trees, shrubbery, and flowers running riot in a neglected portion of the garden. The shaft of light through the arch, the profusion of greenery, and the towering trees in the distance provide a suitably lush and vibrant setting for the passionate embrace of the disheveled lovers. — JB

Fig. 1. Nicolaas van Frankendaal after Hubert François Gravelot, *Le premier baiser de l'amour,* illustration in Jean-Jacques Rousseau, *Lettres de deux amans, habitans d'une petite ville au pieds des Alpes,* Amsterdam, 1761, The Morgan Library & Museum

J. MÉRIGOT FILS (active 1772–1816)

42 ✒ *L'Isle des peupliers*

Etching and aquatint. Plate in *Promenade, ou itinéraire des jardins d'Ermenonville, auquel on a joint vingt-cinq de leurs principales vues*. Paris: Chez Mérigot père, Gattey, Guyot, et à Ermenonville chez Murray, 1788.

Bequest of Julia P. Wightman, 1994; PML 151002

From 1763 to 1775, the Marquis René Louis de Girardin (1735–1808), aided by two hundred English and Scottish gardeners, reconfigured the park at Ermenonville as a landscape garden. A fervent admirer of Rousseau, he incorporated elements from *Julie* into his garden designs and invited the philosopher to take up residence. Rousseau died at Ermenonville in 1778. As a Protestant, he could not be buried in the churchyard, so his remains were placed in a circle of poplar trees on an island in the park and were soon enshrined in a tomb designed by Hubert Robert. This quickly became a place of pilgrimage and the icon of the French Romantic garden.

Mérigot's guidebook instructs visitors to venerate this tableau from the Bench of Mothers, preferably while shedding tears by moonlight. The cult of Rousseau fueled enthusiasm for Romantic garden design, and the Isle of Poplars became a prototype for monuments encircled by trees in European and American landscapes.

The prescribed itinerary through the landscape garden at Ermenonville meanders for three or four hours among grottoes, cascades, lakes and springs, temples and rustic huts, monuments to love, poetic inscriptions, a picturesque brewery, an altar to Reverie, a tasteful hermitage, an obelisk, and a music stand and dance hall for the villagers. Published one year before the French Revolution, the guidebook closes with a tranquil vision of hamlet, mill, and abbey in an idyllic landscape perfected by a progressive nobleman.   ESE

43 ✒ *Maison du philosophe dans le desert d'Ermenonville*

Etched plate in vol. 1, *cahier* 3, of Georges-Louis Le Rouge, *Détail des nouveaux jardins à la mode*. Paris: Chez Le Rouge [1773 or 1774–89]. 4 vols.

Gift of Mrs. Christian H. Aall, 1983; PML 77830–33

LITERATURE: *Wiebenson 1978, p. 84, fig. 64; Hays 2000, vol. 1, pp. 86–134; Korzus 2004; Royet 2004, p. 109, no. 71 (catalogued as cahier III, plate 22, [1776]).*

Military "engineer-geographer" Georges-Louis Le Rouge also drew estate surveys and established a business publishing, importing and distributing maps and prints. Following a personal financial crisis in 1773, he began to issue *cahiers*—fascicles of about twenty-four sheets—presenting plans, views, and architectural details of fashionable European gardens, recording a revolution in style. Commercial success perpetuated the series, eventually producing 492 plates containing over 1,500 designs, the most extensive visual record of mid-to-late-eighteenth-century gardens.

After meeting William Chambers in Paris, Le Rouge

broadcast the concept of the *jardin anglochinois* beginning in 1775, later integrating a French translation of Chambers's treatise on Chinese design into his series. Late installments of his series reproduced Chinese views of the emperor's gardens.

Le Rouge himself drew a precise survey of Ermenonville for his thirteenth *cahier* published in 1776, before the residence and death of Rousseau. In plate 22, the conventional architectural formula of plan, elevation, and section is applied to a primitive hut set in the wilderness park for that most unworldly of secular creatures, a philosopher. This was the first garden building constructed for the Marquis de Girardin at Ermenonville. ESE

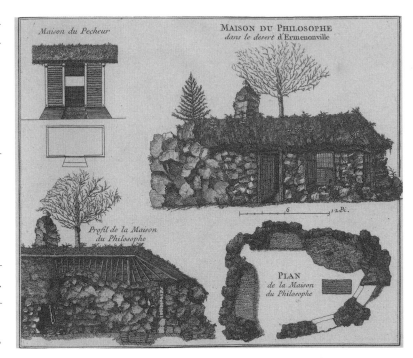

MICHEL, ENGRAVER

44 ✍ *Rocher vûe de l'interieur du jardin faisant l'entrée du desert par la forêt de Marly*

Etched plate in vol. 3, *cahier* 13, of Georges-Louis Le Rouge, *Détail des nouveaux jardins à la mode*. Paris: Chez Le Rouge [1773 or 1774–89]. 4 vols.

Gift of Mrs. Christian H. Aall, 1983; PML 77830–33

LITERATURE: *Ketcham 1994*.

François Racine de Monville (1734–1797) created the gardens of the Désert de Retz from 1774 to 1789, immediately prior to the French Revolution. A fashionable "sybarite"—so-called in his arrest warrant during the Reign of Terror—he designed the landscape garden himself as a compendium of world architecture, horticulture, and history. Twenty follies and innumerable rare botanical species from four continents were arranged on about 95 acres approached through the royal Forest of Marly.

Visitors could walk into this artificial "wilderness" through a cavern fabricated of plaster rocks and guarded by torch-bearing tin satyrs, symbolic figures indicating the entrance to a world of uninhibited fantasy. This design fits Hirschfeld's requirements for a *jardin romanesque*, a wild garden of dramatic rocks and magical grottoes enhanced by imaginary creatures: "the extravagant and the fabulous, condemnable everywhere else, can find their true place here" (see No. 54). Published in 1785, two years after Hirschfeld's comments on the Romantic garden, this nocturnal scene with a full moon is the most fancifully Romantic plate in the entire series. ESE

J. MÉRIGOT FILS (active 1772–1816)

45 ✣ *Le Moulin*

Hand-colored aquatint in *Promenades, ou itinéraire des jardins de Chantilly, orné d'un plan et de vingt estampes qui en représentent les principales vues.* Paris: Chez Mérigot, Brunot-Labbe, Le Normant, et M. Legat à Chantilly, 1791.

Collection of Elizabeth Barlow Rogers
LITERATURE: *Lambin 1972; Wiebenson 1978; Le Ménahèze 2001, pp. 192–94.*

Louis-Joseph de Bourbon (1736–1818), Prince of Condé, inherited Chantilly as a child in 1740, with one of the greatest French classical gardens designed by André Le Nôtre. Upon reaching adulthood, he commissioned architect Jean-François Leroy to transform a marshy area of the park into an English landscape garden. Leroy's designs included a *jardin anglais* with meandering rivulets, a kiosk at the center of a labyrinth, and a deceptively simple hamlet of seven thatched cottages around a green. Inaugurated in 1775,[1] this was the first of the artificially rustic hamlets created for the amusement of a princely court. The half-timbered buildings functioned as dairy, stable, and mill while disguising elegant interiors for suppers and concerts, a reading room, and a billiards hall.

The first published description of the Hamlet, written by architect Nicolas Le Camus de Mézières in 1783, alluded repeatedly to classical figures of mythology and romance who might have dwelled there. By the time this anonymous description illustrated by Mérigot was published in 1791, classical associations with the Hamlet had been abandoned. Generic enchantment replaced myth. Within one of the thatched structures, instead of the banqueting grove for Diana and her nymphs imagined by Le Camus, this guidebook describes the following:

> *a superb dining room, the decoration of which recalls a hunting rendez-vous; one believes oneself transported by a kind of enchantment into the midst of a dense forest. The seats are trunks of trees, carpets of greenery. Flowers spring up from the floor. Some openings arranged here and there in the wall and between the branches of the trees with which the hall is decorated, allow the light of day to penetrate.*

Within a few years, the Hamlet at Chantilly inspired Marie-Antoinette's Hameau at Versailles and similar creations in other fashionable garden parks. In 1789 the prince and his family escaped to Flanders three days after revolutionaries seized the Bastille.   ESE

JACQUES ALIAMET (1726–1788) after CHARLES EISEN (1720–1778)

46 ❧ Allegory of architecture

Etched frontispiece in Marc-Antoine Laugier (1711–1769),
Essai sur l'architecture. Nouvelle édition. Paris: Chez
Duchesne, 1755.

Purchased on the Gordon N. Ray Fund, 2008; PML *195080*
LITERATURE: *Cohen-De Ricci 603.*

A master of Rococo illustration, Eisen understood perfectly the author's arguments against Rococo ornament in architecture—a capricious stylistic aberration to be corrected by a return to nature. A winsome goddess of architecture, holding a straight edge and compass, reclines against the ruins of the classical orders and gestures toward a more truthful and authentic structure, a rustic cabin framed by living trees that support the crossbeams and a pitched roof rising amid the leaves.

The primitive hut imagined by Eisen expresses the spirit rather than the literal meaning of the text, which does not suggest that the earliest buildings were rooted in the soil. But the author surely approved the artist's free interpretation of his theories about the origins of architecture, the true basis of the art not to be found in ingenious decorations but in the simple logic of making shelter with materials readily at hand.

Laugier applied some of the same reasoning to garden design in the last chapter of this influential treatise. He admired the work of Le Nôtre at Versailles but regretted the relentless insistence on regularity and symmetry in this type of formal garden. Instead he commended the elegant simplicity and unaffected veneration of nature in Chinese gardens described by Jesuit missionaries who had visited China and had reported on its art, religion, and culture in the celebrated series of *Lettres édifiantes* (1702–76). The twenty-seventh volume in this series, published in 1745, contains a full account of the imperial gardens in Beijing. The Jesuit Letters were no doubt well known to Laugier, who was a Jesuit himself until he quit the order soon after the publication of this 1755 edition of his *Essai.*   JB

ANNE ATHENA MASSARD after CONSTANT BOURGEOIS (1767–1841)

47 ❧ *Le Belvedere à Morfontaine and La Fontaine Julie à Morfontaine*

Engraved plates in Alexandre, Comte de Laborde (1773–1842), *Description des nouveaux jardins de la France et de ses anciens châteaux.* Paris: De l'imprimerie de Delance, 1808–[15].

Collection of Elizabeth Barlow Rogers
LITERATURE: *Baridon 2004, pp. 5–15.*

The coronation of Napoleon in 1804 ushered in a new era of French opulence, accompanied by a revival of the landscape garden. Four years later, Alexandre de Laborde published the first great postrevolutionary work on gardens, addressed in part to aristocratic proprietors reconstituting their domains. He commis-

Fig. 1. Guyot and Perdoux after Constant Bourgeois, *L'Etang du desert, à Ermenonville*, illustration in Alexandre, comte de Laborde, *Description des nouveaux jardins de la France*, Paris, 1808–15, The Morgan Library & Museum

"Le Belvedere"

"La Fontaine Julie"

sioned the artist Constant Bourgeois, formerly a pupil of Jacques-Louis David, to draw the accompanying views, which provided the first pictorial survey of landscape gardens in France.

Tacitly drawing on Romantic aesthetic theory, Laborde argued that the fundamentally true expression of taste in garden design has been naturalistic throughout history. Magnificent formal gardens have belonged to tyrants, he stated, but periods of excessive formalism always return cyclically to a more profound human response to the nature of a site.

On the other hand, he rejected the extremes of Romanticism, which he associated with affectations of salon society and a denatured nature. With postrevolutionary skepticism, he portrayed Rousseau as a wild man celebrating a wilderness as savage as himself (*sauvage comme lui*; Fig. 1). Instead of unrestrained Romanticism, Laborde recommended a moderate and agreeable heightening of mood in designed landscapes. He described one combination of somber woodland and rushing water as "a sort of laughing melancholy."

In two of his sixteen views of the gardens at Mortefontaine, Bourgeois depicted the deliberately unfinished neo-Gothic belvedere at Mortefontaine and a Fountain of Julie that recalls the naturalistic garden described by Rousseau in *Julie, or the New Héloïse*. Mortefontaine was owned by Napoleon's brother Joseph Bonaparte, King of Naples and of Spain, an enthusiastic garden maker (and, after Napoleon's defeat, a resident of New Jersey).   ESE

CONSTANT BOURGEOIS (1767–1841)

48 ✄ Colored aquatint with overlay

Alexandre, Comte de Laborde (1773–1842), *Teoria dei giardini*. Florence: Fondacci di S. Spirito [ca. 1830].

Collection of Elizabeth Barlow Rogers

Overlay down

Overlay up

Using the before-and-after technique pioneered by Humphry Repton, Laborde proposed the transformation of an old-fashioned garden into a more modern Picturesque style. In this Italian edition of Laborde's remarks on garden design, a rectilinear basin lined with fastigiate trees lifts away to reveal a naturalistic landscape. The reconfigured water resembles a serpentine river set in open meadows with a stone bridge. Laborde compared this proposed landscape to a painting by Poussin or Claude.   ESE

CHARLES GAVARD after PIERRE-FRANÇOIS-LÉONARD FONTAINE (1762–1853)

49 ❧ *Vue du temple de marbre sur la tête de l'ile du pont à l'extrémité de la grande digue*

Engraved plate in Pierre-François-Léonard Fontaine, *Château de Neuilly. Domaine privé du Roi.* Paris: Pihau Delaforest (Morinval), 1836.

Collection of Elizabeth Barlow Rogers

LITERATURE: *Fontaine 1987, vol. 2, pp. 870–71, 890–92, 905–9, 948, and 969–73.*

Following the Bourbon Restoration, Louis Philippe, duc d'Orléans acquired the château and park at Neuilly in 1819. Pierre-François-Léonard Fontaine, architect to every French sovereign through a tumultuous half century, undertook an ambitious expansion of the house and grounds. In 1830 Louis Philippe became the last king of France, projecting an image of comfortable domesticity agreeable to his bourgeois supporters.

In his description of the favorite royal residence, Fontaine gives a history of its development, emphatically repeating that the great expense of the project was entirely reasonable, bringing practical benefits and increased prosperity to the expanding local community. For example, major works on the river improved both navigation and a healthy flow of water, and new construction included the first suspension bridge in the vicinity of Paris. Even the ornamental embellishments at Neuilly "are not the products of a fantastic will, and even less imitations such as one used to see of those rustic cottages, those picturesque rocks, so proudly displayed in the days when the court was placed in the village and the village in the court."[1] Nevertheless the château was burned down during the Revolution of 1848, which ended the monarchy.

Even the printmaking technique of these printed views was considered somewhat populist. In the years immediately preceding the invention of photography, Charles Gavard specialized in mechanical processes of reproduction intended to bring the pictorial arts to a wider audience. This plate is identified as a *pantographe*.

A penciled inscription in this hand-colored copy states that Fontaine gave it to François-Honoré-Georges Jacob-Desmalter, the head of an important Parisian furniture workshop that often collaborated with Fontaine and his partner Charles Percier to execute their designs.   ESE

WILLIAM CALLOW (1812–1908)

50 ❧ *The Garden at Versailles with the Fishing Temple*

Watercolor and gouache on paper, 1837

Purchased on the Sunny Crawford von Bülow Fund 1978; 2007.82

LITERATURE: *Fortoul 1839, pp. 295–99; Gromort 1928; Reynolds 1980, pp. 66–67; Lablaude 1995, pp. 145–61.*

For about seven years, the English artist William Callow taught watercolor painting to the children of Louis Philippe, king of France. In 1837 he received permission to visit private areas of the royal gardens at Versailles in order to draw views for publication. The present drawing was reproduced in both French and English imprints: *Les Fastes de Versailles* by Hippolyte Fortoul, and *Heath's Picturesque Annual for 1839*.

This view of Marie-Antoinette's artificial Hamlet depicts thatched cottages, mill, fishing tower, and two dairies (one functional and one immaculately arranged for refreshments), beside a carefully contoured lake. Vaguely inspired by enthusiasm for Rousseau's ideas of pure and natural country life, it was designed by Richard Mique and Hubert Robert in consultation with the queen during the 1780s. During its construction, a series of harsh winters impoverished the genu-ine peasants of France; and the Petit Hameau de la Reine soon became notorious as the rustic fabrication where Marie-Antoinette played milkmaid. In Callow's resolutely idyllic view, the Romantic qualities of the Hamlet's concept and design, heightened by the tragic death of its originator, infuse the luminous tranquility of the scene.   ESE

Fig. 1. Samuel Fisher after William Callow, *Le village Suisse,* illustration in Hippolyte Fortoul, *Les Fastes de Versailles,* Paris, 1852, The Morgan Library & Museum

CHARLES SAUNIER, ENGRAVER

51 ❧ *Le Père Lachaise*

Steel engraved folding plan in A. Henry, *Le Père Lachaise historique, monumental et biographique.* Paris: Chez l'Auteur, [1852].

Collection of Elizabeth Barlow Rogers

LITERATURE: *Etlin 1984; Linden 2007, pp. 55–79.*

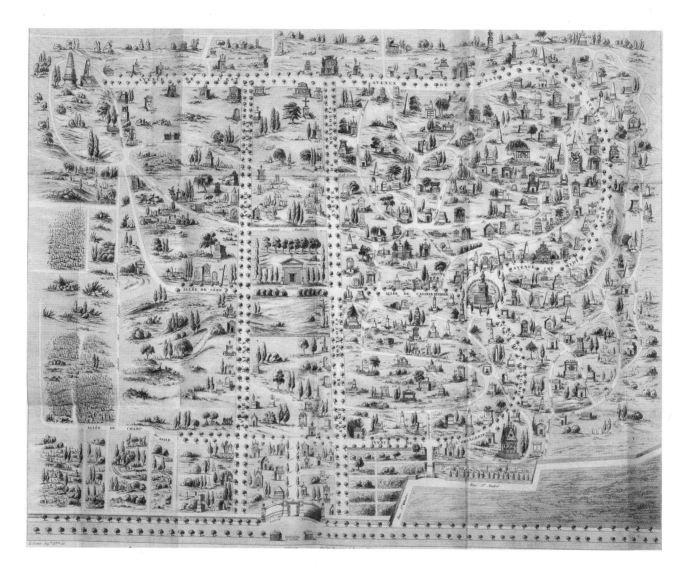

Napoleonic Paris opened four cemeteries outside the city walls, a hygienic improvement also motivated by ideals of religious freedom, individual grave sites, and the permanent commemoration of exemplary lives.[1] The ancien régime garden of Monceau was briefly recommended as "a delectable Elysium" with "the simple epitaph suspended from the foliage of the funerary tree."[2] Instead powerful patriotic, antiquarian, and sentimental impulses combined with Romantic nature worship to produce a new kind of designed landscape.

In 1804 the former residence of Père Lachaise, Jesuit confessor to Louis XIV, became the site of a new cemetery. Architect Alexandre-Théodore Brongniart, who had created a memorial pyramid for the private Elysium of Maupertuis before the Revolution, designed a nonsectarian chapel in the form of a pyramid, never constructed. His tree-lined esplanade became the formal processional axis, outside of which looping drives and footpaths meandered over hilly terrain, their "sinuous" lines supposedly conducive to tranquility. The top of the hill commanded an expansive view of Paris.

Innovative in concept and inconveniently distant from the city, Père Lachaise languished until its appeal was heightened by transfer of the putative remains of La Fontaine, Molière, and Abelard and Héloïse. A Gothic pastiche of architectural fragments housing the medieval lovers compelled Romantic pilgrimage. Soon the newly fashionable burial ground became a magnet for visitors attracted by its landscape design, imposing monuments, and sentimental associations. By 1825 the rapid addition of 26,000 tombs required some orientation. Guidebooks mapped the most notable graves and monuments, offering brief biographies of heroic, artistic, and patriotic personalities.

Travel accounts praised Père Lachaise as a uniquely beautiful setting for the deceased. Mrs. Trollope admired the "fine gloomy funereal shades" of its cypress trees while expressing a disapproving astonishment at public displays of grief by the French.[3] Père Lachaise became an international model, inspiring the creation of garden cemeteries abroad. ESE

EDMOND MORIN (1824–1882) and PIERRE-EUGÈNE GRANDSIRE (1825–1905)

52 ✹ *Parc des Buttes-Chaumont–vue donnant sur le lac* and *Parc des Buttes-Chaumont–vue des falaises*

Steel engravings in Jean-Charles-Adolphe Alphand (1817–1891), *Les promenades de Paris: histoire, description des embellissements, dépenses de création et d'entretien des Bois de Boulogne et de Vincennes, Champs-Élysées, parcs, squares, boulevards, places plantées, étude sur l'art des jardins et arboretum.* Paris: J. Rothschild, 1867–73.

Frances Loeb Library, Graduate School of Design, Harvard University
LITERATURE: *Limido 2002, pp. 124–65.*

Following a period of exile in London, where he particularly admired the new public parks, Napoleon III returned to France and embarked on the transformation of Paris. In 1853 he appointed Baron Georges Eugène Haussmann to modernize the city with clean water, green space, and "strategic embellishments" reducing the potential for barricades. Haussmann enlisted civil engineer Adolphe Alphand to design parks and squares. Fourteen years later, Alphand celebrated their achievement with the first installment of his *Promenades de Paris.*

The newest park presented by Alphand was completed just in time for the Universal Exposition of 1867 in Paris. For three years, a crew of 1,000 men, overseen by Édouard André, converted the infertile quarries and garbage pits of Buttes-Chaumont into a park for the populace of northeastern Paris. The rugged terrain was further exaggerated to create a cliffbound island in an artificial five-acre lake, with bridges, miles of winding footpaths and carriageways. New technologies were used to generate sublime special effects—notably a cascade, pumped by a steam engine, that plunged into a grotto of faux stalactites. About 400,000 trees were planted at Buttes-Chaumont, and exotic species were laid out in a semisystematic arrangement for edification as well as pleasure. ESE

Vue donnant sur le lac

Vue des falaises

Romanticism in Germany

wieder zur Mooshütte geladen, ob sie gleich mit Ottilien in den Zwischenstunden hinauf- geht.

Dadurch müssen wir uns, versetzte Eduard, nicht abschrecken lassen. Wenn ich von et- was Gutem überzeugt bin, was geschehen könnte und sollte, so habe ich keine Ruhe bis ich es gethan sehe. Sind wir doch sonst klug etwas einzuleiten. Laß uns die engli- schen Parkbeschreibungen mit Kupfern zur Abendunterhaltung vornehmen, nachher deine Guts-Charte. Man muß es erst problema- tisch und nur wie zum Scherz behandeln, der Ernst wird sich schon finden.

Nach dieser Verabredung wurden die Bü- cher aufgeschlagen, worin man jedesmal den Grundriß der Gegend und ihre landschaftliche Ansicht in ihrem ersten rohen Naturzustande gezeichnet sah, sodann auf andern Blättern die Veränderung vorgestellt fand, welche die

Kunst daran vorgenommen, um alles das be- stehende Gute zu nutzen und zu steigern. Hie- von war der Uebergang zur eigenen Besitzung, zur eignen Umgebung, und zu dem was man daran ausbilden könnte, sehr leicht.

Die von dem Hauptmann entworfene Charte zum Grunde zu legen war nunmehr eine angenehme Beschäftigung; nur konnte man sich von jener ersten Vorstellung, nach der Charlotte die Sache einmal angefangen hatte, nicht ganz losreißen. Doch erfand man einen leichtern Aufgang auf die Höhe; man wollte oberwärts am Abhange vor einem angenehmen Hölzchen ein Lustgebäude auf- führen; dieses sollte einen Bezug aufs Schloß haben, aus den Schloßfenstern sollte man es übersehen, von dorther Schloß und Gärten wieder bestreichen können.

Der Hauptmann hatte alles wohl über- legt und gemessen, und brachte jenen Dorf-

JOHANN WOLFGANG VON GOETHE (1749–1832)

53 ✒ *Die Wahlverwandtschaften*

Tübingen: J. G. Cotta, 1809. 2 vols. in 1.

Gift of the trustees of the Dannie and Hettie Heineman Collection, 1977; Heineman 662A
LITERATURE: *Gerndt 1981.*

Nature takes its course in this ingeniously plotted *novelle*, best known in English translation as *Elective Affinities.* The title alludes to chemical theories of Goethe's day as well as to romantic impulses that seem to have an irresistible logic of their own, like chemical reactions. An important part of this story takes place in a newly designed park, which also serves as a plot device. In the present passage, the equilibrium of an ideal marriage is already beginning to be disturbed by ambitious plans for landscape improvements highly recommended on the authority of an English publication, probably Repton's *Sketches and Hints on Landscape Gardening.* The husband tends the trees and flowers of a formal garden he inherited with his ancestral estate, the wife designs an outlying park in the sentimental English style, and two houseguests provide advice about these projects, which become a consuming passion in more ways than one.

Goethe described their projects in such fine detail that a literary critic was able to draw a map of the terrain traversed by the love-struck foursome. Goethe had a professional interest in garden design dating back to 1778, when he was helping his patrons develop parkland in Weimar and when he visited Wörlitz, the Garden Realm of Prince Franz of Anhalt-Dessau, a progressive landowner who demonstrated on a grand scale how English precedent could be adapted in Germany. Goethe acknowledged the achievements of that country in an episode signaling the end of *Elective Affinities:* an English connoisseur comes to make a tour of the estate, casts a practiced eye on the recent improvements, and approves of the results while pointing out some places where more work could be done. From start to finish, this *novelle* testifies to the cultural prestige and international influence of Humphry Repton and his followers.   JB

54 ✒ Hermitage

Engraved vignette in Christian Cajus Lorenz Hirschfeld (1742–1792), *Théorie de l'art des jardins.* Traduit de l'allemand. Leipzig: Chez les héritiers de M. G. Weidmann et Reich, 1779–85. 5 vols.

Collection of Elizabeth Barlow Rogers

As professor of philosophy and aesthetics at the University of Kiel in Germany, C. C. L. Hirschfeld wrote the first systematic theory of aesthetics applied to the landscape garden. He argued that the naturalistic landscape garden is an art form superior to painting with transformative potential for the individual, the nation, and the world. The experience of the garden can become transcendent, inspiring, emotional, educational, refining, and

morally improving when the "garden artist" clarifies distinct kinds of character in the landscape to heighten its effects. The programmed character can be gay, gently melancholic, romantic, or majestic, prompting predictably related moods in any sensitive soul. The spontaneous but programmed response to simulations of nature in the landscape garden restores the soul—distorted by society and commerce—to its free, natural state.

In assigning components to each kind of landscape character, Hirschfeld designated the hermitage as a resting point that would reinforce peaceful impressions of sweet melancholy. The contemplative solitude of the hermitage disqualifies it as a part of his definition of the Romantic garden, which requires wild and rustic forms of strange irregularity, such as contorted rocks, cataracts, and grottoes.   ESE

IVAN ZASCHE (1826–1863)

55 ✣ *Aussicht vom Bellevue im Parke Jurjavés nächst Agram in Croatien*

Hand-colored lithograph in *Park Jurjavés*. Vienna: Carl Gerold & Sohn, 1853.

Collection of Elizabeth Barlow Rogers
Literature: Dochnahl 1861, p. 80; Maruševski and Jurković 1993.

One of the first public parks in Europe was initiated by Maksimilijan von Vrhovac soon after he became bishop of Zagreb in 1787. Park Maksimir opened in 1794, but allegations that Bishop Vrhovac sympathized with a Jacobin plot to overthrow the imperial government

brought work to an abrupt halt. Cited as evidence of his subversive tendencies was his lavish expenditure on landscape design in the French style for a progressive civic amenity.

When a successor, Bishop Juraj Haulik de Varallya

(1788–1869, r. 1837–69), revived work on the park in 1839, he imported landscape architect, artists, and horticulturists from Vienna to create a diverse landscape garden with a model farm. Bishop Haulik was head of the new Croatian Slavonic Agricultural Society, which declared farming to be "soul ennobling" as well as economically important. In 1843 he described the rededicated Jurjavés Park as a paragon of farming, an embellishment of the town, and a place where the populace could "invigorate their souls with innocent pleasure of nature."[1]

In 1852, the same year that Zagreb was elevated to an archdiocese, Archbishop Haulik invited Slovak artist Ivan Zasche to leave Vienna and settle in Croatia. Zasche painted the preparatory views for this print series. The Bellevue, also referred to as the Nature Pavilion, was a rustic structure with a conical thatched roof located in a remote area of the park on the edge of the Nightingale Grove.   ESE

Prince Pückler at Muskau

Following his early years in Moravian schools, at the University of Leipzig, and as a military officer allied with the English against the French, Count Hermann Ludwig Heinrich von Pückler-Muskau (1785–1871) inherited a barony with his ancestral seat at Muskau. In 1815 he proclaimed to the residents his determination to lay out an ideal landscape with civic improvements and embellishments on the grand scale. His utopian objective was to improve the environment, the economy, quality of life, and the consciousness of residents and visitors. Seven years later he received the Prussian title of prince, one of the last generation of absolute sovereigns in Europe.

Inspired by the Garden Realm surrounding Wörlitz and strongly influenced by landscape gardens and innovative green civic plans in England, Pückler spent thirty years and most of his assets on creating a regional park of almost 1,500 acres (about 2.3 square miles), integrating castle, town, industry, ornamental gardens, and agriculture within a unified aesthetic design. He razed the old fortifications of his *Schloss*, converted the moat into a lake, diverted streams, and replaced the agricultural fields around the castle with a park. New paths connected planned vistas with focal points, such as a Gothic chapel, the Flower Bridge, Turkish pavilions, and an orangery. Introducing colorful patterned beds of exotic flowers into the foreground of views from the castle, he also planted native species throughout the park and disguised new weirs in the river with naturalistic planting and rockwork.

Pückler attempted to finance the enterprise by amicably divorcing his wife to make way for a wealthier alliance—an unrealized solution to perpetual debt as no suitably wealthy heiress would consent to the arrangement. With the abolition of the old feudal system of compulsory labor service by tenant farmers, he was forced to sell Muskau in 1845.

At the height of his ambition, Pückler published the *Andeutungen über Landschaftsgärtnerei verbunden mit der Beschreibung ihrer praktischen Anwendung in Muskau* (Hints on Landscape Gardening Together with an Account of Their Practical Application at Muskau) in 1834.[1] Modeled to a great extent on the works of Humphry Repton, the *Andeutungen* recommend the English model of refined country life to Prussian gentlemen with "property embellished by the cabbage garden," whose "chief view looks on the manure heap." Pückler wrote in Romantic terms of a "poetical ideal" of "Nature-painting" with hills, woods and meadows, streams, and light and shadow harmoniously designed over time by one governing "artist." Like Repton, he insisted that comfort take precedence over a strictly picturesque aesthetic and inserted elaborate embellishments into the "pleasure ground," forming a transition from the house to the lonely majesty of surrounding nature.

American landscape architects and horticulturists later visited and studied Muskau as a model for estate gardening and town planning integrated into an ideal landscape. As late as 1885, Frederick Law Olmsted advised his young associate Charles Eliot to travel there. Eliot's cogent account of Pückler's accomplishments is quoted in the introduction to the first English translation of the *Andeutungen*, published in 1917 under the title of *Hints on Landscape Gardening*. This publication attests to Pückler's continuing influence in the twentieth century.

No. 56

No. 57

AUGUST WILHELM SCHIRMER (1802–1866)

56 ⚹ *The Neisse Water Meadow at Muskau by Moonlight*

Watercolor and pencil, preparatory drawing for plate 11 of the *Andeutungen über Landschaftsgärtnerei* (Stuttgart, 1834).

Fürst-Pückler-Museum Schloss Branitz; acc. no. VIII 1.168/P

Schirmer painted flowers and views on porcelain at Prussia's Royal Porcelain Manufacture before studying in Berlin and Rome to become a landscape painter. Introduced to Pückler by the prince's architect Karl Friedrich Schinkel in 1832, he was commissioned to draw preparatory views and intentional visions of Muskau for an atlas of lithographs illustrating the prince's *Andeutungen*. Schirmer brought the precision of porcelain painting and a Romantic taste for nocturnal reflections to this watery dream of an idealized landscape.　ESE

HEINRICH MÜTZEL (1797–1868) after AUGUST WILHELM SCHIRMER (1802–1866)

57 ⚹ *The Neisse Water Meadow at Muskau by Moonlight*

Hand-colored lithograph with overlay, plate 11 in the *Andeutungen über Landschaftsgärtnerei* (Stuttgart, 1834)

Stiftung Fürst-Pückler-Park Bad Muskau

This published before-and-after illustration corresponds to the preceding drawing. With the overlay down, the lithograph presents a view from the Schloss Muskau to a street before that part of town was redesigned by Pückler. When the flap is lifted, the street dissolves into a moonlit landscape of tranquil beauty centered on the historic church. A remnant of the old embankment survives on the left.　ESE

O. HERMANN after AUGUST WILHELM SCHIRMER (1802–1866)

58 ⚹ *View of the Manor and Park from the Temple of Perseverance*

Lithograph, plate 22 in the *Andeutungen über Landschaftsgärtnerei* (Stuttgart, 1834)

Purchased on the Gordon N. Ray Fund, 2008; PML 195276

Prince Pückler arranged for the publication of an oblong folio atlas of plans and lithographs, including forty-five views after Schirmer, to accompany an octavo volume of his text on landscape gardening. He traveled widely with his atlas, showing it to the future Kaiser Wilhelm and Napoleon III, both of whom involved him in landscape design projects.　ESE

AUGUST WILHELM SCHIRMER (1802–1866)

59 ❧ *View of the Manor and Park from the Temple of Perseverance*

Watercolor and pencil on paper, preparatory drawing for plate 22 of the *Andeutungen über Landschaftsgärtnerei* (Stuttgart, 1834)

Fürst-Pückler-Museum Schloss Branitz; acc. no. VIII 1.171/P

Following "an exceptionally *lonely* path" through "thickets of beech so dense that the sun has room only to gild the green dome of leaves"—or riding more cheerfully in a carriage—one arrives at the Temple of Perseverance. This high ground, on what is now Polish soil, commands a wide view of the castle, river, mill, dam, and waterfall.

"The perfection of landscape art is reached only in the region where it again appears to be untrammeled Nature, but in her noblest manifestation." Comparing garden art to "growing music" (as opposed to the Romantic description of architecture as "frozen music"), Pückler orchestrated a composition that could "stir the senses with vague but powerful emotions . . . [working] the scattered parts into a beautiful whole, whose melody flatters the senses, but unfolds its highest powers and yields the greatest enjoyment only when harmony has breathed true soul into the work."[1]   ESE

60 ❧ *Flower Garden Beside the Castle at Muskau*

Watercolor and pencil on paper, preparatory drawing for plate 12 of the *Andeutungen über Landschaftsgärtnerei* (Stuttgart, 1834)

Fürst-Pückler-Museum Schloss Branitz; acc. no. VIII 1.217/P

Pückler believed in creating the strongest possible contrast between the embellishment of a pleasure ground immediately surrounding the house and the appearance of wild nature in the distance.[1] This view from the balcony of Schloss Muskau surveys a flower garden in which, "I have allowed my fancy free play and have boldly combined regularity with irregularity without, I hope, having ruined the harmony of the whole. . . . As a matter of fact, the effect is quite rich and original."

The fan-shaped bed around a letter *H* was to be re-planted three times yearly with yellow crocus, carnations, and asters in succession. The mouth of the cornucopia mixes pumpkins with moss and brightly colored flowers, a detail unrecorded by Schirmer. Multicolored parrots animate the background.   ESE

No. 60

61 ❧ *View from the Gloriette to the Park and Lake with Fisherman's Hut*

Watercolor and pencil on paper, preparatory drawing for plate 17 of the *Andeutungen über Landschaftsgärtnerei* (Stuttgart, 1834).

Fürst-Pückler-Museum Schloss Branitz; acc. no. VIII 1.173/P

A fisherman's hut beside a newly created lake at Muskau was thatched to blend in with the roofs of a nearby wax bleachery, icehouse, park keeper's lodge, English cottage, and village. "Thus, the plot appears as one integral part of the park . . . inhabited by well-to-do villagers. I have thus produced unity out of multiplicity." Here Pückler adapted the Romantic aspiration to create unity out of the chaotic diversity of the world to the practical objectives of the landscape designer.   ESE

62 ✒ *View from the English Cottage*

Watercolor and pencil on paper, preparatory drawing for plate 27 of the *Andeutungen über Landschaftsgärtnerei* (Stuttgart, 1834)

Fürst-Pückler-Museum Schloss Branitz; acc. no. VIII 1.166/P

The English cottage "presents the characteristics of gay rural social life" with a covered bowling alley, outdoor seats, a café, a shooting range, a small dance hall, and two rooms for games.

"On a hill opposite stands an isolated salon in the shrubbery, built of rough logs and bark, which is . . . reserved for the gentry, and from which the whole tableau of the crowd enjoying themselves below may be viewed just as one may choose without coming into closer contact."

From this vantage point, "lovers of the idyllic" could also watch shepherds with their flocks and laborers "hastening home with song" at dusk.   ESE

63 ✤ *Pleasure Ground at the Spa, Made in the Style of an Oriental Garden*

Watercolor and pencil on paper, preparatory drawing for plate 33 of the *Andeutungen über Landschaftsgärtnerei* (Stuttgart, 1834)

Fürst-Pückler-Museum Schloss Branitz; acc. no. VIII 1.158/P

LITERATURE: *Pückler 1917; Parshall 2004; Duempelmann 2007.*

Beyond the town, alum works, coal mine, and foundries are situated public baths and mineral waters. "The lover of free, untrammeled Nature will . . . be most pleased with this region. It will be easy for him to find deepest solitude in dense forest and glade, where there is nothing to disturb his thoughts."

Beside the health spa, an oriental garden, "designed to suit all tastes," was planted for late summer bloom during the principal bathing season, with exotic pavilions placed on steep, contorted bluffs.　　ESE

CASPAR DAVID FRIEDRICH (1774–1840)

64 ❧ *Moonlit Landscape*

Watercolor on paper; moon cut out and inserted on a separate piece of paper; laid down on cardboard, [ca. 1830]

Thaw Collection; 1996.150

LITERATURE: *Koerner 1990; Vaughan 2004.*

EXHIBITIONS: *New York 1994, no. 52; New York 2001, no. 9; New York 2006, no. 56.*

Fig. 1. Caspar David Friedrich, *Morning*, Niedersächsisches Landesmuseum, Hannover

Fig. 2. Caspar David Friedrich, *Coastal Landscape*, Kupferstichkabinett, Staatliche Museen zu Berlin

Inspired by his belief that "the divine is everywhere," Friedrich painted landscapes of immersion in nature as a mystical experience. His first requirement of a work of art was that it should engage the mind and put the viewer into a "soulful" mood.

> The picture should only suggest, but above all it should excite the spirit and create room for the play of fantasy. . . . The painter's task is not the faithful representation of air, water, rocks and trees, but his soul and his feelings should be reflected therein. Perceiving the spirit of nature, penetrating, absorbing, and reproducing it with the whole of one's heart and mind: that is the task of a work of art.[1]

Friedrich's friend Carus credited him with rescuing landscape painting from banal insignificance through his melancholic but "distinctively new and radiant poetic tendency."[2] The present watercolor is one of Friedrich's two known surviving "transparencies"—images intended to be lit from behind by pulsing lamplight in a dark and silenced room, sometimes accompanied by music. The moon is a cutout filled with translucent paper. Birgit Verwiebe has related Friedrich's transparencies to Romantic fascination with light as the antithesis of matter, an emanation of divinity and inspiration. She points out that they followed the popular reception of illuminated, semitransparent dioramas introduced by Louis Jacques Mandé Daguerre in 1822 and imitated in Berlin in 1827. But Friedrich made it clear that his experiments with painting on a translucent surface are not to be dismissed as peep show entertainments.[3]

The composition of *Moonlit Landscape* closely re-sembles that of an oil painting called *Morning,* one of a cycle of the Times of Day painted by Friedrich in 1820 and 1821 (Fig. 1). Both works are structured as an arrangement of horizontal bands, with a watery foreground contained by slightly rising terrain that partially hides a building, probably a farmhouse, further obscured by darkness or mist. Rounded hills rise behind an unseen valley. A large area of sky just above the terrestrial crest draws the viewer's attention with remarkable effects of light.

Iconographically, however, this work more closely relates to Friedrich's sepia *Coastal Landscape,* circa 1830, in which a similarly robed and postured statue occupies a pedestal beside a rustic path (Fig. 2). In both pictures, there is a strong sense of connection between the statue and a higher symbolic source of spiritual energy—the moon in one, a cross in the other. This connection is not conveyed by the direction of a sculpted gaze. Instead the cross and the moon radiate a mysterious power that touches a surrogate human figure.[4]

In 1830 Friedrich proposed a transparency in hybrid terms, applying the older romantic idea of magic to a nature regarded as divine by the Romantic movement: a scene in a wood "where through magic power, a treasure is extracted from the earth and heavenly goods are exchanged for earthly ones."[5] In *Moonlit Landscape,* the pantheistic communion of dynamic moon and hallowed humanity also suggests an exchange, triangulated by the spectator standing in the shoes of the reverent artist. ESE

CARL GUSTAV CARUS (1789–1869)

65 ❧ *Fountain Before a Temple*

Charcoal, heightened with white gouache, on blue-gray paper [1854–57]

Thaw Collection; EVT 205
LITERATURE: *Wat 1998, pp. 16–20, 44–47, 83–85, and 129.*
EXHIBITION: *New York 2009, no. 33.*

Carus, professor of gynecology at Dresden, royal physician to the court of Saxony, natural scientist, early psychologist, and landscape artist, was a pupil and friend of Friedrich as well as a fervent admirer of Alexander von Humboldt and Johann Wolfgang von Goethe. He developed a theory of landscape art inspired by Schelling's concept of nature as a "world soul" that unifies the cosmos into a single infinite organism permeated and sustained by a harmonious equilibrium. "All that we feel and think, all that is, and all that we are, rests on an eternal, supreme, infinite unity."[1] In 1831 he published *Nine Letters on Landscape Painting* (Neun Briefe über Landschaftsmalerei), an important statement of Romantic art theory. Reversing the eighteenth-century idea expressed by Sir Joshua Reynolds[2] that drawing from nature was mere imitation compared to the more admirable originality of studio work, Carus argued that "earth-life" was the highest subject for painting. He rejected both formulaic and inaccurate landscape painting as a desecration, particularly belittling Hogarth's idea that beauty could be determined by the serpentine line and dismissing views captured in a Claude glass.[3] Instead, he defined the principal task of landscape painting as "the representation of a certain mood of mental life (meaning) through reproduction of a corresponding mood of natural life (truth)."[4]

Carus believed that the landscape artist must have a "consecrated heart" and a "pure mind" conducive to "the birth of divine ideas." In order to achieve the technical ability to convey "the true and wondrous life of nature," the young artist was to study natural history and roam outdoors to practice scientific drawing of the landscape as carefully as studio painters would study anatomy. Then:

> When the soul is saturated with the inner meaning of all these different forms; when it has clear intimations of the mysterious, divine life of nature; when the hand has taught itself to represent securely, and the eye to see purely and acutely; and when the artist's heart is purely and entirely a consecrated, joyous vessel in which to receive the light from above: then there will infallibly be earth-life paintings, of a new and higher kind, which will uplift the viewer into a higher contemplation of nature. These works will truly deserve to be named mystic and orphic; and earth-life painting will have attained its culmination.[5]

In a late charcoal drawing from the Thaw Collection, Carus continued his lifelong attempt to capture inner mood and meaning through the depiction of carefully selected objects. The full moon so often depicted by Carus and other Romantic artists shines on a nocturnal garden, illuminating marble architecture and dynamic water. A Neoclassical temple pediment in the background quietly presides over the brightest component of the picture, a jet of water shooting up from a fountain toward the moon. Carus vested the typically Romantic sense of contemplative solitude with an optimistic serenity. His brief essay "On the Effect of Individual Landscape Objects on the Mind" aids the interpretation of mood in this drawing:

> Let the veil of cloud break into silvery cloudlets, or disperse in the steady glow of the rising moon or of the sun, and our inner gloom is dispelled; we are uplifted by the thought that the infinite has prevailed over the finite. . . . Finally, water, the fourth basic element of natural life, from which all earth-life emerges, and which reflects the infinity of the sky (heaven on earth, indeed), exerts a twofold attraction on us: its lively turbulence excites and enlivens our feelings, and its still surface, whether light or dark, moves us to infinite longing.[6]

Fragments from the artist's journal describe moonlit walks in Dresden, including several to the Großer Garten; one to the Brühl Terrace, with its iron balustrade; another to the theater on the Zwinger, with its great pediment; and another to the fountain near the Frauenkirche.[7] An actual site for this picture has yet to be identified.   ESE

Romanticism in
America

more excellent qualities in the student than preciseness and infallibility; that a guess is often more fruitful than an indisputable affirmation, and that a dream may let us deeper into the secret of nature than a hundred concerted experiments.

For, the problems to be solved are precisely those which the physiologist and the naturalist omit to state. It is not so pertinent to man to know all the individuals of the animal kingdom, as it is to know whence and whereto is this tyrannizing unity in his constitution, which evermore separates and classifies things, endeavouring to reduce the most diverse to one form. When I behold a rich landscape, it is less to my purpose to recite correctly the order and superposition of the strata, than to know why all thought of multitude is lost in a tranquil sense of unity. I cannot greatly honor minuteness in details, so long as there is no hint to explain the relation between things and thoughts; no ray upon the *metaphysics* of conchology, of botany, of the arts, to show the relation of the forms of

RALPH WALDO EMERSON (1803–1882)

66 ✄ *Nature*

Boston: James Munroe and Company, 1836

Purchased by Pierpont Morgan, 1908; PML *18077*
LITERATURE: *Robinson 1980; Brown 1997.*

Nature was Emerson's first major publication, an important step forward in his career as an essayist, lecturer, and a public intellectual. Soon he would be recognized as the leader of the Transcendentalist movement, which was composed of like-minded progressive thinkers and politically active social reformers in the Boston area. European Romanticism clearly influenced his views on nature—a source of joy and wonder, a basis of religious belief, and a link with the "Universal Being," best perceived instinctively with a childlike awe of the complexity and coherence of the material world. He thought that empirical science was good in itself but that the "untaught sallies of the spirit" would be better for understanding the origins and significance of nature.

Like some of his Transcendentalist colleagues, Emerson was trained as a Unitarian minister with a rationalist outlook more likely to accept the tenets of natural theology than the precepts of revealed religion. He grew increasingly impatient with his ministerial duties and with conventional ideas about religious authority, which he found in the work of God's creation rather than in miracles and scripture. In 1832 he resigned his position as junior pastor in the Second Church of Boston and embarked on a trip to Europe, where he met Romantics, such as Wordsworth and Coleridge, and saw the sights in London, Paris, and Rome. In Paris he visited the Jardin des Plantes, where he particularly admired the astonishing variety of animal, mineral, and plant specimens displayed in the botanical garden, the menagerie, and the Cabinet of Natural History—a scientific spectacle all the more impressive because the specimens were organized in accordance with the intricate classification systems developed by French naturalists Georges Cuvier and Antoine Laurent de Jussieu. Inspired by their example, Emerson announced in his journals that he too would be a naturalist, and indeed he lectured on natural history after he returned to the United States. Science, however, was not his calling. The most memorable part of his visit to the Jardin des Plantes was not the myriad species, families, and orders he viewed in the botanical garden but the garden itself as an all-inclusive aesthetic experience and philosophical revelation. The garden was designed so that the visitor could take it all in at first glance when entering through the gateway and at greater leisure when walking along English-style winding paths on a hilly area above the parterres in which the horticultural specimens were displayed. The importance of observing nature in its totality is a recurring theme in this tract. "When I behold a rich landscape," he noted in the passage displayed here, "all thought of multitude is lost in a tranquil sense of unity."   JB

JOHN HILL (1770–1850) after JOSHUA SHAW (ca. 1777–1860)

67 ✄ *View near the Falls of Schuylkill*

Hand-colored aquatint in *Picturesque Views of American Scenery.* Philadelphia: Published by M. Carey & Son, 1820.

Princeton University Library, Department of Rare Books and Special Collections, Graphic Arts Collection, gift of Leonard L. Milberg, Class of 1953
LITERATURE: *Fowble 1987, nos. 275–76; Koke 1961, no. 41.*

There is an important English ingredient in *Picturesque Views of American Scenery,* a collaboration between two artists who had learned their skills and formed their style in England before they emigrated to America. The landscape painter Joshua Shaw had exhibited his work at the Royal Academy and had obtained the patronage of its American-born president, Benjamin West. The engraver John Hill had earned his living by making aquatints after Turner, Rowlandson, and other artists for London publishers of prints and illustrated books. Both Hill and Shaw brought with them notions of Romanticism and ideas about landscape art that enabled them to make the most of the scenic attractions in America. This view of the Schuylkill is easily the equal of English aquatints of the period, yet it also touches on uniquely American themes, the lure of the wilderness and the untapped resources of territories in the hinterland. Local pride may have played a part in the choice of this "uncommonly romantic and picturesque" scene, just a few miles outside of Philadelphia, where this portfolio was published.

Other parts of the county also had something to offer, according to the author of the introduction, who declared that nowhere else in the world could one see forests, prairies, mountains, and rivers exhibiting such a "variety of the beautiful and sublime." This is the first great collection of American views, even though it was not a commercial success and was never completed, a victim of the depression following the Panic of 1819. After the original publisher went out of business, *Picturesque Views* passed into the hands of Mathew Carey & Son, who prudently decided not to invest any more in this publication. It was sufficiently well received, however, to merit reprinting in 1829 and 1835.   JB

No. 67

JOHN HILL (1770–1850) after JOSHUA SHAW (ca. 1777–1860)

68 ✶ *Washington's Sepulchre, Mount Vernon*

Hand-colored aquatint in *Picturesque Views of American Scenery*. Philadelphia: Published by M. Carey & Son, 1820.

Princeton University Library, Department of Rare Books and Special Collections, Graphic Arts Collection, gift of Leonard L. Milberg, Class of 1953

LITERATURE: *Koke 1961, no. 38.*

The symbolic significance of this highly Romantic locale was not lost on Joshua Shaw, who availed himself of a "painter's license" to make it even more wild, overgrown, and desolate than it actually was. In fact Washington was buried in these humble circumstances only until 1831, when his remains were removed to more prepossessing quarters elsewhere on the Mount Vernon estate. Nonetheless, patriotic Americans who made a pilgrimage to this spot would have thought that it was a singularly appropriate resting place for the father of their country, a paragon of republican virtue, who famously renounced the trappings of power after performing his civic duties.

Sometimes landscape art can be viewed as a political metaphor, but this is an unusually explicit example. The letterpress commentary accompanying this aquatint laments the sorry state of Washington's tomb and advises the reader, "if you would seek his monument look at the country he served, at the republican institutions he loved and fostered, and at the humble farm to which he retired when ambition had no influence and power no charms."　　JB

WILLIAM CULLEN BRYANT (1794–1878)

69 ✶ *Monument Mountain*

Autograph manuscript, 1824

Purchased by Pierpont Morgan, 1909; MA 686
LITERATURE: *Heckscher 2008, p. 11; Muller 2008.*

America's first celebrity poet and editor of the *New-York Evening Post*, William Cullen Bryant helped to muster popular support for the construction of "an extensive pleasure ground" in the city of New York. He could advocate a public park all the more eloquently as a poet who had celebrated nature in much of his work, including this prime example of American Romanticism, a story of forbidden love in a suitably wild, lonesome, and majestic setting. This vivid account of a lover's leap in the Berkshires inspired a landscape painting by Asher Durand, who alluded to Bryant's nature poetry in at least five of his paintings.

Monument Mountain.

Durand was not the only one to have been deeply moved by *Monument Mountain*. Soon after it was published in 1824, Elizabeth Dwight Sedgwick, the wife of one of Bryant's closest friends, asked him for a copy in his hand, which was later inserted in this album along with other Bryant manuscripts and some contemporary portraits. Among the manuscripts are autograph letters to her husband, Charles Sedgwick, including one referring to the pronouncements of a critic "*Wordsworthian* enough . . . to speak of the tie that associates natural and moral beauty, and of the voice of divinity issuing from eloquent places of nature." Bryant knew his Wordsworth but, like other American Romantics, was less introspective in his response to nature and more likely to see it as a source of moral purpose and religious insights.   JB

WILLIAM CULLEN BRYANT (1794–1878), EDITOR

70 ༈ *Picturesque America; or, The Land We Live In. A Delineation by Pen and Pencil of the Mountains, Rivers, Lakes, Forests, Water-Falls, Shores, Cañons, Valleys, Cities, and Other Picturesque Features of Our Country*

New York: D. Appleton and Company, 1872–74. 2 vols.

Collection of Elizabeth Barlow Rogers
LITERATURE: *Wolfe 1981, pp. 102–8; Rainey 1994.*

Like the *Picturesque Views* of 1820, *Picturesque America* extolled the scenic splendors of America, which, however, had greatly increased in size and wealth during the intervening fifty years and had recently completed a transcontinental railroad that made it possible to see the sights in the newly acquired western territories. "Art sighs to carry her conquests into new realms," said Bryant in the preface, noting that

Turner himself had done just about all he could with the stale attractions of the Old World.

The steel-engraved title page shows an American artist at work on a promontory overlooking a waterfall in Virginia. This plate may be a self-portrait of the artist Harry Fenn, who was born and trained in England but settled in New York, where he became one of the most prominent illustrators of his day. He was the chief

Fig. 1. Part-issues, William Cullen Bryant, ed., *Picturesque America*, New York, 1872–74, The Morgan Library & Museum

Fig. 2. Morocco binding, William Cullen Bryant, ed., *Picturesque America*, New York, 1872–74, collection of Elizabeth Barlow Rogers

illustrator of *Picturesque America*, which was so successful that the publishers hired him to work on two sequels, *Picturesque Europe* (1875–79) and *Picturesque Palestine, Sinai and Egypt* (1881–83).

The publishers succeeded in selling nearly half a million copies of *Picturesque America*, an impressive achievement, but they had to produce a large edition to recoup their investment in these two massive volumes containing nearly fifty steel engravings and more than nine hundred wood engravings. Their total outlay on artwork amounted to $138,000. They were able to mitigate these costs by using mass production techniques, which brought the unit cost down to a level accept-

able to consumers and profitable to themselves as well as their colleagues in the book trade who took care of production and distribution. Thriftily, they made the engravings do double duty, first publishing them in their weekly magazine, *Appletons' Journal*, and then reusing them in the part-issues of this work, delivered to subscribers twice a month over the course of two years (Fig. 1). The parts cost fifty cents each—plus $2.50 if a subscriber wanted a muslin box to protect them before sending them off to the binder and an extra $20 if a subscriber wanted to show off this parlor-table book in bindings of "Full Turkey Morocco Antique, Gilt." This is one of the copies in special bindings (Fig. 2). JB

FREDERIC EDWIN CHURCH (1826–1900)

71 🦢 *Horseshoe Falls*

Oil on two joined pieces of paper mounted on canvas, [1856].

Olana State Historic Site; inv. OL.1981.15A and B (P524)

LITERATURE: *Huntington 1983; McKinsey 1985, pp. 243–47; Jeremy E. Adamson, "Nature's Grandest Scene in Art," in Buffalo, Washington, and New York 1985, p. 135, and pp. 62–70 (on Church and Niagara); Carr 1994, pp. 230–33, no. 371; Gail S. Davidson, "Landscape Icons, Tourism, and Land Development in the Northeast," in New York 2006a, pp. 3–22, on Niagara Falls.*

EXHIBITION: *Dallas 1998, pp. 162–63, no. 27.*

As the sublime icon of the American landscape, Niagara Falls had become the subject of numerous popular views by the 1850s. Church visited the site in 1856, inspired by the writings of John Ruskin, who had recast the Sublime as the highest kind of beauty because of its morally uplifting effect.[1] He was particularly impelled by Ruskin's declaration of the "truth of water" as the most wonderful substance:

> *the best emblem of unwearied, unconquerable power . . . what shall we compare to this mighty, this universal element, for glory and for beauty? or how shall we follow its eternal changefulness of feeling? It is like trying to paint a soul.*[2]

Church's on-site drawings culminated in the present oil sketch, a radical reorientation of the usual composition, which typically emphasized the vertical plunge of pounding waters. Balancing impressions of surging power and poised suspension, he stretched his view horizontally along the edge of the rapids, creating a foreground in motion from an imaginary viewpoint over Table Rock on the western edge of the Horseshoe Falls.

This was the final detailed study painted at Niagara in preparation for a seven-foot-long oil painting on canvas. Even before completion of the final work, the preparatory sketch met with critical enthusiasm. In characteristically Ruskinian language, *The Crayon* wrote, "Mr. Church . . .

exhibits a sketch of Niagara Falls, which more fully renders the 'might and majesty' of this difficult subject than we ever remember to have seen . . . on canvas. . . . [T]he eye is not diverted, led away, as it were, from the soul of the scene by the diffuse representation of surrounding features."[3] The *Boston Weekly Traveller* later reported that Church had spent many days at Niagara "not busily sketching all the time, but wandering about with his eyes and his heart brooding upon the Cataract."[4] A rhetoric of emotion and transcendence characterized the rhapsodic reception of the final painting, now in the Corcoran Gallery, exalting Church as the greatest American landscape painter of the era. Even Ruskin himself approved.[5]

Distressed by industrial and commercial encroachments that required him to idealize his views of Niagara, Church initiated a campaign for the preservation of the Falls during the 1860s and 1870s. He exhorted his fellow members of the Century Association to support the cause, and instigated a proposal to Lord Dufferin, the governor general of Canada, urging the establishment of a public park as a cooperative venture between Canada and the United States. Frederick Law Olmsted took up the cause independently in 1869 and with Calvert Vaux designed the New York State Reservation at Niagara two years after its establishment in 1885.[6]   ESE

72 ✒ *Olana from the Southwest*

Oil on paperboard, ca. 1873?

Gift of Louis P. Church, Cooper-Hewitt, National Design Museum, Smithsonian Institution; inv. 1917-4-666

LITERATURE: ; *Novak 1980; Aslet 1990, pp. 34–47; Ryan 2001; Howat 2005; Gerald L. Carr, "Church's Olana: A New Eden," in New York 2007a, pp. 111–23, fig. 63.*

EXHIBITION: *New York 2006a, fig. 36.*

By 1860 Church had become the most famous painter in America, best known for vast canvases depicting landscapes from Niagara Falls to the Andes. That year Church purchased a farm on a hill overlooking the Hudson River. After a lengthy tour of Europe and the Near East, he collaborated with architect Calvert Vaux on the design for a new mansion called Olana, a polychrome fantasy of Persian architecture. His "feudal castle" in the air was completed in 1872. Church also consulted Olmsted, Vaux and Company on the grounds.[1]

But Olana was truly envisioned by Church. Three decades of his devotion resulted in an environmental version of the Romantic *Gesamtkunstwerk,* integrating architecture, decoration, and landscape to fully engage the senses, emotion, and spirit. Church opened views, set the house in an expansive lawn, and laid out more than five miles of drives curving through the estate. "I can make more and better landscapes in this way than by tampering with canvas and paint in the studio."[2] He resisted the gaudy flower beds and subtropical foliage plantings that by this time had come to rival the divinized nature garden aesthetic and instead planted thousands of trees: ". . . for several seasons after I selected this spot as my home, I thought of hardly anything but planting trees. . . ." In *Walden,* Thoreau had recently praised lakes as pure "Sky water," as "earth's eye" and "the landscape's most beautiful and expressive feature."[3] Now Church excavated a lake that echoed the shape of the Hudson River and reflected trees, house, and sky.

Church referred to Olana as an Eden, and as "the Center of the World." Here he portrays the glowing house as nexus, a rarefied work of art crowning earth and touching heaven, framed by the foliage of nature. ESE

H. JORDAN after ALEXANDER JACKSON DAVIS (1803–1892)

73 ⚘ *View in the Grounds at Blithewood, Dutchess Co. N.Y., the Residence of Robert Donaldson Esq.*

Engraved plate in Andrew Jackson Downing (1815–1852), *A Treatise on the Theory and Practice of Landscape Gardening, Adapted to North America*, 6th edition. New York: A. O. Moore & Co., 1859.

Collection of Elizabeth Barlow Rogers

LITERATURE: *Tatum and MacDougall 1989; Schuyler 1996; Sweeting 1996; Major 1997.*

Downing was a nurseryman and horticulturist from Newburgh, New York, tutored in the appreciation of picturesque landscape design by the English artist Raphael Hoyle and in natural history by the Austrian consul Baron Alois von Lederer.[1] From his initial forays into horticultural journalism, he branched out to promote the importance of an aesthetic approach to garden design, a message eagerly received by the burgeoning audience of suburban home and country villa residents. First published in 1841, his treatise on landscape gardening for Americans made him famous at the age of twenty-five; it was issued in nine editions over the next thirty-five years.[2]

Downing followed Thomas Cole and Washington Irving in asserting the moral importance of the arts, including gardening, for the formation of a civilized American landscape and a virtuous national character.[3] On the home front, he advocated the largest possible lawn, up to twenty acres; curving drives and footpaths; flower beds around sundials, urns, or fountains; specimen trees; and an ornamental temple or summerhouse.

His illustrations include this scene of refined country life at Blithewood, on the Hudson River, drawn by architect Alexander J. Davis. This part of Blithewood fits Downing's definition of a beautiful landscape, "always captivating to persons of pure and correct taste."[4] At Blithewood he began an informal collaboration with Davis that continued through the 1840s.

As editor of *The Horticulturist*, Downing became the leading popular advocate for home gardening, agricultural education, village improvement societies, rural cemeteries, public parks (including a national park in Washington, D.C., and a central park in New York City), and suburban life. His Byronic published portrait and his early death in a steamboat accident confirmed his status as the first Romantic hero of American horticulture.   ESE

ALEXANDER JACKSON DAVIS (1803–1892)

74 ✦ *Ravine Walk, Blithewood*

Watercolor on paper, 1847

Avery Library, Columbia University; acc. no. 1955.001.00048
LITERATURE: *Haley 1988; Peck 1992.*

From 1836 to 1851, Davis designed the architectural structures of Blithewood at Annandale-on-Hudson for Robert Donaldson. The project continued onto the adjacent property of Montgomery Place from 1841 to 1873. Together Donaldson and Louis Livingston of Montgomery Place pursued a program of land acquisition to preserve the Saw Kill River, their common boundary, from industrial development. Ultimately, miles of carriage drives and footpaths extended over both estates, punctuated with a variety of Davis's rustic constructions.

In the course of these developments, Davis began to work with the young horticulturist Andrew Jackson Downing. Following the success of Downing's treatise on landscape gardening, their ongoing collaboration strongly influenced American taste in house and garden design throughout the 1840s, advancing a Romantic ideal of country life for a prosperous democratic society.[1]

In 1847 Davis drew a series of watercolors of Blithewood and Montgomery Place to illustrate a description by Downing in *The Horticulturist*. This view represents a rustic bridge and thatched belvedere along the Wilderness Walk on the Blithewood bank overlooking a cataract in the river. Downing described the scene from the opposite bank in the language of popular Romanticism:

Coming from the solemn depths of the wood, [the visitor] is astonished at the noise and volume of the stream, which here rushes in wild foam and confusion over a rocky fall, forty feet in depth. . . .

There is a secret charm which binds us to these haunts of the water spirits. The spot is filled with the music of the falling water. Its echoes pervade the air, and beget a kind of dreamy revery. The memory of the world's toil gradually becomes fainter and fainter, under the spell of the soothing monotone; until at last one begins to doubt the existence of towns and cities, full of busy fellow beings, and to fancy the true happiness of life lies in a more simple existence, where man, the dreamy silence of thick forests, the lulling tones of babbling brooks, and the whole heart of nature, make one sensation, full of quiet harmony and joy.[2]

ESE

75 ✠ *Ericstan for John J. Herrick, Tarrytown, New York*

Watercolor, ink and graphite on paper, [1855]

The Metropolitan Museum of Art, Harris Brisbane Dick Fund; acc. no. 24.66.10
LITERATURE: *Snadon 1988; Peck 1992, pp. 76–77, pl. 49 and fig. 3.28.*

Beginning in the 1830s, Davis was a leading architect of picturesque houses, including the first Gothic Revival residences in the United States. He introduced the castellated villa to America and constructed at least fifteen of the "castlettes" he designed between 1832 and 1857, more than any other architect in Britain or America.[1] Ericstan, overlooking the Hudson River near Tarrytown, was one of the last in the series, built for flour merchant John J. Herrick from 1855 to 1859.

Davis's young collaborator Andrew Downing described this style as Romantic in a chapter called Landscape or Rural Architecture:

The ideas connected in our minds with Gothic architecture are of a highly romantic and poetical nature. . . . Although our own country is nearly destitute of ruins and ancient time-worn edifices, yet the literature of Europe . . . is so much our own, that we form a kind of delightful ideal acquaintance with the venerable castles, abbeys, and strongholds of the middle ages. Romantic as is the real history of those times and places, to our minds their charm is greatly enhanced by distance, by the poetry of legendary superstition, and the fascination of fictitious narrative. A castellated residence, therefore, in a wild and picturesque situation, may be interesting, not only from its being perfectly in keeping with surrounding nature, but from the delightful manner in which it awakens associations fraught with the most enticing history of the past.[2]

At the height of his association with Davis, Downing added the following statement to the 1844 edition of his treatise: "The Castellated style never appears completely at home except in wild and romantic scenery. . . ."[3] Downing associated the style with English heritage, refined minds, and the genius of authors from Shakespeare to Pope to Sir Walter Scott. Nevertheless, with rare exceptions, he expressed doubts regarding the suitability of domestic castles to the American republic.[4]

Davis insisted that American homes needed a stronger connection to their site, enhanced by trees, shrubs, and vines. He often designed the landscapes around his houses, and he published some of the first designs for American domestic architecture to be presented as views in landscape settings.[5] This drawing sets the bijoux fortress in a naturalistic landscape garden, heightening the Romanticism of the scene with the full moon in a nocturnal sky.

ESE

ROBERT HINSHELWOOD (1812–after 1875) after JAMES SMILLIE (1807–1885)

76 ✳ *Lowell's Monument, Willow Avenue*

Steel-engraved plate in Cornelia W. Walter (1813–1898), *Mount Auburn Illustrated.* New York: R. Martin, 1851.

Collection of Elizabeth Barlow Rogers
LITERATURE: *Linden 2007.*

Preceded only by Père Lachaise in Paris, Mount Auburn Cemetery in Cambridge, Massachusetts, initiated a new kind of garden cemetery in 1831 that set monuments in picturesque landscapes of rolling ground, winding paths, ponds, and groves. Intended in part for public health, to reduce the dreaded "miasma" emanating from urban graveyards, the new rural cemeteries also reflected a positive transformation in ideas of salvation and the moral influence of nature. Leading cemeteries also provided inspirational monuments to instill reverence and patriotism.

In this volume, Cornelia Walter, the first American woman to edit a daily newspaper, quoted Romantic poetry throughout her description of Mount Auburn Cemetery. She represented this new kind of cemetery as something greater than an aesthetic amenity, connecting the human spirit to God through an emotionally charged landscape. "To the true imagination, God should be *seen* in the bright light which beams in the noontide over those wavy forest-trees; he should be *heard* in the wind-murmurings which make the leaves rustle, and sway the tender grass; he should be *felt* 'in the sorrows which, to the heart of sympathy, are living all around us. . . .'"[1]

Before the first public parks were established, Mount Auburn inadvertently attracted overwhelming throngs of visitors. Desecration of garden cemeteries by "persons in pursuit of pleasure" became a compelling argument for the creation of public parks.

ESE

J. W. WINDER (active 1855–74), PHOTOGRAPHER

77 ⚘ *Winter Scene, Spring Grove Cemetery*

Mounted plate in *Spring Grove Cemetery, Its History and Improvements, with Observations on Ancient and Modern Places of Sepulture*. Cincinnati: Robert Clarke & Co., 1869.

Collection of Elizabeth S. Eustis

LITERATURE: *Vernon 2000; Linden 1995; Linden 2006.*

Following an apprenticeship in the imperial Hapsburg gardens, Adolph Strauch (1822–1883) was employed, mentored, and educated in landscape design by Prince Pückler-Muskau. After further travels and experience in the Royal Botanic Garden at Regent's Park in London, Strauch brought European precepts of the Romantic era to America, where his landscape design at Spring Grove Cemetery in Cincinnati after 1854 became a national model. To create an ideal site for "contemplative recreation," he converted five acres of wetland into lakes, planted an important arboretum and introduced the influential "lawn plan," eliminating plot enclosures and reducing "ornamental puerilities" in order to imitate "the thoughts of God" expressed in nature.

In the present publication, Strauch set out guidelines for "the ornamental burial ground [that] will become indispensable to every city of any importance, where people of culture reside and aesthetic tastes prevail." A diverse site with undulating ground and mature forest trees should be planned and consistently developed by one executive designer to combine cheerfulness with calm solitude in an environment of "grandeur and simplicity," where elegant monuments are carefully placed amid open lawns and luxuriant vegetation. As recommended by Prince Pückler, "only the well-kept roads and the judiciously scattered buildings" indicate human intervention in a landscape park approximating "the character of untrammeled Nature."[1] Frederick Law Olmsted praised the results: "I know of no cemetery in the country in which there are any natural effects of landscape gardening, properly so called, except at Spring Grove."[2]

ESE

78 ✂ Autograph letter to Elizabeth Baldwin Whitney, 16 December 1890

Frederick Law Olmsted Papers, Manuscript Division, Library of Congress, Washington, D.C.
LITERATURE: *Roper 1983.*

In this letter to a childhood sweetheart, the elderly Olmsted reminisced about the formative influences of his youth that "afterwards determined my profession." Daughter and sister of governors of Connecticut, the charming and cultivated Lizzie Baldwin was his muse at a time when he had not yet decided on a career. Here he gives her credit for encouraging him to study the works of "Emerson, Lowell and Ruskin, and other real prophets." He also recognized the influence of his father, who read to him travel literature that extolled the beauties of nature, which he and his father viewed on vacation trips in New York and New England. In his local public library he discovered theoretical works on landscape art and design, among them William Gilpin's *Remarks on Forest Scenery* and Uvedale Price's *Essay on the Picturesque.* Both works were first published in the 1790s, and yet, in Olmsted's opinion, they were still required reading for students who wished to learn the basic principles of his business. He told Whitney that he would commend Gilpin and Price to junior colleagues in no uncertain terms: "You are to read these seriously, as a student of Law would read Blackstone." He himself had read them seriously at an early age and then again twenty years later when he was just beginning to find his calling under the influence of Andrew Jackson Downing and in collaboration with Calvert Vaux. Frequently quoted by biographers, this letter attests to the important role theoretical publications played in the dissemination of stylistic ideas as well as in the formation of the landscape architecture profession.　JB

79 ⚘ Frederick Law Olmsted and John Olmsted in a camping scene

Frontispiece in Frederick Law Olmsted (1822–1903), *A Journey Through Texas; or, A Saddle-Trip on the Southwestern Frontier.* New York: Dix, Edwards & Co.; London: Sampson Low, Son & Co.; Edinburgh: Thos. Constable & Co., 1857.

Princeton University Library, Department of Rare Books and Special Collections, Philip Ashton Rollins Collection of Western Americana
LITERATURE: *Rogers 1972, pp. 14–15.*

In 1850, amid the turmoil over the Fugitive Slave Law, which required runaway slaves be returned to their owners, *The New York Times* commissioned Olmsted to travel through the South in order to give a series of firsthand reports on the social and economic conditions consequent to slavery. After his return to New York, he published the dispatches he had written under the pen name Yeoman in three volumes: *A Journey in the Seaboard Slave States*, *A Journey Through Texas*, and *A Journey in the Back Country*.

During his travels in the company of his brother John—all the time gathering facts, compiling statistics, reporting conversations—Olmsted managed to observe and comment on the scenery he saw from train windows,

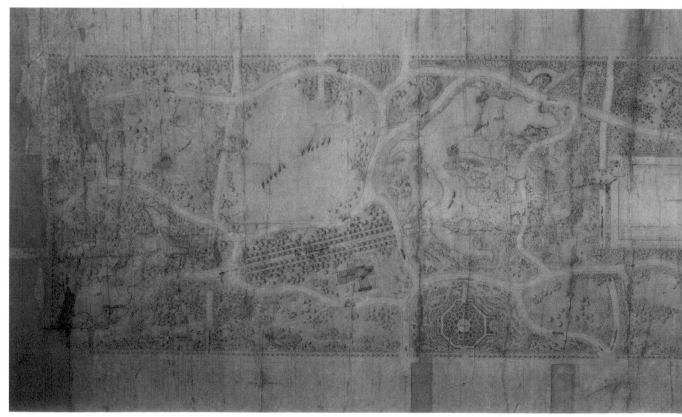

No. 80

steamboat decks, and coaches as well as on mule and horseback. The Romantic impression made on him by the kind of scenery represented in the foreground of this frontispiece —"the rank luxuriance of a semi-tropical vegetation; great trees, . . . their limbs intricately interlaced with vines; . . . dwarf palm, with dark, glossy evergreen shrubs, . . . the sunshine but feebly penetrating through the thick waving canopy of dark gray moss"[1] —carried over into his later work as a landscape architect. For example, on the island in the Lake in Central Park, he sought to create a "tropical effect" using temperate-climate vegetation.

In the background of the two brothers' campsite is a broad, open prairie dotted with trees. Moving farther west and into the Texas Hill Country as he progressed through the great grasslands, Olmsted rhapsodized, "The live-oaks, standing alone or in picturesque groups near and far upon the clean sward, which rolled in long waves that took, on their various slopes, bright light or half shadows from the afternoon sun, contributed mainly to an effect which was very new and striking, though still natural, like a happy melody." [2] This kind of seemingly endless greensward provided an enduring ideal in his future career as a landscape architect. It is easy to apply a similar description to several pieces of park scenery he created, most notably perhaps the Long Meadow in Prospect Park.   EBR

FREDERICK LAW OLMSTED (1822–1903) and CALVERT VAUX (1824–1895)

80 ⚘ *Central Park Competition Entry No. 33: The Greensward Plan of Central Park*, 1858

Brown ink on paper

City of New York/Parks & Recreation

LITERATURE: *Fein 1967; Olmsted and Kimball 1970; Rogers 1972, pp. 17–25; Olmsted 1977, vol. 3; Rogers 2001, pp. 337–44; Miller 2003; Heckscher 2008.*

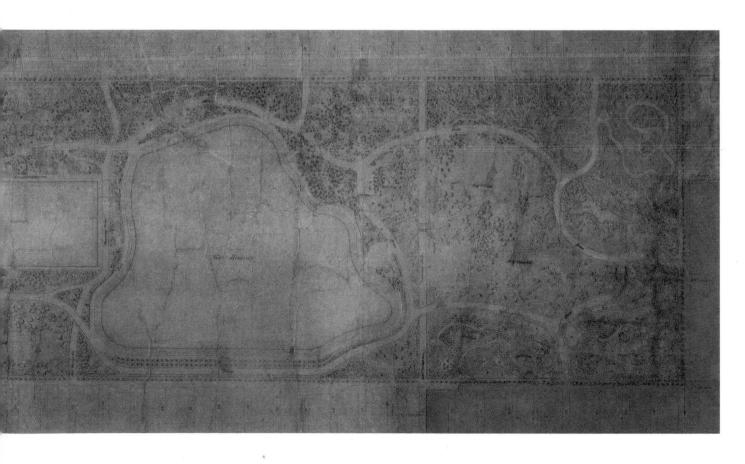

Olmsted and Vaux wrote a *Description of a Plan for the Improvement of the Central Park: "Greensward"* (1858) to accompany their submission in the design competition for the park. Professing the same Romantic attitude toward nature as Ralph Waldo Emerson, William Cullen Bryant, Thomas Cole, and Frederic Church, they declared, "It is one great purpose of the Park to supply to the hundreds of thousands of tired workers, who have not opportunity to spend their summers in the country, a specimen of God's handiwork that shall be to them, inexpensively, what a month or two in the White Mountains or the Adirondacks is, at great cost, to those in easier circumstances."[1] In preparing their plan, which they submitted on the day of the competition deadline, 31 March 1858, they did much of their collaboration after their regular workday, walking the grounds of the future park in the moonlight, appreciating the scenic potential of its bold outcroppings of Manhattan schist, proposing certain topographical alterations in order to transform swamps into lakes and mound soil into rolling meadows. They studied where to place drainage lines and discussed the configuration of carriage drives and the best vantage points for vistas. Friends gathered in the evenings at Vaux's house at 136 East 18th Street to assist in the preparation of the pen and ink drawing depicting their plan. According to Vaux's son Downing, "There was a great deal of grass to be put in by the usual small dots and dashes, and it became the friendly thing for callers to help in the work by joining in and 'adding some grass to Central Park.'"[2] On 28 April, the commissioners announced their decision to award first prize to "Greensward." Thus began the fruitful partnership that created the prototype that launched the parks movement in America.

The element that more than any other defines an Olmsted-Vaux park is a spacious greensward with gentle rises and vistas through the scattered clumps of trees around the edges. By obscuring the boundaries of long meadows as well as those of the park's perimeter, they sought to create an illusory landscape of indeterminate dimensions along with an immediate one for scenic recreation. Because of Central Park's broken topography and narrow rectangular shape, it was difficult to find suitable expanses of ground for this purpose. Above 98th Street, however, there is a piece of tableland that lent itself to becoming the North and East Meadows. In the southern end of the park, the designers proposed blasting away bedrock and grading a six-acre site in

order to create the meadowlike Ball Ground required by the design competition guidelines. To the north they fulfilled another requirement by designating a fifteen-acre open space the Parade Ground. The latter, however, was never used as such, and in implementing the Greensward plan, Olmsted and Vaux were able to cover the surface of the proposed Parade Ground with two feet of topsoil in order to create a thick mat of turf that was to be kept short by grazing sheep, thus adding a pastoral dimension to the park scenery. By visually uniting the Ball Ground and the bucolic Sheep Meadow, they achieved the impression of a single grassy expanse. Realizing that houses would rise on the lots around the park's perimeter, they graded it and planted its borders in a manner that screened out the urban environs. In these and other ways, they executed an impressive act of legerdemain with regard to optical space.

From an engineering perspective, the most ingenious aspect of the Greensward Plan and an enormous boon to the visitor's safety and recreational experience was the sinking below grade of the four transverse roads needed to accommodate east-west city traffic across the park. Here again Olmsted and Vaux considered their design in optical terms. Seven-foot-high planted berms adjacent to the transverse roads allowed for continuous sightlines to the other side, with no notice of the carts and draft animals—and later, taxis, buses, and cars—moving beneath. Although not presented as part of the Greensward plan, they later carried the principle of grade separation of traffic one step further in the construction of paths, carriage drives, and bridle trails. This gave Vaux, often in association with his architectural collaborator Jacob Wrey Mould, the opportunity to design a number of beautiful stone arches to allow strollers to pass safely beneath the drives. Cast-iron bridges to carry foot traffic over the bridle trails further enhanced the ornamental beauty of the park's landscape. Also built of cast iron, Bow Bridge, at the narrow neck between the two lobes of the lake, constitutes Vaux's masterwork in this mid-nineteenth-century building material.

The designers were no doubt relieved that the ornamental flower garden put forth as one of the requirements in the design competition and inserted into the Greensward Plan at the edge of the park adjacent to Fifth Avenue at 74th Street was never built. In his description of their plan, Olmsted maintained that "The Park throughout is a single work of art, and as such subject to the primary law of every work of art, namely, that it shall be framed upon a single, noble motive, to which the design of all its parts, in some more or less subtle way, shall be confluent and helpful."[3] To achieve this end, he shunned the Gardenesque style advocated by John Claudius Loudon. Instead he looked backward to the eighteenth-century theorists of the Picturesque. In his later years, acknowledging the influence of these preceptors, Olmsted wrote in "An Autobiographic Fragment," "While yet a school boy I came to . . . the works of Price and the two Gilpins which my father . . . took out of the Public Library. They are yet the most educative books on park-making in our language or in any language."[4]

The Greensward plan contains one principal element that deviates from the rest of Central Park's romantically picturesque design: the Mall—the wide axial promenade lined on either side with a double row of American elm trees. Olmsted explained: "Although averse on general principles to a symmetrical arrangement of trees, we consider it an essential feature of a metropolitan park, that it should contain a grand promenade, level, spacious, and thoroughly shaded."[5] The promenade's diagonal orientation derived from the designers' desire to make its visual climax the outcrop of Manhattan schist called Vista Rock, "the most prominent point in the landscape of the lower park." In this way they hoped "to withdraw attention in every possible way" from the boundary lines of the narrow rectilinear park site and direct the visitor's gaze to the picturesque scenery of the Ramble.

In all of these ways the Greensward plan illustrates the two fundamental premises of nineteenth-century Romanticism in park design: 1) real and illusory space, often combined in one expansive view, as the chief means of stimulating emotion and 2) experience of the landscape's overall composition by movement through a sequence of picturesque and pastoral scenes. According to Olmsted:

> The main object and justification [of Central Park] is simply to produce a certain influence in the minds of people and through this to make life in the city healthier and happier. The character of this influence is a poetic one and it is to be produced by means of scenes, through observation of which the mind may be more or less lifted out of moods and habits into which it is, under the ordinary conditions of life in the city, likely to fall.[6]   EBR

FREDERICK LAW OLMSTED (1822–1903) and CALVERT VAUX (1824–1895), DESIGNERS

Photograph attributed to Mathew B. Brady (1822–1896); artwork by Calvert Vaux

81 ✂ *No. 4: From Point D* (across the Lake toward Vista Rock)

Greensward plan presentation board with "Present Outlines" (above) and "Effect Proposed" (below). Albumen silver print from glass negative and oil on paper, 1858.

NYC Department of Records/Municipal Archives
LITERATURE: *Miller 2003, pp. 88–95; Heckscher 2008, pp. 28–36.*

By accompanying the Greensward plan with presentation boards showing "before" and "after" perspectives of the same scene, Olmsted and Vaux hoped to help the park commissioners judging the Central Park design competition to visualize the landscape as it would be when their plan was executed. This strategy of contrasting the view of existing conditions with a vision of the prospective landscape recalls the technique originated during the eighteenth century by Humphry Repton in the Red Books he presented to his clients. Although other Greensward presentation boards display paired sketches, in this instance the designers took advantage of the recently available technology of photography to contrast the barren character of the park site as depicted through the lens of the camera in their image of "Present Outlines" with an oil-on-paper rendering of the same scene as it would appear when transformed according to their plan. The lush Romantic beauty of the "Effect Proposed" painting (as well as the park's appearance today) indicates the boldness of their imagination. Its comparison with the photograph hints at the extraordinary feats of earth moving, hydrological engineering, shrub and tree planting, and sheer brute labor needed to create a man-made landscape resembling a work of nature.

Nos. 81 and 82

Olmsted and Vaux's use of topography to determine the parts of their design is apparent here. While outside the park the bold outcrops of Manhattan schist were being blasted away to level the ground where a grid of streets was being laid out, inside the park the thrusting, glacier-polished gray forms were integral parts of the Greensward plan. In their description of the plan, they asserted that the most important feature in the lower half of the park was the long rocky and wooded hillside lying immediately south of the Reservoir. Its highest elevation, Vista Rock, was to be a major focal point, the object of the view from the Mall as well as *From Point D* illustrated here on presentation board *No. 4.*

In the photograph a wooden tower sits atop Vista Rock, functioning as a beacon in the landscape. In the painting one can discern the outlines of the future Belvedere, a handsome Victorian Gothic structure that would be designed in 1865 by Vaux and Jacob Wrey Mould (1825–1886). Because Vista Rock is the second-tallest point in the park, the Belvedere, a stone tower crowned by a steeply pitched roof, sits high above the Old Reser-

voir (now the Great Lawn). Seen from this vantage point, its foundations appear to have emerged organically from the upthrust Manhattan schist bedrock. The tower and the loggias on its surrounding terrace offered the visitor panoramic views, which then extended all the way to the Hudson Palisades and Long Island Sound.

Although architecturally impressive, the Belvedere is quite small in scale relative to its surroundings. Here as elsewhere, Olmsted and Vaux intended for conspicuously sited buildings to serve as mere grace notes within the park's Romantic scenery, while utilitarian structures were to be placed in low-lying areas, screened from view. The subservience of architecture to landscape is also evident in the placement of the compositionally decorative summerhouse seen here in the "Effect Proposed" painting. This ornamental gazebo occupies the spot on the little peninsula the designers named Hernshead, where the cast-iron Ladies' Pavilion now stands. On the hillside depicted on the opposite shore, Olmsted and Vaux created the Ramble, a naturalistic woodland that is much enjoyed by bird watchers today.   EBR

FREDERICK LAW OLMSTED (1822–1903) and CALVERT VAUX (1824–1895), DESIGNERS

Photograph attributed to Mathew B. Brady (1822–1896); artwork by Calvert Vaux

82 ✤ *No. 5: From Point E* (across the Lake from Vista Rock)

Greensward plan presentation board with "Present Outlines" (above) and "Effect Proposed" (below). Albumen silver print from glass negative and oil on paper, 1858.

NYC Department of Records/Municipal Archives
LITERATURE: *Miller 2003, pp. 88–95; Heckscher 2008, pp. 28–36.*

The paired views of this presentation board accompanying the Greensward plan are the reverse of the ones in No. 81. The photograph taken from Vista Rock, looking southwest across the low ground soon to be excavated in order to create the Lake, depicts a treeless landscape in which two small structures, possibly squatters' cabins, can be discerned. The fine miniature oil painting attributed to Vaux shows a clear affinity with the Romantic aesthetic of the artists of the Hudson River school. Vaux was, in fact, directly linked to them. He belonged to the Century Association, the club founded by artists and writers that served as the one of the city's few exhibition venues at the time. He was also a member of the National Academy of Design, where many prominent Hudson River

school artists also showed their work. His sister Mary was married to Jervis McIntee (1828–1891), a student of Frederic Church. It is possible that McIntee, who painted *View from the Terrace Site* in 1858, a landscape embracing Vista Rock and the slope that would become the Ramble, may have had a hand in the creation of the small gem of Romantic art seen here. Another candidate for speculation in this regard is the architect Jacob Wrey Mould, who was also a noted illustrator. Mould was Vaux's full-time collaborator beginning in 1857, when the Greensward plan was being prepared, and in his role as assistant city architect he continued to work on the design and construction of Central Park for almost his entire career.   EBR

CALVERT VAUX (1824–1895) and E. C. MILLER

83 ❧ *Bridge for Carriage Drive*

Lithograph, frontispiece in *Third Annual Report of the Board of Commissioners of the Central Park. January 1860.*
New York: Wm. C. Bryant & Co., 1860.

Collection of Elizabeth Barlow Rogers

LITERATURE: *Reed, McGee, and Mipaas 1990, pp. 32–33; Rogers 2001, p. 341; Miller 2003, pp. 41, 69, and 102–3.*

This lithograph depicts Balcony Bridge, so named because of a pair of corbeled bays forming small balconies with stone seats, which were intended to provide views of the Ramble and Bethesda Terrace at the point where the West Carriage Drive spans an arm of the Lake that once terminated in Ladies' Pond. Designed by Vaux, the open quatrefoil pattern of the bridge's carved parapet is evidence of the popularity of the Gothic Revival style at this time.

Like the rest of the stone arches and cast-iron bridges of Central Park designed by Vaux, often in collaboration with Jacob Wrey Mould, Balcony Bridge expresses the decorative complexity characteristic of a period in which eclecticism knew no bounds. Its carved stonework is but one of the ornamental elements in Central Park that demonstrate the pervasive influence of the English architect and decorative artist Owen Jones (1820–1877), with whom Mould had studied. As an apprentice architect, Mould had assisted Jones in drawing details of the

Alhambra in Spain and in designing the Crystal Palace in London. Jones's magnum opus, *The Grammar of Ornament* (1856), was instrumental in revolutionizing the design arts with the addition of both Ruskinian forms derived from nature and decorative motifs of Italian Gothic, Celtic, Arabian, Turkish, Moresque, and Persian origin. Wall mosaics, tile work, and tessellated pavements were incorporated into architecture, and carved stone assumed a richly ornamental character absent in the preceding Georgian, Federal, and Neoclassical styles. This revolution in the decorative arts and architecture also influenced industrial manufacturers, including Minton & Company of Stoke-on-Trent, the purveyors of the polychrome tiles for the ceiling of the Bethesda Terrace Arcade, and the J. B. and W. W. Cornell Ironworks, which fabricated most of Vaux's cast-iron bridges in Central Park.

After the middle of the nineteenth century, when faraway travel became less fraught with danger, the artists and architects who went beyond the traditional destinations of Grand Tourists saw non-Western imagery firsthand, which helped to foster the enthusiasm for exotic ornament. The Hudson River school artist Frederic Church was particularly notable in this regard. In the architecture and decor of Olana, his Romantically sited home overlooking the Hudson River, Middle Eastern ornamental motifs were reinterpreted in both form and pattern. It is probable that, in choosing Vaux as the architect of Olana, Church had admired his work in Central Park.   EBR

FREDERICK LAW OLMSTED (1822–1903)

84 ✠ Autograph letter to Mary Perkins Olmsted, 25 September 1863

Frederick Law Olmsted Papers, Manuscript Division, Library of Congress, Washington, D.C.
LITERATURE: *Olmsted 1977, vol. 5, pp. 80–92; Roper 1983.*

Olmsted was on his way to California and had just crossed the Isthmus of Panama when he wrote this letter to his wife with a lyrical account of the tropical scenery he had seen along the way. Here, and in a letter to Ignaz Pilat, the head gardener of Central Park, he examined the emotions he had experienced at the sight of luxuriant jungle foliage and concluded that his feelings had arisen from a "sense of the bounteousness of Nature." He hoped to evoke a similar emotional response to parts of Central Park by planting trees, shrubs, and vines that might grow to be equally lush and dense.

Landscaping ideas were still on Olmsted's mind, even though he had resigned his position in the park to manage a mining estate southeast of San Francisco. Pilat loyally endorsed his ideas and promised to implement them in his absence—which, as it turned out, was brief. The mining venture did not succeed, and Olmsted returned east at Vaux's urging to help him design Prospect Park in Brooklyn. It could be said, however, that his visit to the tropics influenced his later work in the Picturesque style, which featured a profusion of foliage, depths of shade, and an extra layer of greenery on trees covered by creepers and vines.   JB

CALVERT VAUX (1824–1895) and JACOB WREY MOULD (1825–1886)

85 ⚹ *The Terrace*

Lithograph, folding frontispiece in *Sixth Annual Report of the Board of Commissioners of the Central Park. January 1863*. New York: Wm. C. Bryant & Co., 1863.

Collection of Elizabeth Barlow Rogers

LITERATURE: *Rogers 2001, pp. 342–43; Miller 2003, pp. 36–69.*

In the *Sixth Annual Report*, Vaux described the new terrace at the terminus of the Mall: "In the general design for the Park the Mall may be considered, with its accessories, an open air hall of reception for dress promenade." For this reason it was to be the most ornamental part of the park. In the report Vaux suggested an elaborate sculptural program that he hoped would be carried out "either through the liberality of individuals, or in some other way."

At the head of the two stairs descending from the Mall he called for bronze statues symbolizing day, night, starlight, and twilight; at the intermediate landing there were to be four pedestals reserved for figures representing winter, spring, autumn, and summer; while statues of science and art would occupy the lower terrace directly opposite the foot of each stair. In addition, he envisioned three other quadruple groupings: one emblematic of childhood, youth, maturity, and old age; another, the mountain, the valley, the river, and the lake; and a third, the agricultural goddesses Flora, Pomona, Sylva, and Ceres, which collectively stood for nature. This last grouping was to occupy a space in the center of the Terrace Arcade, where it would be illuminated by a skylight. The climax of this iconographic composition was to be a large fountain near the Lake that "should suggest both earnestly and playfully the idea of that central spirit of 'Love' that is for ever active, and for ever bringing nature, science, and art, summer and winter, youth and age, day and night, into harmonious accord."

The notions of seasonal alteration and the separate stages of human existence suggest a favorite Romantic theme: the mutability of all phenomena. Thomas Cole's *Voyage of Life* cycle depicting the four ages of man, Jasper Cropsey's cycle of the four seasons, and Asher B. Durand's cycle of the four times of the day are well-known Hudson River school examples. Although the array of allegorical figures Vaux suggested for the Bethesda Terrace never materialized, some of the iconography he called for is evident in Jacob Wrey Mould's designs for the beautiful stonework carving of the two staircase panels leading from the terrace overlook to the Lower Terrace beside the Lake. This rich carving of vines, leaves, fruits, flowers, animals, and birds follows Ruskin's theory of nature as the source of all art, and their arrangement according to seasonal themes is an example of the metaphorical side of Romanticism as well as the premium it put on nature's fecundity.

The figure of the angel crowning the Bethesda Fountain, as seen in the lithograph here, is by Emma Stebbins, the sister of Henry Stebbins, the president of the park's board of commissioners. The name of the fountain recalls the biblical pool of Bethesda in John 5:4, where "an angel went down at a certain season . . . and troubled the water: whosoever then first after the troubling of the water stepped in was made whole of whatsoever disease he had." Stebbins intended the fountain and its attendant angel to symbolize the public health benefit bestowed on New York City with the construction of the Croton Aqueduct, ensuring the abundance of pure water that enabled the nineteenth-century city to become populous and grow to metropolitan dimensions.

The double rows of American elms lining the Mall above the terrace created, as they still do today, an overarching navelike canopy. Together, the Mall and the Bethesda Terrace constitute, as Vaux stated in the 1863 *Report*, "the central point of the plan of the Park." EBR

NOTES

MATTEO RIPA

2. *Etched view of a pavilion by a lake at Jehol*

   1. Yu 2008, p. 85.

   2. Ripa 1861, p. 62.

PIERRE FOURDRINIER

3. *Tuscum*

   1. Pierre de la Ruffinière du Prey has discussed Castell's search for universal rules of architecture in his history of interpretations of the villas described by Pliny.

   2. Castell 1728, pp. 116–17.

   3. Robin Middleton in Millard 1993–2000, vol. 2, pp. 64–66, noted the significance of Castell's linkage of classical authority to new experiments in landscape gardening.

JOHN SERLE

4. *A Plan of Mr. Pope's Garden*

   1. Alexander Pope, letter to Edward Blount, summer 1725, cited in Willson 1998, p. 37.

   2. John Evelyn, diary, 3 August 1654, in Evelyn 1955, vol. 3, p. 121.

   3. John Evelyn, diary, 23 July 1679, in Evelyn 1955, vol. 4, p. 177.

   4. Joseph Addison, in *The Spectator*, no. 37, 12 April 1711, in Hunt and Willis 1988, p. 141.

   5. Alexander Pope to Lady Mary Wortley Montagu, 10 November 1716, in Pope 1956, vol. 1, p. 367.

   6. Alexander Pope to Martha Blount, 22 June [1724?], in Pope 1956, vol. 2, pp. 238–39.

   7. Alexander Pope, "Eloisa to Abelard," in Pope 1954, p. 300.

   8. Pope 1745, p. 5.

   9. "An Epistolary Description of the Late Mr. Pope's House and Gardens at Twickenham," (1747) in *The General Magazine*, Newcastle, January 1748, reprinted in Hunt and Willis 1988, pp. 247–53, and Batey 1999, p. 57.

PIERRE-PHILIPPE CHOFFARD

5. *Approchez, contemplez ce monument*

   1. *Voici le bois secret, voici l'obscure allée*
Où s'échauffoit sa verve en beaux vers exhalée:
Approchez, contemplez ce monument pieux
Où pleuroit en silence un fils religieux:
Là, repose sa mere, et des touffes plus sombres
Sur ce saint mausolée ont redoublé leurs ombres;
Là, du Parnasse anglais le chantre favori
Se fit porter mourant sous son bosquet chéri;
Et son oeil, que déja couvroit l'ombre éternelle,
Vint saluer encor la tombe maternelle.

G. L. SMITH after BENTON SEELEY

7. *The Temple of British Worthies*

   1. Gilpin 1748, p. 22.

   2. By 1788 Seeley's guidebook would describe the grotto as follows: "The trees which stretch across the water, together with those which back it, and others which hang over the cavern, form a scene singularly perfect in its kind. The front of it is composed of the roughest stones, with no other decoration than that of some few spars and broken flints; from the lower cavern the water flows, and from the opening above this a small stream drops into the river. The inside is finished with a variety of shells, spars, fossils, petrifactions, and broken glass, which reflect the rays of light. At the upper end is a circular recess in which are two basons of white marble: In the upper is placed a fine marble statue of VENUS rising from her bath, and from this water falls into the lower bason, from whence it is conveyed under the floor to the front, where it falls into the river."

GIOVANNI FRANCESCO VENTURINI

8. *Veduta della cascata*

   1. Berger 1974, p. 304.

CHARLES-JOSEPH NATOIRE

9. *The Cascade at the Villa Aldobrandini, Frascati*

   1. Charles-Joseph Natoire to Vandières [later de Marigny], June 1752, quoted in Montpellier 1961, *"je souhaiterais beaucoup que parmi nos élèves quand il s'en trouverait quelqu'un qui n'aurait pas tout celui qu'il faut pour arriver à l'histoire avec distinction, de prendre celui du paysage qui est si agreeable et si nécessaire car nous en manquons; mais la plupart croyant se degrader dans ce parti aiment mieux à ramper dans l'un que de chercher à se distinguer dans l'autre."*

JEAN-HONORÉ FRAGONARD

10. *Le Petit Parc*

   1. Charles-Joseph Natoire to Marigny, 27 August 1760, in Montaiglon 1887–1908, vol. 6, p. 354, no. 5459.

   2. Mariette 1851/53–1859/60, vol. 4, p. 26, no. 1.

   3. Multiple sources agree that this cannot be identified as a view in the gardens of the Villa d'Este at Tivoli. By 1988 Pierre Rosenberg published a corresponding etching as *Le Petit Parc* (Paris and New York 1988, no. 66). Eunice Williams asserted in her entry on a related drawing (in New York 1990, p. 188) that the *Petit Parc* title "now extends to all representations of the subject." Jean Massengale, too, calls the painting in The Wallace Collection *Le Petit Parc* in his monograph (Massengale 1993, p. 70).

   4. Jean Massengale (1993, p. 70) points to Fragonard's close study of works by Jacob van Ruisdael in Paris collections following his return from Rome.

   5. Paris and New York 1988, pp. 94–96 and 153–54; Baltimore and Minneapolis 1984, no. 46.

SAMUEL PALMER

12. *Villa d'Este at Tivoli*

1. Samuel Palmer to Miss Linnell, 2 December 1838, in Palmer 1974, vol. 1, p. 249. The drawing referred to is in the Ashmolean Museum, Oxford.

2. Hannah Palmer to John and Mary Ann Linnell, 16 December 1838, in Palmer 1974, vol. 1, p. 252.

3. Samuel Palmer to John Linnell, 9 June 1839, in Palmer 1974, vol. 1, p. 344.

4. Samuel Palmer to John Linnell, 14 September 1839, in Palmer 1974, vol. 1, p. 386.

5. Ruskin 1903–12, vol. 3, pp. 604–5. The complete quotation is cited in Scott Wilcox, "Poetic Feeling and Chromatic Madness: Palmer and Victorian Watercolour Painting," in London and New York 2005, p. 43.

6. Ruskin 1903–12, vol. 3, p. 605.

NICOLAS-HENRY TARDIEU

13. *Winter*

1. Walpole 1785, p. 55.

THOMAS BOWLES

14. *Merlins Cave*

1. Colton 1976; Colton notes on p. 2 that Merlin's Cave was built during one of Caroline's four active regencies while her disengaged husband was in Hannover, Germany. Richard H. Drayton adds further insight into the correspondence of garden structures at Richmond and Stowe as dueling rhetorical devices (Drayton 2000, pp. 38–40).

2. The term *Garden Gothic* apparently was coined by W. D. Robson-Scott in Robson-Scott 1965, pp. 28–33.

EDWARD ROOKER

20. *A View of the Wilderness*

1. Chambers 1757, b1r–v.

2. Chambers 1757, p. 15.

3. Ibid.

4. Chambers 1772, pp. 38–42

5. Chambers 1772, p. 94.

6. Chambers 1772, p. 19.

WILLIAM GILPIN

22. *River-Views, Bays & Sea Coasts*

1. Barbier 1963, pp. 91–92. The Morgan album has not been recorded in monographs on William Gilpin.

23. View of Goodrich Castle

1. Templeman 1939, pp. 34–35 and 117–28 on *A Dialogue upon the Gardens . . . at Stow* (1748).

2. Gilpin 1782, p. 18.

3. Henry David Thoreau, Journal, 21 June 1852, quoted in Boudreau 1973.

4. Gilpin 1782, p. 40.

JOHN HEAVISIDE CLARK

24. *Lightning*

1. John Ruskin, manuscript lecture notes, 1878, quoted in Orestano 2003, pp. 163–64.

BENJAMIN THOMAS POUNCY after
THOMAS HEARNE

26. Folding plates in Richard Payne Knight, *The Landscape*

1. Hearne also exhibited at the Royal Academy views of Knight's landscape garden at Downton Castle.

JOSEPH CONSTANTINE STADLER after
HUMPHRY REPTON

29. *The General View from the Pavillon*

1. Daniels 1999, p. 197. On the same page, Daniels correlates parts of Repton's proposed design with particular plates in the first volume of *Oriental Scenery*.

WILLIAM WORDSWORTH

31. Plan for a winter garden at Coleorton Hall

1. Wordsworth 1983, p. 149.

FRANCIS DANBY

35. *The Procession of Cristna*

1. Francis Danby to John Gibbons, 26 August 1825, quoted in Bristol and London 1988, p. 25.

2. Francis Danby to John Gibbons, quoted in Bristol and London 1988, p. 156. Francis Greenacre first associated this drawing with the poem.

3. John Gibbons to William Powell Frith, quoted in Bristol and London 1988, p. 23.

JOHN CONSTABLE

37. *View of Cathanger, near Petworth*

1. Reported anecdotally by C. R. Leslie in Leslie 1845, p. 307.

2. John Constable to John Dunthorne, 29 May 1802, in Constable 1962–68, vol. 2, p. 32.

3. John Constable to John Fisher, 23 October 1821, in Constable 1962–68, vol. 6, p. 78.

4. John Constable to John Fisher, 29 May 1824, in Leslie 1845, p. 135.

5. John Constable to C. R. Leslie, 16 July 1834, in Constable 1962–68, vol. 3, pp. 111–12.

6. John Constable to John Fisher, 23 October 1821, in Constable 1962–68, vol. 6, p. 77.

SAMUEL PALMER

38. *The Haunted Stream*

1. Samuel Palmer to Philip Gilbert Hamerton, 26 January 1872, in Palmer 1974, vol. 2, p. 835.

J. MÉRIGOT FILS

45. *Le Moulin*

1. The date of construction is often given as 1774. See Wiebenson 1978, p. 100, n. 99.

CHARLES GAVARD after PIERRE-FRANÇOIS-LÉONARD FONTAINE

49. *Vue du temple de marbre*

1. "*[Les embellissements] ne sont pas les produits d'une volonté fantastique, et encore moins des imitations, comme on a pu en voir ailleurs, de ces maisons rustiques, de ces rochers pittoresques, tant vantés autrefois, quand on avait mis la cour au village, et le village à la cour*" (p. 20).

CHARLES SAUNIER

51. *Le Père Lachaise*

1. Bernardin de Saint-Pierre detailed the first proposal for a cemetery of the virtuous in a natural landscape on an island in the Seine in his *Études de la nature* (1784).

2. Etlin 1984, p. 227. Nicolas-Thérèse-Benoist Frochot, prefect of Paris and the Seine, proposed Monceau as a cemetery in 1801.

3. Trollope 1836, vol. 1, pp. 189-95 (Letter XXII on Père Lachaise).

IVAN ZASCHE

55. *Aussicht vom Bellevue im Parke Jurjavés*

1. Maruševski and Jurković 1993, p. 62.

PRINCE PÜCKLER AT MUSKAU

1. The *Andeutungen über Landschaftsgärtnerei* was first published in Stuttgart at the Hallberger'sche Verlagshandlung in 1834. The first printing of the text volume appeared with ten pages of preliminary matter, 282 pages of text, and a page of errata; the corrected second printing contains six preliminary leaves and 272 pages of text. The atlas volume contains forty-four [i.e., forty-five] plates and four plans. The first printing of the text volume has been posted on line by the library of the University of Heidelberg at http://diglit.ub.uni-heidelberg.de/diglit/pueckler1834a; the second printing is available through Google Books. The University of Heidelberg's atlas volume can be seen at http://diglit.ub.uni-heidelberg.de/diglit/pueckler1834b.

AUGUST WILHELM SCHIRMER

59. *View of the Manor and Park*

1. Pückler 1917, pp. 117–18. Some quotations from this translation of the *Andeutungen über Landschaftsgärtnerei* have been slightly modified.

AUGUST WILHELM SCHIRMER

60. *Flower Garden Beside the Castle at Muskau*

1. Pückler stated this explicitly in comments on the landscape garden at Babelsberg, as discussed by Susan M. Peik in Peik 2001, pp. 79–80.

CASPAR DAVID FRIEDRICH

64. *Moonlit Landscape*

1. Caspar David Friedrich, manuscript journal, 1803, Kupferstich-Kabinett, Staatlichen Kunstsammlungen Dresden; excerpts published in Hofmann 2000, pp. 269–72.

2. Carus wrote Friedrich's obituary published in *Kunst-Blatt*, 1840; cited by Oskar Bätschmann, "Carl Gustav Carus (1789–1869): Physician, Naturalist, Painter, and Theoretician of Landscape Painting," in Carus 2002, pp. 3–4.

3. Birgit Verwiebe, "Transparent Painting and the Romantic Spirit," translated by David Britt in Edinburgh and London 1994, pp. 171–77. Verwiebe cites Novalis on page 171.

4. Kupferstichkabinett, Staatliche Museen zu Berlin. The date circa 1830, within a cycle of seven sepias created sometime between 1826 and 1834, is given in Hofmann 2000, pp. 213–14, fig. 142.

5. Caspar David Friedrich to Vasily Andreyevich Zhukovsky, Dresden, 9 February 1830, published in Hofmann 2000, p. 266.

CARL GUSTAV CARUS

65. *Fountain Before a Temple*

1. Carus 2002, p. 89 (Letter 3).

2. Sir Joshua Reynolds, Discourse IV, 1771, in Reynolds 1959, pp. 55–73.

3. Carus 2002, pp. 91 (Letter 3) and 125–27 (Letter 8).

4. Carus 2002, pp. 91 (Letter 3).

5. Carus 2002, pp. 130–31 (Letter 8).

6. Carus 2002, pp. 94–95 (Letter 3, Enclosure 2).

7. Carus 2002, pp. 141–46 ("Fragments from a Painter's Journal").

FREDERIC EDWIN CHURCH

71. *Horseshoe Falls*

1. Ruskin 1903–12, vol. 3, pp. 128–30.

2. Ruskin 1903–12, vol. 3, p. 494.

3. *The Crayon* 4, Feb. 1857, p. 54; cited in Carr 1994, vol. 1, p. 232.

4. Quoted in Williams 1857.

5. Huntington 1983, p. 101.

6. See Francis R. Kowsky, "In Defense of Niagara: Frederick Law Olmsted and the Niagara Reservation," in Niagara Falls 1985, p. 5, on the original attempt by Frederic Church to preserve the Falls. This essay is also posted online by the Preservation Coalition of Erie County.

72. *Olana from the Southwest*

1. A payment to the firm of Olmsted and Vaux is noted in Alex and Tatum 1994, pp. 68–69. For more extensive discussions of the creation of Olana, see Ryan 2001 and New York 2007a, pp. 111–23.

2. Letter to Erastus Dow Palmer, 18 October 1884, cited in Aslet 1990, p. 43.

3. Thoreau 1971, pp. 186 and 188. The first edition of *Walden* was published in 1854.

H. JORDAN after ALEXANDER JACKSON DAVIS

73. *View in the Grounds at Blithewood*

1. On Downing's education, see Schuyler 1996, pp. 15–17.

2. For an analysis of Downing's evolving views on landscape gardening in subsequent editions of his treatise and in his editorials, see Major 1997.

3. Adam Sweeting places Downing's beliefs in their American cultural context in his chapter on "Architecture, Morality, and Gentility" in Sweeting 1996, pp. 93–121.

4. Downing 1852, p. 210.

ALEXANDER JACKSON DAVIS

74. *Ravine Walk. Blithewood*

1. On this collaboration, see Jane B. Davies, "Davis and Downing: Collaborators in the Picturesque" in Tatum and MacDougall 1989, pp. 81–123. Davies called Davis "the most brilliant American romantic architectural designer of the period [and] also the finest architectural draftsman" (p. 83).

2. Andrew Jackson Downing, [A Visit to Montgomery Place], *The Horticulturist, and Journal of Rural Art and Rural Taste* 2, Oct. 1847, pp. 153–60; reprinted with reproductions of drawings by A. J. Davis in Haley 1988.

75. *Ericstan for John J. Herrick*

1. Snadon 1988, p. 17. Davis introduced the type with his early partner Ithiel Town at Belmead in Virginia in 1832. Snadon discusses Ericstan on pp. 265–75 and reproduces several views.

2. Downing 1841, pp. 330–31.

3. Downing 1844, p. 368.

4. Downing 1850, p. 262; noted in Snadon 1988, p. 19.

5. Davis 1837.

ROBERT HINSHELWOOD after JAMES SMILLIE

76. *Lowell's Monument, Willow Avenue*

1. Walter 1851, p. 9.

J. W. WINDER

77. *Winter Scene. Spring Grove Cemetery*

1. Pückler 1917, pp. 38–39, 80. Sickert's English translation of the *Andeutungen* appeared long after Strauch's introduction of Pückler's style to America.

2. Quoted in Linden 1995, p. 45.

FREDERICK LAW OLMSTED

79. Camping scene

1. Olmsted 1857, p. 97.

2. Olmsted 1857, pp. 129–30.

FREDERICK LAW OLMSTED and CALVERT VAUX

80. *Central Park Competition Entry No. 33*

1. Olmsted and Kimball 1970, vol. 2, p. 46.

2. "Historical Notes," in *Transactions of the American Society of Landscape Architects from its Inception in 1899 to the End of 1908*, Harrisburg, PA, 1912, p. 81, as quoted in Olmsted and Kimball 1970, vol. 2, p. 43, and Heckscher 2008, p. 26.

3. Olmsted and Kimball 1970, vol. 2, p. 45.

4. Olmsted 1977, supplementary series, vol. 1, p. 40.

5. "Document II: Description of a Plan for the Improvement of the Central Park: 'Greensward' (1858 [1868 reprint])," in Fein 1967, p. 73.

6. Rogers 1972, p. 25.

WORKS CITED IN ABBREVIATED FORM

Adams 1973
Eric Adams, *Francis Danby: Varieties of Poetic Landscape*, New Haven and London, 1973.

Alex and Tatum 1994
William Alex and George B. Tatum, *Calvert Vaux: Architect and Planner*, New York, 1994.

Andrews 1989
Malcolm Andrews, *The Search for the Picturesque: Landscape Aesthetics and Tourism in Britain, 1760–1800*, Stanford, CA, 1989.

Aslet 1990
Clive Aslet, *The American Country House*, New Haven and London, 1990.

Austen 1818
Jane Austen, *Northanger Abbey and Persuasion*, 4 vols., London, 1818.

Ballantyne 1997
Andrew Ballantyne, *Architecture, Landscape and Liberty: Richard Payne Knight and the Picturesque*, Cambridge and New York, 1997.

Balston 1947
Thomas Balston, *John Martin, 1789–1854: His Life and Works*, London, 1947.

Barbier 1963
Carl Paul Barbier, *William Gilpin: His Drawings, Teaching, and Theory of the Picturesque*, Oxford, 1963.

Baridon 2004
Michel Baridon, preface to the facsimile edition of Alexandre de Laborde, *Description des nouveaux jardins de la France et de ses anciens châteaux*, Paris, 2004.

Batey 1999
Mavis Batey, *Alexander Pope, The Poet and the Landscape*, London, 1999.

Beiswanger 1983
William L. Beiswanger, "The Temple in the Garden: Thomas Jefferson's Vision of the Monticello Landscape," *Eighteenth-Century Life* [8], January 1983, pp. 170–88.

Berger 1974
Robert W. Berger, "Garden Cascades in Italy and France, 1565–1665," *Journal of the Society of Architectural Historians* 33, 1974, pp. 304–22.

Bermingham 2000
Ann Bermingham, *Learning to Draw: Studies in the Cultural History of a Polite and Useful Art*, New Haven and London, 2000.

Betjeman 1931
John Betjeman, "Sezincote, Moreton-in-Marsh, Gloucestershire: Its Situation, History, and Architecture," *Architectural Review* 69, May 1931, pp. 161–66.

Birch 1999
Dinah Birch, "Elegiac Voices: Wordsworth, Turner, and Ruskin," *The Review of English Studies* [50], 1999, pp. 332–44.

Boudreau 1973
Gordon V. Boudreau, "H. D. Thoreau, William Gilpin, and the Metaphysical Ground of the Picturesque," *American Literature* 45, 1973, pp. 357–69.

Bracher 1949
Frederick Bracher, "Pope's Grotto, The Maze of Fancy," *The Huntington Library Quarterly* 12, 1949, pp. 141–62.

Brown 1997
Lee Rust Brown, *The Emerson Museum: Practical Romanticism and the Pursuit of the Whole*, Cambridge, MA, and London, 1997.

Brownell 1978
Morris R. Brownell, *Alexander Pope & the Arts of Georgian England*, Oxford, 1978.

Brownell 1982
Morris R. Brownell, introduction to the facsimile edition of John Serle, *A Plan of Mr. Pope's Garden as It Was Left at His Death*, Los Angeles, 1982.

Bryant 1875
William Cullen Bryant, *The Poetical Works of William Cullen Bryant*, edited by Henry C. Sturges, New York, 1875.

Buchanan 2001
Carol Buchanan, *Wordsworth's Gardens*, Lubbock, TX, 2001.

Carr 1994
Gerald L. Carr, *Frederic Edwin Church: Catalogue Raisonné of Works of Art at Olana State Historic Site*, 2 vols., Cambridge and New York, 1994.

Carus 2002
Carl Gustav Carus, *Nine Letters on Landscape Painting*,

Written in the Years 1815–1824, translated by David Britt, Los Angeles, 2002.

Castell 1728

Robert Castell, *The Villas of the Ancients Illustrated*, London, 1728.

Chambers 1757

William Chambers, *Designs of Chinese Buildings, Furniture, Dresses, Machines and Utensils*, London, 1757.

Chambers 1772

William Chambers, *A Dissertation on Oriental Gardening*, London, 1772.

Chase 1943

Isabel Wakelin Urban Chase, *Horace Walpole, Gardenist*, Princeton, 1943.

Clark 1943

H. F. Clark, "Eighteenth-Century Elysiums: The Rôle of 'Association' in the Landscape Movement," *Journal of the Warburg and Courtauld Institutes* 6, 1943, pp. 165–89.

Clarke 1977

George B. Clarke, introduction to the facsimile edition of George Bickham, *The Beauties of Stow*, Los Angeles, 1977.

Clarke 1992

George B. Clarke, "The Moving Temples of Stowe: Aesthetics of Change in an English Landscape over Four Generations," *The Huntington Library Quarterly* 55, 1992, pp. 501–9.

Clarke and Penny 1982

Michael Clarke and Nicholas Penny, eds., *The Arrogant Connoisseur: Richard Payne Knight, 1751–1824: Essays on Richard Payne Knight Together with a Catalogue of Works Exhibited at the Whitworth Art Gallery, 1982,* Manchester, 1982.

Cohen-De Ricci

Henri Cohen, *Guide de l'amateur de livres à gravures du XVIIIᵉ siècle*, sixth edition, edited, corrected and enlarged by Seymour de Ricci, Paris, 1912.

Colton 1976

Judith Colton, "Merlin's Cave and Queen Caroline: Garden Art as Political Propaganda," in *Eighteenth-Century Studies* 10, 1976, pp. 1–20.

Colvin 1954

Howard Colvin, *A Biographical Dictionary of English Architects 1660–1840*, London, 1954.

Conner 1978

Patrick Conner, "Unexecuted Designs for the Royal Pavilion at Brighton," *Apollo* 107, 1978, pp. 192–99.

Constable 1962–68

John Constable, *John Constable's Correspondence*, edited by R. B. Beckett, 6 vols., Ipswich, 1962–68.

Daniels 1999

Stephen Daniels, *Humphry Repton: Landscape Gardening and the Geography of Georgian England*, New Haven and London, 1999.

Davis 1837

Alexander Jackson Davis, *Rural Residences, etc., Consisting of Designs, Original and Selected, for Cottages, Farm-Houses, Villas, and Village Churches*, New York, 1837.

Dernie 1996

David Dernie, *The Villa d'Este at Tivoli*, London and Lanham, MD, 1996.

Desmond 1995

Ray Desmond, *Kew: The History of the Royal Botanic Gardens*, London, 1995.

Dinkel 1983

John Dinkel, *The Royal Pavilion Brighton*, London, 1983.

Dochnahl 1861

Friedrich Jakob Dochnahl, *Bibliotheca hortensis: Vollständige Garten-Bibliothek; oder, Alphabetisches Verzeichniss aller Bücher, welche über Gärtnerei, Blumen- und Gemüsezucht, Obst- und Weinbau, Gartenbotanik und bildende Gartenkunst von 1750 bis 1860 in Deutschland erschienen sind*, Nuremberg, 1861.

Downing 1841

Andrew Jackson Downing, *A Treatise on the Theory and Practice of Landscape Gardening, Adapted to North America*, New York, London, and Boston, 1841.

Downing 1844

Andrew Jackson Downing, *A Treatise on the Theory and Practice of Landscape Gardening, Adapted to North America*, second edition, enlarged, revised, and newly illustrated, New York and London, 1844.

Downing 1850

Andrew Jackson Downing, *The Architecture of Country Houses; Including Designs for Cottages, Farm Houses, and Villas*, New York and Philadelphia, 1850.

Downing 1852

Andrew Jackson Downing, *Cottage Residences; or, A Series of Designs for Rural Cottages and Cottage Villas, and Their Gardens and Grounds, Adapted to North America*, fourth edition, revised, New York, 1852.

Downing 1856

Andrew Jackson Downing, *Rural Essays*, edited by George William Curtis, New York, 1856.

Drayton 2000

Richard Harry Drayton, *Nature's Government: Science, Imperial Britain, and the "Improvement" of the World*, New Haven, 2000.

Duempelmann 2007

Sonja Duempelmann, ed., *Pückler and America*, German Historical Institute, *Bulletin*, supplement 4, Washington, DC, 2007.

Du Prey 1994

Pierre de la Ruffinière du Prey, *The Villas of Pliny from Antiquity to Posterity*, Chicago, 1994.

Emerson 1983

Ralph Waldo Emerson, *Essays & Lectures*, edited by Joel Porte, New York, 1983.

Etlin 1984

Richard A. Etlin, *The Architecture of Death: The Transformation of the Cemetery in Eighteenth-Century Paris*, Cambridge, MA, 1984.

Evelyn 1955

John Evelyn, *The Diary of John Evelyn*, edited by E. S. de Beer, 6 vols., Oxford, 1955.

Fein 1967

Albert Fein, ed., *Landscape into Cityscape: Frederick Law Olmsted's Plans for a Greater New York City*, Ithaca, NY, 1967.

Fontaine 1987

Pierre-François-Léonard Fontaine, *Journal, 1799–1853*, 2 vols., Paris, 1987.

Fortoul 1839

Hippolyte Fortoul, *Les fastes de Versailles, depuis son origine jusqu'à nos jours*, Paris, 1839.

Fowble 1987

E. McSherry Fowble, *Two Centuries of Prints in America, 1680–1880: A Selective Catalogue of the Winterthur Museum Collection*, Charlottesville, VA, 1987.

Fowler 1961

The Fowler Architectural Collection of the Johns Hopkins University, catalogue compiled by Lawrence Hall Fowler and Elizabeth Baer, Baltimore, 1961.

Gerndt 1981

Siegmar Gerndt, *Idealisierte Natur: Die literarische Kontroverse um den Landschaftsgarten des 18. and frühen 19. Jahrhunderts in Deutschland*, Stuttgart, 1981.

Gilpin 1748

William Gilpin, *A Dialogue upon the Gardens of the Right Honourable the Lord Viscount Cobham, at Stow in Buckinghamshire*, London, 1748.

Gilpin 1782

William Gilpin, *Observations on the River Wye, and Several Parts of South Wales . . . Made in the Summer of the Year 1770*, London, 1782.

Gilpin 1789

William Gilpin, *Observations, Relative Chiefly to Picturesque Beauty, Made in the Year 1776, on Several Parts of Great Britain, Particularly the Highlands of Scotland*, 2 vols., London, 1789.

Girardin 1783

René-Louis de Girardin, *An Essay on Landscape; or, On the Means of Improving and Embellishing the Country Round our Habitations*, London, 1783.

Girtin and Loshak 1954

Thomas Girtin and David Loshak, *The Art of Thomas Girtin*, London, 1954.

Goethe 1971

Johann Wolfgang von Goethe, *Elective Affinities*, translated by R. J. Hollingdale, Harmondsworth, 1971.

Gray 1960

Basil Gray, "Lord Burlington and Father Ripa's Chinese Engravings," *The British Museum Quarterly* 22, 1960, pp. 40–43.

Gromort 1928

Georges Gromort, *Le hameau de Trianon: histoire et description*, Paris, 1928.

Haley 1988

Jacquetta M. Haley, ed., *Pleasure Grounds: Andrew Jackson Downing and Montgomery Place*, Tarrytown, NY, 1988.

Harris 1968

John Harris, "English Country House Guides, 1740–1840,"

in *Concerning Architecture: Essays on Architectural Writers and Writing Presented to Nikolaus Pevsner*, edited by John Summerson, London, 1968, pp. 58–74.

Harris 1970

Eileen Harris, "Designs of Chinese Buildings and the Dissertation on Oriental Gardening," in John Harris, *Sir William Chambers, Knight of the Polar Star*, University Park, PA, 1970, pp. 144–62.

Harris and Savage 1990

Eileen Harris and Nicholas Savage, *British Architectural Books and Writers, 1556–1785*, Cambridge and New York, 1990.

Hays 2000

David Lyle Hays, *The Irregular Garden in Late Eighteenth-Century France*, Ph.D. dissertation, Yale University, 2 vols., 2000.

Heckscher 2008

Morrison H. Heckscher, "Creating Central Park," *The Metropolitan Museum of Art Bulletin* 65, no. 3, winter 2008.

Helsinger 1982

Elizabeth K. Helsinger, *Ruskin and the Art of the Beholder*, Cambridge, MA, and London, 1982.

Hipple 1957

Walter John Hipple, *The Beautiful, the Sublime, & the Picturesque in Eighteenth-Century British Aesthetic Theory*, Carbondale, IL, 1957.

Hirschfeld 2001

Christian Cajus Lorenz Hirschfeld, *Theory of Garden Art*, edited and translated by Linda B. Parshall, Philadelphia, 2001.

Hofmann 2000

Werner Hofmann, *Caspar David Friedrich*, translated by Mary Whittall, London, 2000.

Honour 1979

Hugh Honour, *Romanticism*, New York, 1979.

Howat 2005

John K. Howat, *Frederic Church*, New Haven and London, 2005.

Hunt 1987

John Dixon Hunt, *William Kent, Landscape Designer: An Assessment and Catalogue of His Designs*, London, 1987.

Hunt and Willis 1988

John Dixon Hunt and Peter Willis, eds., *The Genius of the Place: The English Landscape Garden 1620–1820*, Cambridge, MA, and London, 1988.

Huntington 1983

David C. Huntington, "Frederic Church's Niagara: Nature and the Nation's Type," *Texas Studies in Literature and Language* 25, 1983, pp. 100–38.

Illingworth 1994

John Illingworth, "Ruskin and Gardening," *Garden History* 22, 1994, pp. 218–33.

Jefferson 1950

Thomas Jefferson, *The Papers of Thomas Jefferson*, edited by Julian P. Boyd et al., Princeton, 1950–.

Jones 2005

Mike Jones, *Set for a King: 200 Years of Gardening at the Royal Pavilion*, Brighton, 2005.

Kant 1960

Immanuel Kant, *Observations on the Feeling of the Beautiful and Sublime*, translated by John T. Goldthwait, Berkeley, 1960.

Ketcham 1994

Diana Ketcham, *Le Désert de Retz: A Late Eighteenth-Century French Folly Garden, The Artful Landscape of Monsieur de Monville*, revised edition, Cambridge, MA, and London, 1994.

Knight 1887

William Knight, ed., *Memorials of Coleorton; Being Letters from Coleridge, Wordsworth and His Sister, Southey, and Sir Walter Scott to Sir George and Lady Beaumont of Coleorton, Leicestershire, 1803 to 1834*, 2 vols., Edinburgh, 1887.

Koerner 1990

Joseph Leo Koerner, *Caspar David Friedrich and the Subject of Landscape*, New Haven and London, 1990.

Koke 1961

Richard J. Koke. *A Checklist of the American Engravings of John Hill (1770–1850), Master of Aquatint*, New York, 1961.

Korzus 2004

Bernard Korzus, "Georges Louis Le Rouge: un cartographe franco-allemand du XVIIIe siècle," in Véronique Royet et al., *Georges Louis Le Rouge: Jardins anglo-chinois*, Bibliothèque nationale de France, Inventaire du fonds français, graveurs du XVIIIe siècle, 15, Paris, 2004, pp. 45–55.

Lablaude 1995

Pierre-André Lablaude, *The Gardens of Versailles*, translated by Fiona Biddulph, London and Wappingers Falls, NY, 1995.

Lambert 2005

Ray Lambert, *John Constable and the Theory of Landscape Painting*, Cambridge and New York, 2005.

Lambin 1972

Denis Lambin, "A Note on Chantilly," *The Garden History Society Newsletter*, 17, May 1972, pp. 11–12.

Le Ménahèze 2001

Sophie Le Ménahèze, *L'Invention du jardin romantique en France 1761–1808*, Neuilly-sur-Seine, 2001.

Leslie 1845

C. R. Leslie, *Memoirs of the Life of John Constable*, second edition, London, 1845.

Leslie 1995

C. R. Leslie, *Memoirs of the Life of John Constable*, third edition, edited by Jonathan Mayne, London, 1995.

Limido 2002

Luisa Limido, *L'Art des jardins sous le Second Empire: Jean-Pierre Barillet-Deschamps, 1824–1873*, Seyssel, 2002.

Linden 1995

Blanche M. G. Linden, *Spring Grove: Celebrating 150 Years*, Cincinnati, 1995.

Linden 2006

Blanche M. G. Linden, "Nineteenth-Century German-American Landscape Designers," *Site/Lines* 1, spring 2006, pp. 9–11.

Linden 2007

Blanche M. G. Linden, *Silent City on a Hill: Picturesque Landscapes of Memory and Boston's Mount Auburn Cemetery*, revised edition, Amherst, MA, 2007.

Lister 1985

Raymond Lister, *The Paintings of Samuel Palmer*, Cambridge and New York, 1985.

Loudon 1850

John Claudius Loudon, *The Villa Gardener: Comprising the Choice of a Suburban Villa Residence, the Laying Out, Planting, and Culture of the Garden and Grounds, and the Management of the Villa Farm, Including the Dairy and Poultry-Yard*, second edition, London, 1850.

Mack 1965

Maynard Mack, "A Poet in His Landscape: Pope at Twickenham," in *From Sensibility to Romanticism: Essays Presented to Frederick A. Pottle*, edited by Frederick W. Hilles and Harold Bloom, New York, 1965, pp. 3–29.

Maggs cat. 1212

Maggs Bros. *Bookbinding in the British Isles, Sixteenth to the Twentieth Century*, catalogue 1212, London, 1996.

Major 1997

Judith K. Major, *To Live in the New World: A. J. Downing and American Landscape Gardening*, Cambridge, MA, and London, 1997.

Malins 1968

Edward Malins, *Samuel Palmer's Italian Honeymoon*, London, 1968.

Malins 1980

Edward Malins, "Indian Influences on English Houses and Gardens at the Beginning of the Nineteenth Century," *Garden History* 8, 1980, pp. 46–66.

Manwaring 1925

Elizabeth Wheeler Manwaring, *Italian Landscape in Eighteenth Century England: A Study Chiefly of the Influence of Claude Lorrain and Salvator Rosa on English Taste, 1700–1800*, New York, 1925.

Mariette 1851/53–1859/60

Pierre-Jean Mariette, *Abecedario de P.J. Mariette et autres notes inédites de cet amateur sur les arts et les artistes*, edited by Ph. de Chennevières and A. de Montaiglon, 6 vols., Paris, 1851/53–1859/60.

Martin 1976

Peter E. Martin, "Intimations of the New Gardening: Alexander Pope's Reaction to the 'Uncommon' Landscape at Sherborne," *Garden History* 4, 1976, pp. 57–87.

Maruševski and Jurković 1993

Olga Maruševski and Sonja Jurković, *Maksimir: The Famed Croatian Landscaped Garden*, Zagreb, 1993.

Massengale 1993

Jean Montague Massengale, *Jean-Honoré Fragonard*, New York, 1993.

May 1962

Georges May, "Rousseau's Literary Writings: An Important New Edition," *MLN* 77, 1962, pp. 519–28.

McEachern 1989–93

Jo-Ann E. McEachern, *Bibliography of the Writings of Jean Jacques Rousseau to 1800*, 2 vols., Oxford, 1989–93.

McKinsey 1985

Elizabeth R. McKinsey, *Niagara Falls: Icon of the American Sublime*, Cambridge and New York, 1985.

Metropolitan Bulletin 2008

"Recent Acquisitions: A Selection, 2007–2008," *The Metropolitan Museum of Art Bulletin* 66, fall 2008, p. 30.

Millard 1993–2000

National Gallery of Art. Washington, DC, *The Mark J. Millard Architectural Collection*, 4 vols., Washington, DC, and New York, 1993–2000.

Miller 2003

Sara Cedar Miller, *Central Park, An American Masterpiece*, New York, 2003.

Montaiglon 1887–1908

Anatole Montaiglon et al., eds., *Correspondance des directeurs de l'Académie de France à Rome avec les surintendants des bâtiments*, 17 vols., Paris, 1887–1908.

Morgan Library 1955

The Pierpont Morgan Library, *Sixth Annual Report to the Fellows of the Pierpont Morgan Library*, compiled by Frederick B. Adams, Jr., New York, 1955.

Morgan Library 1964

The Pierpont Morgan Library, *Thirteenth Report to the Fellows of the Pierpont Morgan Library*, compiled by Frederick B. Adams, Jr., New York, 1964.

Morgan Library 1981

The Pierpont Morgan Library, *Nineteenth Report to the Fellows of the Pierpont Morgan Library*, edited by Charles Ryskamp, New York, 1981.

Muir 1912

John Muir, *The Yosemite*, New York, 1912.

Muller 2008

Gilbert H. Muller, *William Cullen Bryant: Author of America*, Albany, NY, 2008.

Nash 1982

Roderick Nash, *Wilderness and the American Mind*, third edition, New Haven, 1982.

Neumeyer 1947

Eva Maria Neumeyer, "The Landscape Garden as a Symbol in Rousseau, Goethe, and Flaubert," *Journal of the History of Ideas* 8, 1947, pp. 187–217.

Norton 1963

Paul F. Norton, "Daylesford: S. P. Cockerell's Residence for Warren Hastings," *The Journal of the Society of Architectural Historians* 22, October 1963, pp. 127–33.

Novak 1980

Barbara Novak, *Nature and Culture: American Landscape and Painting, 1825–1875*, New York and Toronto, 1980.

Olmsted 1857

Frederick Law Olmsted, *A Journey Through Texas; or, A Saddle-Trip on the Southwestern Frontier*, New York, London, and Edinburgh, 1857.

Olmsted 1977

The Papers of Frederick Law Olmsted, Baltimore and London, 1977– .

Olmsted and Kimball 1970

Frederick Law Olmsted, Jr., and Theodora Kimball, *Frederick Law Olmsted, Landscape Architect, 1822–1903*, 2 vols., New York and London, 1922–1928; reprinted New York, 1970.

Orestano 2003

Francesca Orestano, "The Revd William Gilpin and the Picturesque; or, Who's Afraid of Doctor Syntax?" *Garden History* 31, 2003, pp. 163–79.

Palmer 1974

The Letters of Samuel Palmer, edited by Raymond Lister, 2 vols., Oxford, 1974.

Parshall 2004

Linda Parshall, "Landscape as History: Pückler-Muskau, The 'Green Prince' of Germany," in *Nature in German History*, edited by Christof Mauch, New York, 2004, pp. 48–73.

Paulson 1972

Ronald Paulson, *Rowlandson: A New Interpretation*. London, 1972.

Peake 2004

David Peake and Susanna Peake, *Sezincote*, Stow-on-the-Wold, ca. 2004.

Peck 1992

Amelia Peck, ed., *Alexander Jackson Davis, American Architect 1803–1892*, New York, 1992.

Peik 2001

Susan M. Peik, ed., *Karl Friedrich Schinkel: Aspects of His Work*, Stuttgart, 2001.

Pelliot 1923

Paul Pelliot, "La gravure sur cuivre en Chine au xviiie siè-cle," *Byblis*, 1923, pp. 103–8.

Pope 1745

Alexander Pope, "Verses on a Grotto by the River Thames, at Twickenham, composed of Marbles, Spars, and Minerals," written in a letter to Bolingbroke, 3 September 1740, published in *Gentleman's Magazine*, January 1741 and again in October 1743, reprinted in John Serle, *A Plan of Mr. Pope's Garden as It Was Left at His Death*, London, 1745.

Pope 1954

Alexander Pope, *The Rape of the Lock and Other Poems*, edited by Geoffrey Tillotson, second edition, The Twickenham Edition of the Poems of Alexander Pope II, London and New Haven, 1954.

Pope 1956

Alexander Pope, *Correspondence*, edited by George Sherburn, 5 vols., Oxford, 1956.

Pope 1961

Alexander Pope, *Epistles to Several Persons (Moral Essays)*, edited by F. W. Bateson, second edition, The Twickenham Edition of the Poems of Alexander Pope, vol. III, ii, London and New Haven, 1961.

Pückler 1833

Hermann Fürst von Pückler-Muskau, *Tour in England, Ireland, and France in the Years 1828, 1829, with Remarks on the Manners and Customs of the Inhabitants, and Anecdotes of Distinguished Public Characters*, translated by Sarah Austin, Philadelphia, 1833.

Pückler 1917

Hermann Fürst von Pückler-Muskau, *Hints on Landscape Gardening*, translated by Bernhard Sickert, edited by Samuel Parsons, Boston and New York, 1917.

Rainey 1994

Sue Rainey, *Creating Picturesque America: Monument to the Natural and Cultural Landscape*, Nashville and London, 1994.

Reed, McGee, and Mipaas 1990

Henry Hope Reed, Robert M. McGee, and Esther Mipaas, *Bridges of Central Park*, New York, 1990.

Repton 2005

Humphry Repton, *Humphry Repton's Memoirs*, edited by Ann Gore and George Carter, Norwich, 2005.

Reynolds 1959

Sir Joshua Reynolds, *Discourses on Art*, edited by Robert R. Wark, San Marino, CA, 1959.

Reynolds 1980

Jan Reynolds, *William Callow, R.W.S.*, London, 1980.

Reynolds 1984

Graham Reynolds, *The Later Paintings and Drawings of John Constable*, 2 vols., New Haven and London, 1984.

RIBA *Early Printed Books*

Early Printed Books, 1478–1840: Catalogue of the British Architectural Library Early Imprints Collection, British Architectural Library, Royal Institute of British Architects, compiled by Nicholas Savage et al., 5 vols., London and New Jersey, 1994–2003.

Ripa 1861

Matteo Ripa, *Memoirs of Father Ripa During Thirteen Years' Residence at the Court of Peking in the Service of the Emperor of China*, London, 1861.

Robinson 1869

William Robinson, *The Parks, Promenades, & Gardens of Paris Described and Considered in Relation to the Wants of Our Own Cities and the Public and Private Gardens*, London, 1869.

Robinson 1980

David Robinson, "Emerson's Natural Theology and the Paris Naturalists: Toward a Theory of Animated Nature," *Journal of the History of Ideas* 41, 1980, pp. 69–88.

Robson-Scott 1965

W. D. Robson-Scott, *The Literary Background of the Gothic Revival in Germany: A Chapter in the History of Taste*, Oxford, 1965.

Rogers 1972

Elizabeth Barlow Rogers, *Frederick Law Olmsted's New York*, New York, 1972.

Rogers 2001

Elizabeth Barlow Rogers, *Landscape Design: A Cultural and Architectural History*, New York, 2001.

Roper 1983

Laura Wood Roper, *FLO: A Biography of Frederick Law Olmsted*, Baltimore, 1983.

Rousseau 1997

Jean-Jacques Rousseau, *Julie, or the New Héloïse: Letters of Two Lovers Who Live in a Small Town at the Foot of the Alps*, translated and annotated by Philip Stewart and Jean Vaché, *The Collected Writings of Rousseau*, vol. 6, Hanover, NH, and London, 1997.

Royet 2004

Véronique Royet et al., *Georges Louis Le Rouge: Jardins anglo-chinois*, Bibliothèque nationale de France, Inventaire du fonds français, graveurs du XVIIIᵉ siècle, 15, Paris, 2004.

Ruskin 1903–12

John Ruskin, *The Works of John Ruskin*, edited by E. T. Cook and Alexander Wedderburn, 39 vols., London and New York, 1903–12.

Ryan 2001

James Anthony Ryan, *Frederic Church's Olana: Architecture and Landscape as Art*, Hensonville, NY, 2001.

Savory 1997

Jerold J. Savory, *Thomas Rowlandson's Doctor Syntax Drawings: An Introduction and Guide for Collectors*, London and Madison, NJ, 1997.

Schmid 1998

F. Carlo Schmid, *Naturansichten und Ideallandschaften: Die Landschaftsgraphik von Johann Christian Reinhart und seinem Umkreis*, Berlin, 1998.

Schuyler 1996

David Schuyler, *Apostle of Taste: Andrew Jackson Downing 1815–1852*, Baltimore and London, 1996.

Sirén 1990

Osvald Sirén, *China and Gardens of Europe of the Eighteenth Century*, Washington, DC, 1990.

Sitwell 1909

Sir George Sitwell, *On the Making of Gardens*, London, 1909.

Smith 2002

Greg Smith, *Thomas Girtin: The Art of Watercolour*, London, 2002.

Snadon 1988

Patrick A. Snadon, *A. J. Davis and the Gothic Revival Castle in America, 1832–1865*, Ph.D. dissertation, Cornell University, 1988.

Story 1831

Joseph Story, *An Address Delivered on the Dedication of the Cemetery at Mount Auburn*, 24 September 1831, Boston, 1831.

Sutton 1954

Thomas Sutton, *The Daniells, Artists and Travellers*, London, 1954.

Sweeting 1996

Adam Sweeting, *Reading Houses and Building Books: Andrew Jackson Downing and the Architecture of Popular Antebellum Literature, 1835–1855*, Hanover, NH, and London, 1996.

Tatum and MacDougall 1989

George B. Tatum and Elisabeth B. MacDougall, eds., *Prophet with Honor: The Career of Andrew Jackson Downing 1815–1852*, Washington, DC, 1989.

Templeman 1939

William D. Templeman, *The Life and Work of William Gilpin (1724–1804): Master of the Picturesque and Vicar of Boldre*, Urbana, IL, 1939.

Thomson 1730

James Thomson, *The Seasons*, London, 1730.

Thoreau 1971

Henry David Thoreau, *Walden*, edited by J. Lyndon Shanley, Princeton, 1971.

Torrance 1998

Robert M. Torrance, ed., *Encompassing Nature: A Sourcebook*, Washington, DC, 1998.

Trollope 1836

Frances Trollope, *Paris and the Parisians in 1835*, 2 vols., London, 1836.

Vaughan 2004

William Vaughan, *Friedrich*, London and New York, 2004.

Vernon 2000

Noël D. Vernon, "Adolph Strauch: Cincinnati and the Legacy of Spring Grove Cemetery," in *Midwestern Landscape Architecture*, edited by William H. Tishler, Urbana, IL, and Chicago, 2000, pp. 6–24.

Walpole 1785

Horace Walpole, *Essay on Modern Gardening; Essai sur l'art des jardins modernes*, Twickenham, Middlesex, 1785.

Walter 1851

Cornelia W. Walter, *Mount Auburn Illustrated*, New York, 1851.

Wat 1998

Pierre Wat, *Naissance de l'art romantique: Peinture et*

théorie de l'imitation en allemagne et en angleterre, Paris, 1998.

Weinhardt 1958

Carl J. Weinhardt, Jr., "The Indian Taste," *Metropolitan Museum of Art Bulletin* 16, March 1958, pp. 208–16.

Wiebenson 1978

Dora Wiebenson, *The Picturesque Garden in France*, Princeton, 1978.

Wilcox 2005

Timothy Wilcox, *Samuel Palmer*, London, 2005.

Williams 1857

Williams, Stevens, Williams & Co., *The Great Fall Niagara, Painted by Frederic Edward [i.e., Edwin] Church*, New York, 1857.

Willis 1972

Peter Willis, "Rousseau, Stowe and *Le jardin anglais:* Speculations on Visual Sources for *La Nouvelle Héloïse,*" *Studies on Voltaire and the Eighteenth Century* 90, 1972, pp. 1791–98.

Willson 1998

Anthony B. Willson, "Alexander Pope's Grotto in Twickenham," *Garden History* 26, 1998, pp. 31–59.

Wilton 1976

Andrew Wilton, *Turner in Switzerland*, Dübendorf, 1976.

Wittkower 1969

Rudolf Wittkower, "English Neo-Palladianism, the Landscape Garden, China, and the Enlightenment," *L'Arte* 6, 1969, pp. 18 35.

Wolfe 1981

Gerard R. Wolfe, *The House of Appleton: The History of a Publishing House and Its Relationship to the Cultural, Social, and Political Events that Helped Shape the Destiny of New York City*, Metuchen, NJ, and London, 1981.

Wordsworth 1967-93

William Wordsworth, *The Letters of William and Dorothy Wordsworth*, edited by Ernest de Selincourt, revised by Mary Moorman, second edition, 8 vols., Oxford, 1967–93.

Wordsworth 1983

William Wordsworth, *Poems, in Two Volumes, and Other Poems, 1800–1807*, edited by Jared Curtis, Ithaca, NY, 1983.

Wordsworth 1986

Home at Grasmere: Extracts from the Journal of Dorothy Wordsworth (Written Between 1800 and 1803) and from the Poems of William Wordsworth, edited by Colette Clark, Harmondsworth, 1986.

Wordsworth 1991

William Wordsworth, *The Thirteen-Book Prelude*, edited by Mark L. Reed, 2 vols., Ithaca, NY, and London, 1991.

Wordsworth and Coleridge 1798

William Wordsworth and Samuel Taylor Coleridge, *Lyrical Ballads, with a Few Other Poems*, London, 1798.

Wright 1979

Thomas Wright, *Arbours & Grottos*, edited by Eileen Harris, London, 1979.

Yu 2008

Yu Liu, "Transplanting a Different Gardening Style into England: Matteo Ripa and His Visit to London in 1724," *Diogenes* 55, 2008, pp. 83–96.

❧ Index

(Page references in italics refer to illustrations.)

⚘ ACKNOWLEDGMENTS

The authors are grateful to the following colleagues for their assistance with this publication:

John D. Alexander, Anna Lou Ashby, Barbara Bair, Karen Banks, Adrian Benepe, Charles E. Beveridge, Kenneth Cobb, Sheila Connor, Mary Daniels, Gail S. Davidson, Cara Dufour Denison, Inge Dupont, Rhoda Eitel-Porter, Patricia Emerson, Frederic A. Eustis II, Linda S. Ferber, Maria Fredericks, Susan L. Glover, David R. Godine, Graham Haber, Rachel Hildebrandt, Erin Hyde, Juliette Ibelli, Andrea Immel, Michael Inman, Jerry Kelly, Declan Kiely, Floramae McCarron-Cates, Julie L. Mellby, Sara Cedar Miller, Julia Moore, Marilyn Palmeri, Cord Panning, Janet Parks, Robert Parks, Paula Pineda, John A. Pinto, Reuben M. Rainey, John Reed, Brian Regan, Astrid Roscher, Charles Ryskamp, Anne Schäfer, Beate Schneider, Miriam W. Scott, Lucinda Scott-Kellermeier, Reba F. Snyder, Eva Soos, Theodore Stanley, Gert Streidt, Julie Tozer, Evelyn D. Trebilcock, Frank Trujillo, Stephen H. Van Dyk, and Rachel Waldron.

⚘ CREDITS

Every effort has been made to trace copyright owners and photographers. The Morgan apologizes for any unintentional omissions and would be pleased in such cases to add an acknowledgment in future editions.

Photographic copyright:

No. 74, Avery Architectural and Fine Arts Library, Columbia University, New York; No. 72, Cooper-Hewitt, National Design Museum, Smithsonian Institution / Art Resource, NY; Fig. 53, courtesy of the Century Association Archives Foundation; No. 52, top and bottom, courtesy of Frances Loeb Library, Harvard University Graduate School of Design; Nos. 78, 84, courtesy of the Library of Congress; Fig. 48, Department of the Interior, National Park Service, Yellowstone National Park; Fig. 49, Gilcrease Museum, Tulsa, OK; Figs. 13, 18, 25 © The Frick Collection, New York; Figs. 40–43, Nos. 56, 60, 61, 62, 63, Fürst-Pückler-Museum Schloss Branitz; Fig. 46, gift of the Avalon Foundation, 1965.14.1. (1949) / PA; Image courtesy of the Board of Trustees, National Gallery of Art, Washington; No. 64, Fig. 2 © Kupferstichkabinett. Staatliche Museen zu Berlin; Figs. 9, 12, 26, 38, 39 45, Nos. 11, 75, image © The Metropolitan Museum of Art / Art Resource; Nos. 4–10, 12, No. 12, Fig.1, The Morgan Library & Museum (ML&M); No. 28, ML&M 1954.16; No. 27, ML&M 1954.17; No. 39, ML&M 1978.22; No. 25, ML&M 2006.24:2; Fig. 44, ML&M, bequest of Gordon N. Ray, 1987, PML 143828–75; No. 47, Fig. 1, ML&M, gift of Henry S. Morgan, 1965, PML 55906; Fig. 32, ML&M, gift of Paul Mellon, 1979, PML 76209; No. 2, ML&M, gift of Paul Mellon, 1980, PML 76758; No. 24, ML&M, GNR 5625; No. 33, ML&M MA 393–97; No. 53, ML&M MA 662A; No. 69, ML&M MA 686; No. 40, ML&M MA 6711; No. 31, ML&M MA 1581.20; No. 41, Fig. 1, ML&M PML 17445; No. 30, ML&M PML 50898; Nos. 20, 21, 22, ML&M PML 53027; No. 29, Fig. 1, ML&M PML 75757; No. 43, ML&M PML 77830; No. 44, ML&M PML 77831; No. 32, ML&M PML 133379; No. 41, ML&M PML 140140; No. 70, Fig. 1, ML&M PML 143828–75; No. 15, ML&M PML 150466; No. 42, ML&M PML 151002; No. 29, top and bottom, ML&M PML 152316; No. 66, ML&M PML 18077; No. 46, ML&M PML 195080; No. 58, ML&M PML 195276; Fig. 24, ML&M, purchased as the gift of the Fellows, 1960.10; No. 50, Fig. 1, ML&M REF 544.362 F74; No. 35, ML&M, The Sunny Crawford von Bülow Fund 1978, 2001.18; No. 50, ML&M, The Sunny Crawford von Bülow Fund 1978, 2007.82; No. 64, Fig. 1, Niedersächsisches Landesmuseum Hannover; No. 80, New York City Parks Photo Archive; Nos. 81, 82, NYC Department of Records / Municipal Archives; No. 71, Olana State Historic Site New York State Office of Parks, Recreation and Historic Preservation; No. 70, Princeton University Library; Nos. 67–68, Princeton University Library, Department of Rare Books and Special Collections, Graphic Arts Collection, gift of Leonard L. Milberg, Class of 1953; No. 16, Rare Books Division, The New York Public Library, Astor, Lenox and Tilden Foundations; Fig. 5 © Royal Academy of Arts, London; Figs. 40–43, No. 57, 59, Stiftung Fürst-Pückler-Park Bad Muskau; No. 38, Thaw Collection, ML&M, EVT 125; No. 65, Thaw Collection, ML&M, EVT 205; No. 37, Thaw Collection, ML&M, 1996.146; No. 64, Thaw Collection, ML&M, 1996.150; No. 34, Thaw Collection, ML&M, 2006.52; Fig. 19, Thaw Collection, ML&M, 2006.53. 19; No. 19, Fig. 1, Typ705.54.350 F, Houghton Library, Harvard University; Fig. 3, Widener Collection, image courtesy of the Board of Trustees, National Gallery of Art, Washington; Fig. 17, Yale Center for British Art, Paul Mellon Collection B1978.43.14; page 10, © U. Edelmann-Städel Museum-ARTOTHEK.

Photography:

Fig. 5, Prudence Cuming Associates Limited; No. 72, Matt Flynn; Figs. 1–2, 6, 7, 10, 14–16, 20–23, 27–37, 47, 50–52, Nos. 1–8, No. 12, Fig. 1, Nos. 13–15, 17–27, 30–33, 36, 39–42, 44–47, top and bottom, No. 47, Fig. 1, No. 48, top and bottom, Nos. 49–51, 53–55, 58, 66, 69, 70, No. 70, Figs.1 and 2, No. 73, 76–77, 83, 85, Graham Haber, 2009; Nos. 28–29, top and bottom, 43, Schecter Lee, 2009; Nos. 9, 64, David A. Loggie; Figs. 8 and 11, Elizabeth Barlow Rogers; Fig. 19, No. 29, Fig. 1, Nos. 35, 37–38, 65, Joseph Zehavi.

✎ *PUBLISHED BY THE MORGAN LIBRARY & MUSEUM*

IN ASSOCIATION WITH DAVID R. GODINE

Karen Banks, *Publications Manager*
Patricia Emerson, *Senior Editor*
Marguerite Dabaie, *Editorial Assistant*

✎ *PROJECT STAFF*

Marilyn Palmeri, *Photography and Rights Manager*
Eva Soos, *Photography and Rights Assistant Manager*
Alessandra Merrill, *Administrative Assistant*

Set in Walbaum types
Designed by Jerry Kelly